Netporn

Critical Media Studies
Institutions, Politics, and Culture

Series Editor
Andrew Calabrese, University of Colorado

Advisory Board

Patricia Aufderheide, American University • **Jean-Claude Burgelman**, Institute for Prospective Technological Studies • **Simone Chambers**, University of Toronto • **Nicholas Garnham**, University of Westminster • **Hanno Hardt**, University of Iowa • **Gay Hawkins**, The University of New South Wales • **Maria Heller**, Eötvös Loránd University • **Robert Horwitz**, University of California at San Diego • **Douglas Kellner**, University of California at Los Angeles • **Gary Marx**, Massachusetts Institute of Technology • **Toby Miller**, University of California, Riverside • **Vincent Mosco**, Queen's University • **Janice Peck**, University of Colorado • **Manjunath Pendakur**, Southern Illinois University • **Arvind Rajagopal**, New York University • **Giuseppe Richeri**, Università Svizzera Italiana • **Kevin Robins**, Goldsmiths College • **Saskia Sassen**, University of Chicago • **Dan Schiller**, University of Illinois at Urbana-Champaign • **Colin Sparks**, University of Westminster • **Slavko Splichal**, University of Ljubljana • **Thomas Streeter**, University of Vermont • **Liesbet van Zoonen**, University of Amsterdam • **Janet Wasko**, University of Oregon

For a complete listing of series titles, visit www.rowmanlittlefield.com.

Netporn

DIY Web Culture and Sexual Politics

Katrien Jacobs

ROWMAN & LITTLEFIELD PUBLISHERS, INC.
Lanham • Boulder • New York • Toronto • Plymouth, UK

ROWMAN & LITTLEFIELD PUBLISHERS, INC.

Published in the United States of America
by Rowman & Littlefield Publishers, Inc.
A wholly owned subsidiary of The Rowman & Littlefield Publishing Group, Inc.
4501 Forbes Boulevard, Suite 200, Lanham, Maryland 20706
www.rowmanlittlefield.com

Estover Road, Plymouth PL6 7PY, United Kingdom

British Library Cataloguing in Publication Information Available

Library of Congress Cataloging-in-Publication Data

Jacobs, Katrien.
   Netporn : DIY web culture and sexual politics / Katrien Jacobs.
      p. cm. — (Critical media studies)
   Includes bibliographical references and index.
   ISBN-13: 978-0-7425-5431-3 (cloth : alk. paper)
   ISBN-10: 0-7425-5431-7 (cloth : alk. paper)
   ISBN-13: 978-0-7425-5432-0 (pbk. : alk. paper)
   ISBN-10: 0-7425-5432-5 (pbk. : alk. paper)
   1. Internet pornography. 2. Internet—Censorship. I. Title.
HQ471.J33 2007
306.77—dc22

2007008663

Printed in the United States of America

∞™ The paper used in this publication meets the minimum requirements of
American National Standard for Information Sciences—Permanence of Paper
for Printed Library Materials, ANSI/NISO Z39.48-1992.

To my netporn friends who entertained me
with deep humor and tireless thought

Contents

Acknowledgments

Without the support of my colleagues this book would not have been possible. First of all, Matteo Pasquinelli, Marije Janssen, Geert Lovink, and Sabine Niederer at the Institute of Network Cultures and Paradiso, Amsterdam, who helped me organize the first two international conferences on Internet pornography, The Art and Politics of Netporn (October 2005) and C'lick Me (June 2007). Many of the ideas, materials, and web attitudes would have been inaccessible to me without their help and support. I also would like to give special thanks to all the porn producers and consumers who agreed to be interviewed and cited. Some of them also kindly gave permission to reproduce photographs. Others agreed to be interviewed but wished to remain anonymous. I am grateful to my colleagues at Emerson College and City University of Hong Kong who helped me obtain travel and research money necessary to carry out the interviews. I am indebted to scholars and curators who invited to me to give talks and test-ride porn slideshows, specifically Gina Marchetti, Giorgio Biancorosso, Josephine Ho, Jurgen Bruening, Emil Hrvatin, Dirk Verstockt, Tim Stuttgen, Andreas Broeckman, John Erni, and Hector Rodriguez. I would like to thank all those who gave comments on various drafts and who helped me with editing and proofreading: Paul Desjardins, Becky Ip, Jayne Karolow, Ned Rossiter,

Broderick Fox, and Kimberly Hall. I would also like to thank Brenda Hadenfeldt and Bess Vanrenen at Rowman & Littlefield for taking on this project and for invaluable assistance in the process of writing and producing the book. Thanks to Shujen Wang for sisterly advice and feedback. Thanks to Andrew Guthrie for his continuing support.

Introduction

Internet pornography is changing our knowledge of the body and of digital media, as it enters our lives and media networks with its unique sexual chemistry. Despite the increasingly rigid surveillance of porn sites, digital networks continue to pester or enrich intimacies between people and technologies and support a mutual sharing of products. For instance, the swapping of homemade pornographic images has become a part of our dating strategies, and we may use the web to impress sexual partners and try to show them our looks and sexual desires. This book introduces an expanded definition of pornography based on media theory and presents interviews with a wide range of porn producers. It discusses morphing patterns of arousal in these web-based zones where people chat obsessively during their porn exchange, take on alter egos, swap creative ideas and criticism, and question or emulate the goals of commercial porn industries. How can we grasp the resonance and effect of this kind of Internet pornography? The book argues that the connectivity of micro-porn spaces is beckoning new consumer groups and spawning large behavioral shifts in sexuality for everyday women and men. Rather than placing these specific micro-porn spaces on a pedestal, the book outlines tensions between indie (independent) movements, mainstream culture, and the law. The book also positions the researcher as a person who judges radical-innovative porn productivity and its opponents by using alternative methods to dry or detached media analysis.

One could think of the producers and consumers of micro-porn spaces as sexually active multitudes. The concept of the *multitude* was coined by the Italian post-Marxists who emphasized new forms of collectivity and sought to escape from older concepts and practices of work and the working class. Multitudes create mobility and escape from corporate industries and the exploitation of workers, where they would be seen as dead labor within the exchange economy. Multitudes do not adhere to older definitions of work masses nor critical masses that can overthrow the system. Multitudes are characterized by the transformation of production through the application of technical knowledge and socialized intelligence. Paul Virno, author of *A Grammar of the Multitude*, emphasizes cultivating acts of communication as a significant mode of production.[1] Porn exchange and communication are indeed lubricants for producers and consumers who test new technologies and domains while interacting with each other. Moreover, generations of porn users have helped define sexual tolerance, sex debates, and revolutions in the face of societal backlash.

Steven Shaviro argues in *Connected, or What It Means to Live in a Network Society* that networkers are more than ever experiencing a blurring between selfhood and the ephemeral signs, myths, and pathways of digital culture.[2] Within the fuzzy realm of digital culture and identity, it is no longer possible or desirable for modern citizens to escape into a ghetto of political difference. Porn users build private and noncommercial web zones that are almost instantly threatened or changed by the technological push of consumer culture. Capitalist industries use prepackaged porn domains and release porn spam into the network. Shaviro suggests that we cannot stop these waves of technological-cultural change—and that we cannot help but be immersed in it. He writes about the explosion of spam messages: "When such insect messengers come calling, you cannot choose not to respond. You may swat or shoo away a single fly, but more of them will always show up."[3] Porn spam is now a part of our nature or a part of the ecology of the network. Porn spam announces products; it also appears in our mailbox as seductive email messages sent by somebody with a familiar-sounding name. Corporation spam or debris takes on many guises within the web ecology, at times using the casual flirt as a primary strategy of seduction. This makes it harder for us to plow through our mailboxes and distinguish between fake flirts and real ones. But somehow we do want to stay connected and become more skilled at accepting a loss of faith in radical cultures from past eras.

The web is home for intriguing and uncanny collaborations within booming porn spaces, as commercial operators can more or less peacefully coexist with the fringes, including new artistic work, amateur movements, and subcultural experiments. Hence, we have become part of a second porn boom. The first boom took place at the turn of the twenty-first century and surpassed its major obstacles, such as widening the direct channels of file transfers, known as peer-to-peer (p2p) platforms for pirated porn exchange, and political resistance from conservative governments. People of many cultural backgrounds and sexual tastes have taken e-commerce into their own hands and reworked it as smaller and more humane (or softer) endeavors—indie porn, realcore porn, nerdporn, dyke porn, tranny porn, bear porn, queer porn, pornographic video games, ex-girlfriend porn, web affairs, and porn blogging.

The chemistry of technological innovation and crisis of the subcultural love/sex experiment is exactly what is so powerful about the second netporn boom. Micro-porn spaces have contributed to a uniquely chameleonic or anxious web sphere. Porn experiments have become more possible and more tempting to the deeper soul, as they are built by determined sex seekers and sex workers. Porn is successfully being appropriated and reinterpreted by alternative producers and activist sex workers, younger pro-porn feminists, queer porn networks, aesthetic-technological vanguards, p2p traders, radical sex/perv cultures, and free-speech activists.

These porn spaces are connected in their fantasy to create an alluring web sphere for the masses, even if some of them also have commercial interests. Meanwhile, there have been crude proposals by governments and more aggressive or conservative entrepreneurs to clean up this exact breeding of the porn sphere. For instance, the social network site MySpace has tried to ban sexual self-profiling and image exchange by its members by censoring all erotic and pornographic materials. When creating an account and uploading a picture on MySpace, web users get the following photo policy message: "Photos may not contain nudity, violent or offensive material, or copyrighted images. If you violate these terms, your account will be deleted."⁴ One of the main reasons that MySpace officials take such a rigorous attitude is their fear of losing business. But as this book shows, young people from various cultures, races, and class backgrounds have become technologically skilled networkers and participants in self-aware sexual representation.

This is a trend toward porn culture that ought to be debated by academic researchers, who are lagging behind in understanding popular culture and media activism. Of course, porn research is becoming a more accepted scientific endeavor, but the more radical gender/sex researchers are still being attacked and even lose their funding after denunciations by conservative groups. In a seminal article about the legacy of the legendary eccentric sex researcher Alfred Kinsey in the *New York Times*, "Long after Kinsey, Only the Brave Study Sex," Benedict Carey shows that American sexologists are still actively targeted by government and hence are less eager to continue their research. American sex research has advanced enormously in comparison with other cultures but also suffers in a climate of blacklisting, self-censorship, and stigmatization. As Carey writes: "In a culture awash in sex talk and advice in magazines and movies and on daytime TV, the researchers present their findings in coded language."⁵ Since pornography is still a coded ingredient of sex science within several disciplines, how can researchers truly open up porn culture?

There are different tracks one can take in understanding web culture, from gathering quantitative data about netporn industries to theoretical work and new methods for participatory observation. Regardless, researchers are encountering shifting boundaries between analytical (cold) and experiential-involved (warm) modes of processing data. There is an additional factor of inebriation in the study of porn, since it is an area where researchers might also feel the sweet temptations of their flesh. But this factor has actually been acknowledged and dealt with since the early schools of sexology. Kinsey displayed an unusual urge to extend innovative, artful, and wet methodologies to sex science. He first successfully surveyed masses of American citizens about their private sex affairs. Later on in life, he wanted to observe sex encounters and hired a cameraperson to record sex sessions, some of which were taking place in Kinsey's inner circle and in the attic of his own house. I believe that he was on the right track: He had a deep interest in the unspeakable realms of sexual pleasure within sex science and was always looking for suitable methods and new technologies to gain newer forms of knowledge. The aim of this book is to extend his creative mind-set into a sex-positive study of Internet pornography, where, like Kinsey, we have to become warmer scientists or at least be deeply enough immersed in sexual encounters to understand how people resist and reinvent commercial porn while having sex.

I am a woman, a scholar, an artist, and a curator and I browse and look at porn in my own unique way. Like the clinically and empirically tested group of female porn users, whose profiles I introduce in chapter 3, "Porn Arousal and Gender Morphing in the Twilight Zone," I do get turned on by a wide palette of porn genres. However, my porn experiences stem from years of chatting and having truly intriguing cybersexual encounters. Together with the web crowds, I moved from cybersex to porn, looking for everyday bodies and authentic passionate sex. I personally like lesbian porn, as I love to watch women make love—all types of women including feminine women and butch dykes, as well as FTM trannies (female-to-male transgendered persons). Ever since I started going to the movies, I also felt turned on by the sex and love scenes between men, not to mention the occasional glimpses of beautiful erections. More recently, I like to peek into the sex lives of bears, men with big and burly bodies who have body hair. I like watching transgendered people as I get turned on witnessing the various layers of sexual identity and I am curious to see the transbody. Other than that, I like ordinary movies with intense sex scenes. I like animated porn because it is colorful, wild, humorous, and contains a commotion of flickering fantasy scenes. Apart from all these categories, I have a persistent hankering for a certain type of fetish porn, which classifies me with the "deviants" and separates me from "normal" people.

In my study of Internet pornography, I have tried to open up to as many genres and players as possible, even though I had to play a double role, both checking out spaces and carrying out my research. Just like in the days of Kinsey, scholars are now standing eye-to-eye with a vibrant porn culture. What are we to do with this porn culture? Internet porn is indeed wide open to middlebrows, women and queer users, marginal groups, aesthetic innovators, and intellectuals, even though one may argue that this innovation is still too much dominated by Western intellectual or sex-activist cultures. Therefore, it is also important to look at a wider variety of porn cultures and to analyze the second porn boom from a non-Western point of view.

In July 2005, I had just started writing this book when I moved to Hong Kong to take up a position as assistant professor at City University of Hong Kong. Here I arrived in the densely wired city of Hong Kong, right across the border from the ruthless communist dictatorship, commercial expansionism and spooky Internet surveillance of mainland China. Would I still be able to locate my vanguard culture? Would I find open and progressive porn spaces that puncture corporate porn and can withstand iron-fisted government policies? Of course, I did find patches of tolerant queer porn culture in Hong Kong, but the postcapitalist trading approach and theories of Georges Bataille were perhaps harder to argue. For instance, just twenty-four hours after installing the BitTorrent file-sharing software on my office computer to research p2p trading, my entire network was shut down by the university's IT administrators. I knew that it was illegal to use the BT software in Hong Kong, but I did not know that the university IT department would be so diligent in blocking my efforts. Hong Kong provided a new time and space for me to think. How was I to question my Western mind-set and how would I be able to have a dialogue with Chinese intellectual frameworks? How could I find people in Hong Kong willing to chat about their own need for spaces, their desires for a pornography renaissance?

This book moves from a discussion of Western porn vanguards to its Eastern variations, and thus shows how notions of porn space and chemistry are always culture specific and depend on local politics. For instance, Internet surveillance and piracy have become massive topics of discussion in Hong Kong and greater China. The search engine Google recently sold out to the Chinese government, explaining that it would censor its search services in China in order to gain greater access to China's fast-growing market. The company decided to set up a new site for China that would restrict access to sensitive topics such as the independence of Taiwan and the 1989 Tiananmen Square massacre. It was predicted that the number of Internet users in China would increase from about 100 million in January 2006 to 187 million in the year 2008. A survey conducted in August 2005 revealed that Google was losing market share to Beijing-based rival Baidu.com.[6] Several weeks after the company's decision, a New York legislator filed a suit against Google accusing the company of promoting obscene content, including child pornography. As the complaint states: "Defendant is willing to accede to the demands of the Chinese autocrats to block the search term 'democracy,' but when it comes to the protection and well-being of our nation's innocent children, defendant refuses to spend a dime's worth of resources to block child pornography from reaching children."[7] Even though child porn is illegal in the United States and has been successfully monitored by Internet service providers (ISPs) and the U.S. government, would Google eventually submit to continuing right-wing pressure and censor porn altogether?

In my research, I have asked porn producers and consumers in different cultures to articulate their changing web agencies and have presented the results in different chapters, each of which consists of theoretical views on networks and case studies. In chapter 1, "Netporn Browsing in Small Places and Other Spaces," netporn is shown to permeate physical (sub)urban places and "other spaces" created by web users and collectives. Web users cultivate attachments to their everyday small places and spaces other than the ones they routinely inhabit. These spaces are located in a twilight zone where their different personalities and sexual attitudes intersect, but do not solidify into a moral law or defined porn habit. Developing a theoretical notion of space as unfolding spaces, the chapter presents Internet pornography's cybergeography as dispersed in bodies and cultures, yet also forcefully regulated by global corporations and nation-state governments. The chapter analyzes pornographic self-profiling and user interactivity in indie and altporn sites and social networks such as www.suicidegirls.com, www.burningangel.com, www.bleuproductions.com, and www.cyber-dyke.net. It outlines the boom of queer, feminist, nerdy, and African American–owned porn sites and then outlines a looming crisis or geopolitical conflict between pornography's emancipation and conservative initiatives toward racial hatred, homophobia, and online censorship.

Chapter 2, "Post or Perish: The New Media Schooling of the Amateur Pornographer," details the sexual aesthetics and trading habits of porn amateurs who use peer-to-peer platforms for exchanging home-made porn and pirated products. The *amateur* is a performative user who engages in an alternative gift economy, which allows him or her to develop a sense of identity and status within selected spaces. Traders develop virtual profiles and virtual cash alongside their social networks and trading routes. These behaviors challenge the business goals and performance management of commercial pornography. Even though commercial pornography never stopped expanding as an industry, web users have become more aware of the parallel development of a general economy. Following a theory of virtual trading based on the ideas of Georges Bataille, the chapter discusses the importance of excess energy and luxury activities in network society.[8] Bataille worked with a theory of unproductive expenditure based on the ritual of potlatch, that is, ostentatiously endowing somebody with an overflow of gifts without desiring a return gift. This notion may explain why people become buddies or lovers online after they've devoted time to each other to be joined in sex cults, sex spectacles, sex games, sex arts, or just sexual activities. The gift economy creates special relationships between people that may not be threatened or interchangeable with behaviors created by capitalist markets. This society of gift-giving and excess is witnessed in digital photography experiments with digitally morphed bodies, in the exchange of porn on straight and queer sites and Usenet groups, in the making of porn with political-activist missions, and in amateur groups who gather in art house theaters.

Chapter 3 outlines feminine porn consumption as our outlet to experience and watch diversified bodies and gender-fluid identities. It also posits porn agency as the ability to engage in chat and discussion while consuming porn, or the enjoyment of diversified acts of consumption. It is a post-Kinseyan analysis of porn arousal that argues that the transformative bodies of consumers are an essential stage in the cultural and genetic-biological development of human beings and technology. The chapter first outlines clinical experiments in porn arousal and their dependence on binary concepts of sex and gender. These concepts are flawed in understanding the modern netporn experience, which involves a self-awareness of the spectator and a post-binary conditioning of his/her gaze. The chapter looks at schizoid identities in bear porn and transgender porn sites and how they construct a porn user.

Chapter 4, "Eros in Times of War: From Cross-Cultural Teasings to the Titillation of Torture," moves into muddy political territory and argues that a new phase in netporn history has been written with the creation and circulation of mediated war torture as "warporn." The chapter proposes a reading of warporn in reference to contemporary authoritarian mythologies of gender. In his groundbreaking study of World War II Nazi culture, *Male Fantasies I & II*, Klaus Theweleit shows how the collective-mythic unconscious of Nazi soldiers was primarily characterized by a desire to be freed from all that can be identified with the female body: fluidity, blood, warmth, and sensuality. He describes the visual-performative body grammar of Nazi soldiers as an organization of the armored male self in a world constantly threatening its disintegration. The chapter shows how warporn and related images of violence perpetuate a hatred of ethnic and gay minorities. Finally, following the theories of media activism, the chapter explains that certain media artists, body artists, and s/m (sadomasochism) practitioners comment on the political crisis by appropriating and commenting on violence as warpunks (those who use war images as a defense against war).

Chapter 5, "Post-Revolutionary Glimpses and Radical Silence: Netporn in Hong Kong and Mainland China," carries out an analysis of porn spaces in those countries. Hong Kong and China are flashing nodes in expansionist porn markets, but they are also networked sites of pleasure exchange and porn activism. Besides using local pay sites, large groups of Hong Kong web users are engaged in trading porn on p2p file-sharing systems. Moreover, those users are shown to cultivate multiple identities on anime fan sites and swinger sites and in the subcultural lifestyles, including those of cosplayers (costume players) and Lolitas. The Hong Kong twilight zone is a space where actual lives meet with hypersexual identities and communication patterns. The chapter outlines Hong Kong's sexual identities by looking at hierarchical rules and lawmaking within social networks, as well as the impact of colonial history and a traumatic relationship with the draconian Internet government by mainland China. The Hong Kong twilight zone is the boundary of different cultures, a uniquely rich space of interactivity among Chinese people, migrants, and expats, and a space of collision between free-thinking and traditional citizens. The chapter researches this erotic touch-zone to show how people negotiate race, gender, and power and how they build and govern their largely self-made porn identities.

Since netporn has stirred political turmoil and a new wave of theory and sex activism, the book outlines the major components of porn culture—the networking of micro-niche porn sites and queer activism, the blossoming of noncommercial trading and porn excess, the cultivation of feminine and gender-fluid consumption, and the artistic potential and growing pains of erotic amateurism. Moreover, if we open up netporn culture from a non-Western perspective, it would be hard to avoid discussions of global conflicts and racial tensions around porn culture. The book shows that, regardless of these tensions, we are all changing as sexual beings and scholars and paving the way for a future of pornographic self-representation.

Notes

1. In Paul Virno's view, the locutor could be seen as a performer, or performance artist, who speaks back to signals. *Virtuoso* does not mean a virtuoso performance in the traditional sense, but individuals and collectives communicating as multitudes. See *A Grammar of the Multitude* (Los Angeles: Semiotexte, 2004), 55.

2. See Steven Shaviro's analysis of the aesthetics and cultural impact of digital networks in *Connected, or What It Means to Live in the Network Society* (Minneapolis: University of Minnesota Press, 2003).

3. Shaviro, *Connected*, 23.

4. Myspace.com photo policy, www.myspace.com (June 28, 2006).

5. Benedict Carey, "Long after Kinsey, Only the Brave Study Sex," *New York Times* (November 9, 2004).

6. "Google Censors Itself for China," BBC News Online (May 8, 2006) http://news.bbc.co.uk/1/hi/technology/4645596.stm (retrieved May 16, 2006).

7. See Anne Broache, "Suit Accuses Google of Profiting from Child Porn," CNET News.com (May 5, 2006). http://news.com.com/Suit+accuses+Google+of+profiting+from+child+porn/2100-1030_3-6069014.html (May 13, 2006). See also Nicholas Carr's responses in his *Pandora's Search Engine* http://www.roughtype.com/archives/2006/05/pandoras_naught.php.

8. See Shaviro's discussion of potlatch in *Connected*, 218–38.

CHAPTER ONE

Netporn Browsing in Small Places and Other Spaces

This chapter introduces indie (independent) pornography on the web and theories of porn in cyberspace, while contemplating how new porn spaces are affected by censorship legislation. Commercial pornography has flooded the Internet and pockets of sex activism are budding alongside the porn boom. Pornography moving freely across borders is foremost a capitalist vision, but this mobility is equally defined by web users and artists who visit and maintain alternative spaces and peer-to-peer (p2p) networks for producing and sharing sexually explicit materials. Revisiting Foucault's notion of space as "heterotopia," pornography is shown to permeate physical places and *other* spaces. Web users cultivate attachments to everyday places and spaces *other* than the ones they routinely inhabit. Networked sexual agency materializes desire far beyond the confines of community rituals and commodity industries. Besides the fact that porn industries expand their markets and diversify products, sex communities emerge alongside these markets and play a vital role in negotiating sexuality. Developing a theoretical notion of space as *other* spaces, this chapter unfolds the sexual web as exuberant and dispersed in bodies and cultures, yet forcefully regulated by global corporations and nation-state governments.

Alt/Indie Pornography Seizes the Web

The term *indie* can be loosely defined as the production or distribution of a work outside of the established, traditional system. Despite the rapid commercialization of alternative sex culture as "indieporn" or "altporn," the web hosts vibrant, imaginative, and cross-cultural porn spaces. The most creative web-based pornographers can be thought of as culturally aware media makers or connoisseurs who articulate sexual desires within peer-to-peer networks. Pornography is an object of pleasure and debate among these p2p web users, who test new models of e-commerce as production/consumption alongside intimate personal camaraderie, information sharing, fictional storytelling, and cultural debates.[1] But how can we grasp the maturing of these cultures in light of the corporate media's and porn industry's tendency to control ownership, to consolidate edgy content, and to maintain gender and class divisions as scripted roles for sex workers?

Internet pornography is increasingly produced and consumed as a transnational commodity culture by web users who live in a variety of cultures and places. However, Internet pornography is becoming an organized industry, one of the most pushy, lucrative, technologically audacious, and politically controversial sectors of the expanding digital entertainment industries. It was elucidated in the PBS *Frontline* program "American Porn" (2002) that the money makers of the adult video industry today are not the content makers nor the sex workers, but product distributors who solicit content from companies and prepare it for global distribution. American hotel chains Marriott and Westin are some of the businesses garnering easy benefits from the porn boom. In return for offering in-room X-rated movies, hotel chains receive a profit percentage and become primary beneficiaries of the porn industry. In addition, there are cable and satellite companies and conglomerate owners, such as AT&T and General Motors, which channel porn into millions of homes, taking a huge share of the profit or money spent by consumers.

In "American Porn," Bill Asher, president of the Vivid Entertainment Group, one of the largest adult video production companies in Los Angeles, describes his vision of porn space: "We really have only scratched the surface right now. If you look at how many television homes there are in this world, or there will be, [if you look at] how many total homes there are, versus how many can get adult, we're still a very, very small percentage."[2] Asher adds that he does not believe that the Internet will ever be able to become the primary distributor of adult content. However, in May 2006, Vivid plunged into the web and announced a plan for Internet distribution of its DVDs. In collaboration with www.alladult.com, Vivid launched a "burn to DVD service" that allows customers to create their own DVD copies that will play in any standard DVD player. It is reported that Vivid beat the Hollywood movie industry in bridging the gap between Internet consumption and the living room.[3] Moreover, Vivid took a leap into alternative media culture by signing an agreement with Eon McKai, a twenty-six-year-old graduate of the California Institute of the Arts, to open the Vivid-Alt porn brand.

Eon McKai, front cover of Girls Lie, *Vivid-Alt, 2006.*

Eon McKai, photograph from Neu Wave Hookers, Hustler Video, 2006.

Eon McKai became known for the altporn movies with three volumes of *Kill Girl Kill* before releasing the critically acclaimed *Neu Wave Hookers*, which in February 2006 became the number one video on *AVN*'s Top Twenty-Five Weekly Rentals and Sales Chart. (*AVN* is the industry trade magazine *Adult Video News*.) A witty reviewer of McKai's award-winning movie wrote: "Beautiful, goth-esque girls having lots of nasty sex in a variety of interesting environments. The new wave part is that the music is provided by a bunch of bands that you may have heard of, but we haven't. The New Wave Hookers *homage* part is provided by the sparest of plots involving a bunch of girls getting a copy of that esteemed old classic, becoming intrigued by it, and invading VCA to find out more about it (no, really, that's the plot)."[4] *Neu Wave Hookers* immediately distinguishes itself from other products through its artful cover design. It was carried out by graphic designer Alaska, who studied experimental art and whose style is described by blogger Gelatimotel as being "able to seduce consumers putting together the sparkling energy of pop and the vital impulses of underground."[5] The movie itself opens up to a disjointed scene set with moody music, and a soundtrack of a sexy girl's voice telling funny stories about one of her encounters with men and how she could not find his penis. The scene shows a motel room where a young hipster sex worker is trying to have sex with a shady, retired cab driver, but is feeling sick and appalled and keeps interrupting the session. Their strained prelude to sex is depicted through repetitive dialogue and quick-shifting camera angles, slightly blurry images, and manipulated colors. The viewer is promised flesh and made to feel some affection for the characters. The movie soon fades into an entirely different scene and mood, a small space where a group of sex workers are dancing mechanically to music while looking into the camera. The humorous-

Eon McKai, photograph from Neu Wave Hookers, *Hustler Video, 2006.*

absurd interlude moves into hot kissing sex when we see an encounter between Joanna Angel and her male partner. Their extensive fondling and kissing with soft and real acts reveals a high suspense that is usually absent in porn.

Sex educator and porn blogger Violet Blue gave McKai's *Art School Sluts* a glowing review and believes that the movie indicates a departure from commercial porn: "And the director, Eon McKai, made *Art School Sluts* with such style and great performances that I have to honestly say that I've never seen anything like it. And I want to see more. Bukowski, Japanese broken doll fetish, disaffected trust fund art students—nothing is safe from this incredibly smart porn film. Beautiful girls that dress and act like girls I know in SF art school circles (not like porn chicks *at all*), having sex like I know my generation has it. It's funny, beautifully shot, has a clean fresh look to it, is mysterious and is way hipper than porn. Porn is not cool, but here it is. No fucking fakes, porn nails, Barbies, or fake tits, either."[6]

McKai announced that he would like to promote in his Vivid-Alt movies the kind of creativity and versatility in pornography that is common on the web: "I really want to take what alt has started to become, and take those parentheses that are alt and push them really far to the right and really far to the left. . . . On the web, alt-porn has a much more diverse, eclectic voice. But on video, it's just been us—Rob Rotten, Joanna Angel and me."[7] Joanna Angel is one of McKai's superstars, and the owner of www.burningangel.com, a leading altporn website for tattooed and pierced punk-looking girls, which first emerged as a mixture of pornographic photos and Angel's interviews with music bands. The website has since morphed into a neatly organized pay porn site where members can get access to about forty girls. Visitors can view preview photos and read diaries, while paying members have access to videos and webcams. Angel refers to herself as an alternative porn producer with feminist values. From the beginnings of a topless punk rock girl on the Internet, she chose to be trained as a hardcore porn star and self-pronounced slut, and started working with production company VCA in making altporn videos.[8]

Porn movies such as Eon McKai's and Joanna Angel's aim to perpetuate the eclectic aesthetics and creative peer-to-peer exchanges of netporn. Long before netporn became a cluster of organized pay sites, electronic networks encouraged web users to share sex and formulate their journeys into pornography. These platforms for sexuality are now used within pay sites, as image exchange can be combined with live chat on webcams and discussion boards. Altporn sites such as www.burningangel.com and www.suicidegirls.com have not only incorporated but also perfected the peer-to-peer information architectures of cybersex domains. The sites aim to please nerdy navigators, as they feature daily interviews with culture makers and pop stars, and have newsfeeds to articles about technology, entertainment, and sexual politics. The sites work with weblogs (blogs) where models and members alike can post profiles and write daily journals. Moreover, members are expected to post comments after they access photos or videos, as it is their way of gaining status within the community.

Central to the aesthetics of indieporn is the concept of the "authentic" body, as the sites work with nonprofessional models unmodified by surgery, who are accessible to members through chats, journals, and blogs. As Florian Cramer and Stewart Home write, indieporn sites such as www.suicidegirls.com, www.thatstrangegirl.com, and www .fatalbeauty.com are the pornography of the decade and a significant new cultural movement. Indieporn is the avant-garde of the Internet, or the erotically imaginative branch of the porn industry and, as such, these porn spaces have successfully replaced the queer porn and media activist movements of the 1980s and 1990s. Whereas most altporn sites commission photographers to shoot models, other sites such as www .ishotmyself.com allow models to be their own photographers.[9]

Cramer and Home also denounce the indieporn movement for mimicking the business models of commercial porn sites. The site www .suicidegirls.com welcomes its viewers to one thousand girls and boasts of having gathered fourteen million comments by members. Members get extra brownie points for displaying the SG brand name on stickers, T-shirts, or logos. The names and profiles of the most loyal SG members are displayed on the site. The site is also a social network—models and members can gain status by posting comments on porn shoots and by documenting their ongoing friendships. But the primary objective is making sales, and this objective prevents intimate exchanges between SG models and members. Rather than developing imaginative diaries or passionate exchanges, the indieporn consumer is an absent-minded, lukewarm, and predictable consumer who jots down quick, generic yet friendly remarks to the stars. Even though the site offers channels for models and members to discuss personal affairs and cultural histories, the comments are mostly very short messages and superficial statements of encouragement.

A typical porn story features Mayana from Florida, posing at home in her bathroom, casually undressing and taking a bath. Mayana's photo shoot garners about two hundred comments, which are mostly very short and polite messages of appreciation and encouragement. Reading Mayana's diary and blog, one can see that she is a well-educated girl who loves "foreign films, documentaries, languages, grammar, sociology, reading, going to school, having a butterfly garden, playing with animals, riding bikes, etc."[10] She is a dark-haired and dark-skinned woman who writes about going to college classes and having little diversions in life. She does not reveal her ethnic background. She likes to exhibit her body and wants to be the very definition of a suicidegirl—to be comfortable with her body and to support something that celebrates girls for being different.[11] Even though her diary does not radiate lust or passion, her photo shoots receive many comments from members who like her work and also would like to get to know her in real life.

In another corner of the world, Katya, an Israeli Army girl, contributes to the www.suicidegirls.com site with outdoor scenarios that combine sexual poses with comments on her Jewish identity. For instance, in the story *Leaving Egypt*, Katya is shot naked in a vast desert, showing off her body and pouring sand all over herself. One could see in this story a Jewish emancipation narrative, as Katya makes a reference to the story of Passover. She embodies Israel, the wife of God who according to Jewish tradition makes a journey and transition into freedom by relating to the earth. *Dead Tracks* is a more macabre story and shows Katya awakening from death and showing her skinny, naked body on train tracks. She explains the concept of *Dead Tracks*: "One day I woke up all alone. The last thing I remembered was me and my grandparents on the train in our way to the amusement park. Then there was a big boom. When I woke up all by myself I refused to think that they weren't with me so I just searched around to see if I could find them. And look at that . . . I did."[12] Katya finds the photographs of her grandparents, who are now dead. This story is more complex and arguably points to the Jewish ethnic trauma of the Holocaust and Katya's need to remember her killed ancestors. The story again garners about two hundred comments, but the historical Jewish context for understanding Katya's eroticism is only vaguely touched upon.

Yet, how are we supposed to look at and comment on Katya's pornography? Where are all the models and members of www.suicidegirls.com located, and are they invested in debates on sexual identity, religion, or ethnicity? Indeed, when analyzing the even more imaginative branches of altporn videos or porn on the web, we can see that models express themselves as "neutral" or unmarked ethnic identities. Are the suicide-girls mostly white American girls who try to sell a universal notion of an alternative sex culture? Their profiles, blogs, and message boards make little reference to race, religion, sexual orientation, or cultural difference. Even though the interface design allows for such exchanges, in actuality models and members prefer to shy away from the nerdiness of deeper relationships.

Most Internet porn sites today follow a standardized interface design and sell sex and pornography with attractive graphics and state-of-the-art user interactivity. Internet studies such as Wyatt et al. *Technology and In/Equality: Questioning the Information Society* and Kolko, Rodman, et al. *Race in Cyberspace* have shown that the Internet maintains historical-cultural divisions between people and cultures. These studies have criticized commercialized web platforms such as portals for pampering and pacifying consumers rather than educating or stimulating: "The portal model, and the heavy presence of traditional media organizations, gives impetus to the idea of 'pushing' content—including advertising—at customers rather than waiting for them to pull it down."[13] The presence of traditional broadcast media is an important stage in streamlining Internet content so as to emphasize its commercial function. The communicative exchanges on www.suicidegirls.com are indeed hindered by the consumerist pulse of the website. The creators modeled the site on a pay site and it lures consumers primarily with compartmentalized high-resolution images of the girls. The site also promotes its blogs, but the actual journals and correspondence are lacking in cultural exchanges or intimate communication.

However, as a feminist contribution to porn, the site breaks ground in how it encourages "authentic" models to collaborate with photographers in suggesting photo shoots and stories. The models are mostly conventionally attractive young girls, but their bodies and fictions are not as contrived as those of commercial porn stars. The site also breaks down the typically gendered economy of pornography, as it has attracted a fairly large percentage of female consumers to look at and comment on the work of the suicidegirls.

Web Mistresses and Naked Nerds into the Flow

Two studies on the origins of pornography in modern culture, Walter Kendrick's *The Secret Museum: Pornography in Modern Culture* (1996) and Lynn Hunt's *The Invention of Pornography: Obscenity and the Origins of Modernity, 1500–1800* (1997), have shown that attempts to restrict the distribution of porn have historically been part of a larger objective to limit access to public spaces. Porn emerged within male elite groups, or male domains, which thoroughly feared the democratization of culture and protected porn collections from the lower classes and women's communities. During the last few decades, pornography has undergone a shift in cultural reach as a wider variety of producers and consumers participate in the making of markets. Large companies and small-scale operators coexist in their willingness to construct clusters of micro-niche markets.

Indieporn industries are increasingly influenced by the work of female web personas or *webmistresses* such as Jane Duvall of *Jane's Net Sex Guide*; she is a well-regarded reviewer of porn sites and movies who networks with innovative independent and queer porn producers. Moreover, as a woman who appreciates sadomasochism (s/m) in sex and pornography, Duvall embraces the Internet as a platform for amateur pornography and independent sites. She finds that sex-positive attitudes about the s/m community are still absent from mainstream pornography, and she looks for sites where models can directly control the scenes they shoot and how they present their body images.[14] Even though commercial netporn is morphing into web zones of tactile organization and performativity, the ability for producers to manage their own sites and body images has created new public freedoms. Frederick Lane's study *Obscene Profits: The Entrepreneurs of Pornography in the Cyber Age* cites a new presence of women-owned web sites as a highly significant trend in the porn industry:

> The ability of women to participate in the pornography industry without the intervention of a (typically male) magazine editor or video producer has profound implications for the industry as a whole. . . . The Internet has the effect of suddenly making any woman who chooses to set up her own nude Web site the head of her own *Playboy*-like channel or publisher of her own *Penthouse*-like magazine. Admittedly, the estab-

lished players in the pornography industry have enormous technical, financial, and editorial resources. . . . But amateur Web site operators have their own enormous draw: the very realness of the images they offer and the inherent voyeurism of looking at them.[15]

In the anthology *Naked Ambition: Women Who Are Changing Pornography*, sex worker and porn publicist Carly Milne highlights female sex workers and porn entrepreneurs who have been active players in the porn industries. Carly Milne's anthology came out of her authored meanderings on her blog *pornblography*. In an entry written on March 26, 2004, Milne shares a progressive view on the subject of pornography and parenting. In the same entry, she attaches a variety of "artsy" pictures shot with her webcam, showing how she uses colorful dildos around the anal region.[16] The ease of media making on the Internet has benefited porn amateurs and those aspiring to be megastars. For instance, Danni Ashe opened the uniquely prosperous independently owned website Danni's Hard Drive. Ashe's decision to make Internet pornography came out of her exchanges with web users in the alt.sex and alt.binary Usenet groups. She started participating in online sex forums where people discussed the porn and sex industries at great length: "It was out of these Usenet groups' conversations that the idea for *Danni's Hard Drive* was born, and the day my husband installed a faster modem and showed me his new company's website . . . the proverbial light bulb went on over my head."[17] While Ashe as a geek girl and voluptuous blonde immediately attracted mobs in 1995, other women have also been able to build communities around awkward personal fetishes or alternative body types.

A pioneer in the genre of *nerdporn* was Cloei of www.nekkidnerds .com, a twenty-seven-year-old woman from Cambridge, Massachusetts. Cloei describes herself as "a shy woman who has a fetish for nerds." She first worked as a model for commercial porn sites, but since the mid-1990s started to build her own company and web community that profiles sexy (and mostly female) nerds. Even though the mass media frames nerds and geeks as (mostly male) obsessive intellects with less-than-average bodies, Cloei gives a twist to this stereotype by sexualizing and feminizing it. She constructs a positive image of the sexy nerd by contrasting that image with bluntly manufactured porn stars:

I am sick and tired of searching through the net looking at page after page of tall blonde cookie cutter girls that you know are not true amateurs. These days searching for "adult material" is just site after site of the same girls with a few rare exceptions, and frankly it is giving us wild web chicks a bad name. And that's not fair now is it. So I decided to do something about it. I wanted to capture the girl you see in the back of the class sitting there reading her book not paying attention to anybody. The girl you see on the street walking to work, or the girl who sits in the cube next to you day in/day out coding her little heart out. Girls who have much more than a pretty smile to offer, but also an amazing mind.[18]

Cloei's site also transformed into a pay site but is still a departure from commercial porn in that she works with amateur models rather than professionals. The models are often her friends and acquaintances. In a website area called Geekgurls, Cloei introduces her erotic geek squad and what kind of relationships she has with each of the models. Viewers are encouraged to interact with the models and comment on issues through chat rooms and message boards. They can either talk to girls directly through webcams (web cameras) or post questions and ideas in an online forum. In a Nakkid Nerds blog, posted on www.livejournal.com, we find photographs and diaries of male and female geeks and nerds posing with eroticized computer hardware parts. One of these is a hijacked photograph of the young Bill Gates himself.

"Scrabble," Anna the Nerd, www.nerdpron.com, 2006.

Almost ten years later, nerdporn maintains a link to the altporn/ indieporn cluster, as we see in the recently launched site www.nerdpron .com, owned by webmistress Anna. Her introduction is almost an exact copy from Cloei's mission statement. As she writes: "I am Anna and I'm a nerd. An honest-to-god, real-life nerd, I am the cute girl on the subway with her nose in a comic book and I love getting naked on the Internet. I invite you to watch me play with my computers, books, comics, and more, in frequently updated galleries, and click on the thumbnails to see the full-size images! With membership you can even read my erotica and get a peek inside me or watch me code on my webcam!"[19] Anna is a savvy networker and webmistress who models herself as a smart and sex-positive geek girl. Her portraits as a sexy nerd and

"Cable ball," Anna the Nerd, www.nerdpron.com, 2006.

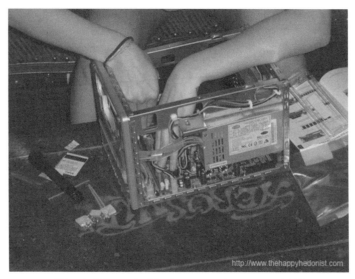

"Shuttle," Anna the Nerd, www.nerdpron.com, 2006.

solo-amateur are indeed different from "cookie-cutter" porn stars and she contributes to the democratization of pornography.

The Internet is fostering the growth of sex-positive women entrepreneurs who work with individually owned sites or collaborate in porn networks. A pioneer of Internet distribution of indie s/m videos is Maria Beatty, who in 1997 founded www.bleuproductions.com to facilitate the Internet distribution of her lesbian fetish and s/m porn productions. Beatty started out as an art house filmmaker and set out to introduce a new type of "playfulness and eroticism" in her porn videos, presenting lesbian s/m in a more "elegant, sensual, feminine film style." She hoped to diversify a commercial adult video market that is too much "focused on easy, gratuitous, and/or blatant, raw sex scenes."[20] Beatty believes that independent producers benefit from Internet distribution, as it enables them to sell works at retail value, have more control over publicity, and gain easy access to international consumers and distributors.

Beatty's productions are a mixture of commercial lesbian s/m porn and art house erotica. Her debut film, *The Elegant Spanking*, is an "erotic noir" that was initially primarily shown at lesbian and gay film festivals, both domestic and international, and sold to a limited wholesale mar-

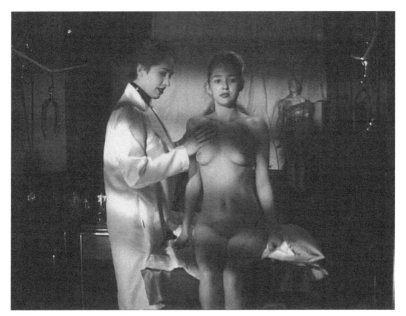

Maria Beatty, www.bleuproductions.com, photograph from Doctor's Orders, 1998.

ket through the art house distributor Outspoken Productions. Once *The Elegant Spanking* was distributed through Bleuproductions, sales quadrupled and audiences came to include male and female heterosexual viewers. Even though Beatty was previously categorized as a lesbian filmmaker, she started to cater her movies to mixed gay/lesbian and straight audiences. Her most popular videos—*The Sassy Schoolgirl* (an underage-looking schoolgirl and female schoolteacher who role-play corporal punishment, 1998), *The Boiler Room* (a very explicit lesbian s/m video with enema and cavity exploration, 1999), and *Doctor's Orders* (nurse-patient medical scenarios, 1999)—cater to "mainstream" heterosexual fantasies, fetishes, and demands, yet Bleuproductions has enabled her to work independently and develop a more personal and experimental film style. Moreover, through her website and email correspondence, Beatty receives feedback about her videos from consumers around the world. She says she believes that Internet distribution allows citizens from more restrictive countries to buy tapes from offshore sites.

Maria Beatty, www.bleuproductions.com, photograph from Doctors Orders, *1998.*

Another sister cluster of altporn/indieporn would be www.cyber-dyke.net, a network featuring a collection of sites made by and for lesbians and queer women. The CyberDyke network invites webmistresses who "are committed to making beautiful and thought-provoking pornographic and erotic sites and who would like to have their own porn sites." The webmistresses of these different porn sites are encouraged to join the network in order to boost their individual memberships, as CyberDyke offers its members a package deal whereby they have access to several sites. The second aim of the network is to help to build a supportive community for lesbians and other queer women on the Internet: "In addition to creating exceptional erotic entertainment that respects women, offered at a fair price with excellent customer service, we are creating a network where the webmistresses can interact, discuss marketing strategies, and support one another."[21] The network currently offers a variety of pornography, such as Serafinasox for those who worship feet and stockings, Posteriority for "ass-loving lesbians," Big Beautiful Heaven featuring BBWs (beautiful big women), and Darkplay for the BDSM (bondage, dominance, sadism, and masochism) community. Sapphosgirl is a site featuring "beautiful girls with an intellectual edge" and offers a selection of artistic photographs of their bodies.

Even though most of these queer porn sites are owned and operated by white Americans, the Internet is also creating opportunities for women of color to contribute to the alternative porn culture. In her essay "Because I'm Sexy and Smart! Black Web Mistresses Hack Cyberporn," Mireille Miller-Young looks at a new generation of African American webmistresses such as Sinnamon Love, Vanessa Blue, and Kim Eternity. Miller-Young openly evokes the racist "cybertypes" of Blackness in most commercial porn sites: "If you have a taste for some brown sugar, smooth, coffee skin, deliciously curvy Black women, you will most likely click your way to one of those corporate, generic, and even totally unrelated sites like www.peepshows.com. Or you may find a site like www.ExploitedBlackTeens.com, another unremarkable, unimaginative netsmut site. Black teenage girls lured into cheap hotel rooms for sex with small-time white boy pornographers."[22] Miller-Young refers to Lisa Nakamura's scholarship on the semiotics of "cybertypes." The concept of the *cybertype* is built upon the nineteenth-century word *stereotype*, which originally referred to a machine that could easily mass reproduce specific images. Nakamura investigates how the Internet propagates, disseminates, and commodifies typical images of race and racism.[23] In the case of Black porn actresses, they are typified as an underclass ready to be dominated by male pimps and customers. Miller-Young shows that the new wave of Black porn stars uses the Internet porn industry to deconstruct cybertypes and gain greater control over their labor and representation. Alongside Asian and Latina women, Black women are using digital technologies to acquire positions of power within the lucrative commerce of netporn. As independent web operators and assertive women, they present their more dynamic and personalized versions of sexiness, control, and cultural identity. Even though they have to compete with slick operations sponsored by large production companies, they can design their own images and stay away from the oblique exploitation of women of color in some of those sites.

The Spawning of Porn Spaces:
Cosmo-Spaces, Small Places, Other Spaces

How can we understand the interplay between alternative bodily aesthetics, progressive ideology, and material porn spaces that have nurtured the altporn and indieporn clusters? First, centers of content production have been mostly located in the historical high-tech urban zones (or cosmo-spaces) with developed infrastructures for labor and permissible standards for the porn trade. Luca Martinazzoli shows that porn innovation and porn culture take place within and around those cosmo-spaces, as companies seek to hire local qualified directors, models, filmmakers, and lawyers to maintain their businesses.

Martinazzoli zooms in on the Los Angeles porn industry, showing that it is subject to competitive pressure that has encouraged a dense specialized cluster. This cluster is the industry's economic geography and is located in the San Fernando Valley of California. Martinazzoli also investigates how altporn/indieporn is participating in this industry. Los Angeles is the most lucrative porn space in the United States and it feeds cultures of alternative creators, distributors, and audiences. For instance, the altporn site www.suicidegirls.com (SG) is primarily located there, even though it spreads a rhetoric of worldwide authenticity and amateurism. The site allows web users from different cultures to participate as models or members. However, SG models and members in actuality have shown little inclination to reveal or discuss cultural difference.

Martinazzoli defines the porn industry as a geographically contained segment of the "creative industries." Creative industries are defined as "industries offering service output that focuses on entertainment or manufactured products through which consumers construct distinctive forms of individuality."[24] The idea of Los Angeles as a cosmo-space of vibrant porn identities and individuals is reinforced by the presence of upscale stores where people can peruse and buy products. The best example is the Hustler Hollywood megastore located on Sunset Boulevard in West Hollywood, surrounded by white upper-middle-class neighborhoods. The boutique-style Hustler store rivals megastores such as Virgin or HMV and attracts youngsters who visit the neighboring music bars and clubs. The store is hyper-visible in the city and its upscale aesthetics and respectability are reflected in the large transparent glass architecture. The store has a clean interior design and abounds with colorful, attractive product branding. The store totally breaks away from shady sex shops; it also houses a high-quality bookstore and various types of shirts and sex toys. People who want to hang out and have coffee there can do so without feeling out of place. The actual porn selections encapsulate the standard categories of porn: ethnic/European, special interests, superstar, gay, and so on. In May 2006, the store highlighted the altporn productions made by Eon McKai and Joanna Angel.

Netporn lives in and around these cosmo-spaces, even though democratization and flows of e-commerce are moving its economic geography to other places. Where are the new locations that were previously excluded and divorced from the hubs of pornography? Are the economic flows different from the older forms of adult entertainment? Cybergeographer Matthew Zook shows that the interaction between older geographies and newer cybergeographies is creating a unique network society. In a network society, an electronically formulated space of flows connects previously disconnected places to a global network of social and economic interactions. Cybergeography promotes a visualization of these flows around web-based industries and nodes of traffic, but it also investigates the concrete materials cultures of network society. In other words, the roles of these agents are not only simply seen as a spaceless logic of cyber-interactions but also as histories and economies of the physical places they inhabit. The *space of flows* cannot be understood without reference to the *space of places* to which it connects.

Zook's cybergeography provides a valuable counterpoint to the power of cosmo-spaces as it highlights the ability of socially marginal and underground agents to connect in global networks. His case study, "Underground Globalization: Mapping the Space of Flows of the Internet Adult Industry," analyzes how new underground nodes are overlaid upon the older geographies.[25] Digital products, low barriers to entry, cost differentials, and sensitivity to regulation have created a pervasive and complex geography of models, webmasters, and consumers. With a series of specially developed datasets investigating the location of content production, websites, and hosting, Zook hopes to prove that the online adult industry indeed offers opportunities in places outside of the major metropolitan areas. It is a challenging task for the cybergeographer to map out these netporn flows. As Zook explains, websites can be hosted in one place, whereas the models are contracted in another place. For instance, in the case of booming Chinese "nudity-chatting" sites, those site owners seek webhosts from outside mainland China to avoid policing, while models and content are produced locally.

As for the creation of web content, Zook finds that a relatively small number of Western-dominated suppliers provide the bulk of content, specifically for websites offering video streaming and live interaction that require expensive equipment and facilities. Since pornography is a socially stigmatized and legally prosecuted product worldwide, the hubs of productivity and networking are still located alongside cosmo-spaces with permissible standards, such as Los Angeles, Amsterdam, and Tokyo.

However, when it comes to distribution and webhosting, Zook uncovers an emerging network of people and places outside the major metropolitan areas. Places like Hungary and Thailand are becoming new centers for the creation of pornographic materials because of the easy availability of sex workers. As far as the percentage of top membership and free sites on the web, an alternative cybergeography is emerging with Eastern European and Caribbean locations playing an important role. The vast majority of adult websites are hosted on computers within the United States, but other clusters can be found in the Czech Republic, Russia, and Bulgaria. These countries provide hosting for relatively more adult websites than mainstream Internet sites. Last but not least, there are places that offer havens from stringent government regulation and foster "hot" (illegal) money flows such as Antigua, the Virgin Islands, Belize, the Bahamas, and Panama.

Despite shifting netporn geographies, Zook concludes that the history of the Internet has served to imprint values strongly associated with the United States, with regard to the presentation of cultures and ethnicities and the promotion of Western values of sexuality. However, one could also argue that new types of web identities and agencies are cultivated by journeying consumers regardless of their documented ethnicity or place of residence. Online journeys dissolve the borders between everyday places and other spaces, enabling complex relationships between cultures and creative fictions to emerge. Hence, another theoretical model to contextualize the web user's desire to "journey" would be Foucault's early definition of space as *other spaces*. In his essay "Of Other

Spaces," Foucault writes that we live in an epoch of space, where space is not a delineated entity but one that constantly fragments and dissolves, re-forming as other spaces.[26] With modernity, the medieval concept of space as emplacement was replaced by that of "heterotopia," a notion of space whose fixed nature and location are constantly disrupted by transience and ever-shifting relations between places. According to Foucault, heterotopias are capable of taking several sites that are incompatible or "foreign to one another" and juxtaposing them within a single space.[27] Foucault uses the example of festivals and fairgrounds where random games and displays are bundled together, but one could also make examples of porn spaces as incompatible websites that impact shifting zones of the psyche. Daniel Defert explains that Foucault's concept of space meant to introduce a carnivalesque order of existence:

> These spatio-temporal units, these space-times, shared the fact of being places where I am and yet I am not, as in the mirror or the cemetery, or where I am another, as in the brothel, the vacation resort, or the festival: carnival transformations of ordinary existence, which ritualize splits, thresholds, and deviations, and localize them as well.[28]

Heterotopia is Foucault's characterization of such disorder and chaos in spatio-temporal units, and how they enable intricate and multiple, often conflicting, workings of thought and gestures. Foucault first defined *heterotopia* as "a disorder in which fragments of a large number of possible orders glitter."[29]

Foucault is perhaps a foreteller of electronic agency in defining space as morphing and disorderly networks, though a newer reading of his concept would include the disorder of bodies and spaces of actual correspondents. Porn spaces cannot be seen as pure emplacement nor as purely disembodied spaces but, rather, as cultural spaces where porn users explore phenomena and intersect with each other's mental, physical, and emotional journeys. Contemporary artists and theorists have developed profiles of the journeying body within the digital media environment. For instance, David Cronenberg's *eXistenZ*, a film about game designers and corporate game wars, depicts people becoming one with game pods that are made of blubbery animal parts. Gamers connect to these parts by means of an umbilical cord straight into their spines and they become psychically immersed in a parallel game reality.

It is as if the game pods are fed brainwave signals by their little cocoon babies while putting the conditioned human body to sleep.

Cyberfeminist artists such as Francesca da Rimini have in recent years developed artful meditations on these types of clinging. Da Rimini's website contains archives of her cybersex correspondence and documents a libidinal search for love as "journeying," showing how sex and fantasies are built, expanded, ruined, and refurbished over time. The site demonstrates web life as journeys into multiple nodes of desire emanating from web-based correspondence. For instance, her "doll yoko" is a character who "swims up from a crater mud pond of dead girls as her pale hands perform gentle inquisitions upon your fleshform as she haunts your imagination." Doll yoko is a character rooted in Japanese folklore and exotic fetishism who embodies da Rimini's personal memories, constructed language, and images. Da Rimini invented doll yoko in a small place near Kyoto, a place where she was on holiday and where, according to local legends, Japanese baby girls had been drowned at birth. The legend of this place entered doll yoko's journey and linked her to other characters such as Gashgirl, a cynical vampire who rips into fleshforms, and the dominant and self-absorbed "puppet mistress" who sees the web as a "global freak show." Da Rimini explains that these alter-ego personas have had a profound impact on her own everyday body and sexuality:

> During the 3–4 years that I was most intensely reconfiguring myself as an online erotic intelligence, as GashGirl and later as doll yoko, a period of my life that was particularly marked by obsession, an addictive relationship to going online, euphoria, wild oscillations of emotions, [and] relentless creative output, I was experiencing my body in new ways, far more sexualized, responsive to suggestion and physically sensitive than it had been before. This went hand in hand with a driving need to write, to write daily, hourly, to never leave the screen, to record the psychic and emotional development of the characters I was inhabiting, and the passages of the relationships they were forming with other minds played out within the liquid space of the nets.[30]

In contrast to a feminine web user who journeys and chats, Cramer and Home propose a traveler-browser who checks out repetitive collections and develops sexual techniques of ecstasy. They believe that modalities of boredom and repetition can still expand the sexual mind of the browser: "Pornography is one of the arts that creates ecstatic perception, triggering arousal only through symbolic codes. . . . Computing and programming have likewise been known in pornography for centuries. In the *120 Days of Sodom*, de Sade imagines a ceaseless execution of coded game rules. There is no single point of originality, but only combinations computed out of a set of sex partners and their organs." Cramer and Home thus propose a theory of "pornographic coding," where endless porn browsing methods are practiced in response to numerous collections. While searching does not have to lead to climax or orgasm, it may consist of out-of-body experiences. Just as the shamans of ancient times took psychedelic mushrooms to cultivate their minds, porn ecstasy techniques can be developed based on porn browsing techniques. Cramer and Home thus evoke the (male) geek's disavowal of the flesh body and the porn browser's levels of bonding with fellow geeks: "Once you go above level Five you don't necessarily need coitus. Indeed, at level Six you are telepathic and sexually combined with your fellow hackers."[31]

A third method of porn consumerism has been posited by Matteo Pasquinelli. His essay was written in response to war cruelties committed by the U.S. military in the Abu Ghraib prison—and the related images that circulated on the net in August 2004, arguably as yet another type of pornographic pop entertainment. In an era determined by a growing polarization between Western corporate media and Islamic prohibitions on media, this option is to make and exchange porn as "videopoesis," or to reclaim, modify, and share porn as art and autonomous media. In this way, people can make do-it-yourself (DIY) porn and acknowledge cultural differences within their communities: "Collective imagery is not affected by the video technology of mass technologies only, but also by the natural instincts of humankind. Let's call them animal narratives." Web users are porn animals or "grinning monkeys" who can reject the porn spaces of popular brands to make and distribute radical kinds of netporn imagery. This imagery attempts to make a stronger imprint on the fantasies of globalized porn viewers. Pasquinelli proposes that web users embrace porn in such a monkey-like manner, using sex drives and autonomous media to create alliance-networks around porn culture.[32]

Netporn Politics:
Days of Rage, Centuries of Repression

Porn empire industries, just like their predecessors in the adult video business, have been focused on distributing products beyond national boundaries. The Internet porn boom has created a vision of commercial expansionism and pornographic "pushiness" that has wreaked havoc among conservative governments and consumer groups, specifically in cultures where sex workers and pornographic products are socially stigmatized or stringently monitored by law. Netporn politics are also part of an intensified geopolitical conflict, as attacks on progressive, sex-positive ideologies, and alternative media are directed not only by Western capitalism and by its alliance with anti-porn crusaders, but also increasingly by fundamentalist anti-porn movements in other cultures.

The opening months of the year 2006 were characterized by days of rage: massive public protests in Islamic nations over offensive images perpetuated by the West. First, there were protests and outbursts of violence over caricatures of the Prophet Muhammad that were published in the Danish journal *Jyllands-Posten* on September 30, 2005. As the controversy heated up, some of the cartoons were reprinted in newspapers in more than fifty other countries. Some critics believe that the cartoons were indeed culturally insulting, Islamophobic, and intended to humiliate a marginalized Danish minority. Supporters of the cartoons claim that they illustrate an important issue and that their publication exercises the right of free speech. The Internet was a crucial medium for people to either organize the protests against the cartoons or exercise the right of free speech in their defense. Some impressive indie media sites were built within days of this global event, with collectively edited information on the events and extensive links to major newspaper stories from around the globe. A remarkable amount of information was compiled on the Wikipedia website under the item Jyllands-Posten Muhammad Cartoons Controversy and on the weblog www.cartoonbodycount .com, a collectively edited archive of quantitative information on the protests, dates, sizes, and casualties.[33]

Another type of conflict that affects netporn politics is the nation-state government control over and censorship of popular Internet search engines. The debates are raging over the role of Google and Yahoo! in handing over information about browsing patterns to the Chinese government. Offering his predictions for 2006, Internet analyst Nicholas Carr wrote, "The culture wars [will] slam into the Internet, as a group of influential evangelicals launch a boycott of Google, demanding that it 'stop distributing pornography' through its search engine." In May 2006, a New York legislator indeed filed a suit against Google, accusing the company of promoting obscene content, including child pornography. The suit accuses Google of acceding to the demands of the Chinese autocrats to block search terms such as *democracy*, while being lenient when it comes to the issue of pornography and the protection and well-being of children. Carr predicts that this will be a big nut to crack for sex and free-speech activists: "The Internet is in the mainstream now, and search engines will not be exempt from society's norms and controversies."[34]

Since netporn is another mainstream transnational industry, its future will be determined by participation of non-Western nation-states, some of which take irrational measures when judging online sex and pornography, even though they would be less inclined to erase collaboration with any other expansionist industry. For instance, in China, where since 2002 the government has vowed to win the war on Internet pornography, new legislation has been passed to prosecute sites for nudity-chatting—webcam performances where web users watch each other perform, while giving textual feedback in a chat box. While the government wants to ban all commercial services using this technology, they have not specified legislation for nudity-chatting as a noncommercial sexual activity.

The first nudity-chatting case was brought in Beijing, Dongcheng, in August 2005. A forty-three-year-old male named Chai was arrested for the crime of disseminating pornographic materials. According to Chai's report, there were five men, one woman, and a married couple interacting on 263.com, when the Beijing City Internet Monitoring Department went through this site and saw their porn activities.[35] Chai became immersed in this chat room through "good Internet friends" who had received the secret code from "good acquaintances." Meanwhile, other police raids of nudity-chatting in China have come to light. In October 2005, the Jiangsu Ministry of Public Security and the Ministry of Information Industry announced that they had appointed hundreds of Internet police to monitor nudity-chatting twenty-four hours a day.[36] One could easily argue that nudity-chatting should be a right of the individual sex-seeker to develop, control, and express one's sexual body. In today's society, many people rely on changing digital technologies to experience sexual needs and relationships. But the government does not make such distinctions and uses standardized obscenity legislation to create an image of control, surveillance, crime, and punishment. Indeed, while Internet policing on all types of nudity chatting has begun and been reported on in the Chinese news, the cultural repercussions of this sex or porn activity are now beyond debate.

Such anti-porn legislation will likely have a negative impact on the work of artists and smaller porn operators, rather than bigger organized industries. Another crucial location of conflict is Indonesia, where in May 2006 the Indonesian government had planned to pass a hard-line conservative anti-pornography bill, as a result of politicians and Muslim groups who were angered by the influx of "degenerate" products through the Internet and pirated DVDs. Indonesian politicians are wary of alienating Indonesia's Muslim majority and are condoning the growing anti-porn movement. In Jakarta, police have seized hundreds of thousands of "erotic" magazines, including *FHM* and *Rolling Stone*, after heeding an edict from Police Chief Sutanto to eradicate pornography.

This rising tide has affected Agus Suwage, one of Indonesia's leading contemporary artists. Suwage's installation *Pinkswing Park*—created with Davy Linggar and depicting multiple pictures of near-naked men and women frolicking in a utopian park—was censored at the Jakarta Biennale of 2005. Moreover, curator Jim Supangkat closed down the entire Biennale exhibition after it was hit by public protests. Suwage and a group of artists and academics have decided to fight the anti-porn law and emphasize sexuality as an everyday cultural phenomenon. As explained by leading feminist professor Gadis Arriva: "Women have always dressed sexily and in tight clothes; this law is something very alien to us, [since] we have bare-breasted women in Bali and Papua [and] this is part of our culture."[37] If the anti-porn law gets passed, it would be difficult for artists and activists to exhibit any type of pornographic, erotic, or sexually explicit art or media.

The censorship climate affects us all and is by no means restricted to non-Western nations. In an attempt to monitor web-based exchanges of illegal types of porn, national governments in Western countries as diverse as the United States, Australia, the United Kingdom, and France have started to issue stringent censorship laws. The fear that the Internet kindles the growth of porn that is violent, harmful, and exploitative of children has produced new policies by legislators and corporations in their desire to control electronic information. For instance, in March 2003, the U.S. Congress initiated the large-scale surveillance of file-sharing programs or p2p networks in response to their distribution of illegal types of porn. The General Accountability Office (GAO) and the House Government Reform Committee issued a report entitled "Child Pornography Is Readily Accessible over Peer-to-Peer Networks." Government officials carried out surveillance tests on the networked computers of individuals in student communities at Ivy League institutions and concluded that web users are at significant risk: "Juvenile users of peer-to-peer networks face a significant risk of inadvertent exposure to pornography when searching or downloading images."[38] To document the risk of inadvertent exposure to pornography, the GAO collaborated with the Customs CyberSmuggling Center of the U.S. Department of Homeland Security to perform searches on the p2p network KaZaA and found that child porn was indeed being traded. The GAO's report also mentioned that the Federal Bureau of Investigation, in the fiscal year of 2002, allocated $38.2 million and 228 agents to an Innocent Images Unit, and wants to solicit the cooperation of peer-to-peer companies in dealing with the issue of child pornography.[39] A similar example of government surveillance took place in the UK with Operation Ore, a piece of legislation that currently enables the police to monitor and arrest web users engaged in acts of child pornography without investigating the social or ethical codes of conduct developed by online correspondents.

John Perry Barlow of the Electronic Frontier Foundation (EFF) in his online article "Censorship 2000" predicted a large networked anti-porn effort in the United States and Europe, arguing that nation-states and international organs such as the G8 (Group of Eight Industrial Nations) would start pressuring ISPs (Internet service providers) to act as legislators of the Internet. ISPs in several countries are now forced by law to report illegal traffic to the police. The UK-based Internet Watch Foundation, made up of Internet industries, government, and consumer representatives, also encourages web users themselves to report on illegal traffic. The Internet Watch Foundation prides itself on encouraging citizens to become familiar with government policies and to become governing bodies using a centralized and user-friendly website. The foundation works in partnership with ISPs, telecom companies, mobile operators, software providers, police, and government agencies. The goal is to minimize the availability of illegal content, particularly child abuse images. As the foundation writes: "Our Internet Hotline can deal with reports of potentially illegal Internet content, such as websites, newsgroups and online groups that contain images of child abuse anywhere in the world; adult material that potentially breaches the Obscene Publications Act in the UK; or criminally racist material in the UK." Self-government and surveillance of fellow citizens are presented as civil duties that lead to results, as the foundation proudly reports: "2450 notifications sent to the police in 2001."[40]

Barlow believes that such alliances between nation-state governments and Internet industries may easily result in the political suppression of marginal groups, as it creates a tide of intolerance: "Within narrower contexts, suppressing the expression of gays, women, heretics, traitors, and troublemakers is politically popular."[41] Efforts to involve netizens (active participants in the Internet community) in Internet governance such as the European Union's Safer Internet forum or the UK's Internet Watch Foundation may lead to a mainstreaming of sexual politics, rather than an understanding of new porn spaces and indie and queer porn movements. An example of such a mainstreaming would be the censorship of online sexual communities by commercial portals—and their eventual removal. In particular, this has been the case for commercial host portals such as Egroups, Yahoo!, Excite, and Visto, which have disabled legal adult websites for gay communities where materials deemed to be "obscene," such as pictures of urinating boys, were exchanged. As those sites were hosted by corporate host portals as free services, the portal managers were "free" to set any terms of service (TOS) they chose. For instance, the Visto.com TOS reads: "We reserve the right to terminate any subscriber, without disclosure of specific reason for said termination, at our own discretion, if we deem that such termination is in the best interest of Visto Corp" (Visto homepage). It is important to note that such control on adult sites is damaging to the educational and social functions that they perform. Some of the moderators of censored sites have maintained extensive discussions about nudity among children and nonparental adults in order to resist a generalized representation of this taboo area of sexuality.[42]

The implications of tightening global censorship and attempts at civic Internet governance is that people may vote for a climate of sexual mainstreaming and react out of fear and paranoia. Hence, there is a growing conflict between the official nation-state watchdogs on pornography, on the one hand, and the spawning of porn culture through altporn/ indieporn producers, activists, and artworks on the other. Moreover, we do have to take into account cultural differences when trying to legislate porn culture. For instance, while depictions of nude minors within gay and lesbian networks spur moral outrage in the United States, these depictions may also be tolerated in other cultures such as Japan. Mark McLelland (2000) notes, for instance, that scatological references may appear obscene to Western audiences, but they are more commonplace in Japanese media. Discussing the website Saki's Room and illustrations with urination and masturbation themes, McLelland suggests that "the most troubling illustrations for a western viewer involve scenes depicting interplay between male minors."[43] For instance, in Massachusetts, a bill has passed that makes it illegal to upload or download images containing the nudity of a person under eighteen, even if the images depict naked babies or children and do not have any pornographic intent at all. McLelland's research reveals that areas of censorship and taboo in one particular culture often go unnoticed in another culture.

The future of global porn may indeed be threatened by censorship measures, as governments and citizens start to apply the most stringent measures of censorship legislation, rather than initiate public debates. An early example of a local culture proposing strict measures against global technologies was the Western Australian Censorship Act of 1996, an ad hoc state law intended to forgo the more lenient mechanisms of the Australian Federal Government.[44] U.S. officials have tried to argue that global technologies are damaging to American community standards. However, in May 2002, the U.S. Supreme Court struck down the Child Online Protection Act (COPA), a bill in which proponents argued that the Internet as global technology by design exposes children to pornographic materials. However, since the 2002 Supreme Court ruling over COPA, other arms of the U.S. government have made serious efforts to monitor and put restrictions on Internet porn traffic. The debate between U.S. Attorney General John Ashcroft and the ACLU (American Civil Liberties Union) revolved around whether community standards of decency could be transferred from one place to another. The ACLU argued on the side of cultural differences and said that a federal censorship law affecting the Internet would result in applying the most conservative community standards to the entire nation. Ashcroft replied that U.S. community and moral standards were in danger and that the Internet would be especially damaging for minors. He argued that community standards for minors are less dependent on cultural difference and more likely to be "reasonably constant" throughout the nation. Even if different adult cultures have numerous ways of digesting pornographic materials, there is no difference in how Internet porn globally affects minors. As Senator N. Haynes states: "If adults and children are mutually given unfettered access to adult and obscene materials via the Internet, a child's computer is essentially converted into an adult bookstore."[45]

In her controversial book, Judith Levine deconstructs the "harmful to minors" obscenity standard used by these proponents of COPA. Her book aims to show that this obscenity standard has been operational in the United States since 1968, and is currently being revamped by the government to phase out sexuality debates rather than promote tolerance and media education. Levine argues that children should be schooled in media literacy and moral intelligence rather than be exposed to censored versions of the Internet: "To give children a fighting chance in navigating the sexual worlds, adults need to saturate it with accurate, realistic information and abundant, varied images of love and sex."[46] The most compelling arguments against COPA came from researchers within the Society for the Scientific Study of Sexuality and the Institute for the Scientific Study of Sexuality, who have found that there is no sufficient evidence that children are harmed by exposure to sexually explicit words or images.[47] Moreover, these researchers have also found that the category of "minors" (eighteen years or younger in the United States) is too broad for the application of a measure of child psychology.

In response to the 1998 Child Internet Protection Act (CIPA), an act that requires public libraries to filter their computers if they want to retain federal funding, Judith Krug of the American Library Association wrote a plea against the mandatory use of filtering software, arguing instead for progressive sex education: "It would be better to educate children and teenagers about the various uses of the Internet rather than rely on software to help them navigate."[48] Educational programs toward Internet literacy and sexual politics in high schools and higher education would be needed to close the gap between top-down government measures and decentralized online communities.

Conclusion

The future of pornography's alternative media spaces is gloomy, as web users are increasingly monitored, moderated, or punished by stricter agreements between nation-state governments and consolidated Internet industries. It would be accurate to think that indieporn movements and ideologies will suffer from this climate. Netporn may be defined by the corporate owners and their illustrious information design, as Frederick Lane observes: "The Internet corollary of a tony address, vast distribution networks, and economy of scale will be the ability to engage in ubiquitous advertising and to develop and implement the latest technological improvements."[49] In other words, technological innovation and a corporate branding of cybersex and social networks may become the new future of netporn.

However, the next chapter will argue that digital media networks have created a robust foundation for amateur porn as homemade expressions of lust and love. Web users are engaged in porn navigation as noncommercial types of consumerism or sexual communication. Porn culture includes mundane sexual adventures (widely defined) and noncommercial p2p porn exchanges, and even allows complex discussion of social and ethical communication issues that are bluntly ignored by the profit-oriented porn industries.

Notes

A previous version of this chapter appeared in *Cultural Studies* 18, no. 1 (January 2004): 66–84.

1. A wide range of sex bloggers can be visited at http://del.icio.us/netporn/ Blogs and www.sexblo.gs, and a good example of "slash fiction" fansites would be http://fictionresource.com/slash/index.php (May 16, 2002).

2. *Frontline*, "American Porn: Interview with Bill Asher," PBS website, www .pbs.org/wgbh/pages/frontline/shows/porn/interviews/asher (May 16, 2002).

3. Vivid Entertainment Group press release: "Vivid Entertainment Launches 'Burn to DVD' Service—Allows Customers to Create Their Own DVD Copies at Home." www.hoovers.com/free/co/news/list.xhtml?ID=51033& Name=Vivid-Entertainment-Group&source_type%5B%5D=pr (June 4, 2006).

4. Description of *Neu Wave Hookers* on Blowfish website. www.blowfish .com/catalog/videos/surreal.html (June 5, 2006).

5. Luca Martinazzoli Interview with Alaska on Gelatimotel weblog www .gelatimotel.com/?p=123 (June 5, 2006).

6. Violet Blue, "Hot Reviews," www.tinynibbles.com/bookmovie.html (June 4, 2006).

7. Dan Miller, "Vivid Signs McKai." February 16, 2006. www.avn.com (June 4, 2006).

8. Joanna Angel, "On Being a Feminist with a Porn Site," in *Naked Ambition: Women Who Are Changing Pornography*, ed. Carly Milne (New York: Carroll and Graf, 2005), 187.

9. Florian Cramer and Stewart Home, "Pornographic Coding," paper presented at the Crash Conference, Feb. 11, 2005; available online at www .netzliteratur.net/cramer/pornography/london-2005/pornographic-coding .html (February 25, 2006).

10. Suicidegirl Mayana's online profile, www.suicidegirls.com (February 25, 2006).

11. Suicidegirl Mayana's Photoshoot *Sequent* http://suicidegirls.com/girls/ Mayana/photos/Sequent (May 15, 2006).

12. Suicidegirl Katya's Photoshoot *Dead Tracks* http://suicidegirls.com/girls/ Katya/photos/Dead_Tracks. The interpretations of Katya's Jewish scenarios were suggested by Tobaron Waxman, private email correspondence (January 15, 2006).

13. Sally Wyatt, Flis Henwood, Nod Miller, and Peter Senker, eds., *Technology and In/Equality: Questioning the Information Society* (London: Routledge, 2000), 37.

14. Jane Duvall, "On Mining the Internet for Good Adult Content," in *Naked Ambition*, ed. Carly Milne, 187.

15. Frederick S. Lane, *Obscene Profits: The Entrepreneurs of Pornography in the Cyber Age* (New York: Routledge, 2000), 113.

16. Carly Milne's porn blog, Pornblography, www.pornblography.com/daily_grind (November 15, 2003).

17. Danni Ashe, "On Learning How to Launch the Most Popular Web Site from Working at a Strip Club," in *Naked Ambition*, ed. Carly Milne, 230.

18. Cloei, homepage greeting, Nakkid Nerds, www.nakkidnerds.com (March 4, 2006).

19. Anna the Nerd, homepage greeting, Nerdpron, www.nerdpron.com (March 4, 2006).

20. Maria Beatty, personal interview with the author (November 15, 2000).

21. CyberDyke Network "Information for Webmistresses," www.cyberdyke.net/cyberdyke-webmasters.html (February 8, 2006).

22. Mireille Mille-Young, "Because I'm Sexy and Smart! Black Web Mistresses Hack Cyberporn," *Cut-Up Media* magazine, www.cut-up.com/news/detail.php?sid=416 (February 6, 2006).

23. Lisa Nakamura, *Cybertypes: Race, Ethnicity, and Identity on the Internet* (New York: Routledge, 2002).

24. Luca Martinazzoli, "Porn Valley: Hardcore Geographical Cluster," paper presented at the My Creativity Conference, Institute of Network Cultures, Amsterdam, November 2006.

25. Matthew Zook, "Underground Globalization: Mapping the Space of Flows of the Internet Adult Industry," *Environment and Planning* 35, no. 7 (2003): 1261–86.

26. The English version of this essay appeared in 1986, but it was originally published in 1967.

27. Michel Foucault, "Of Other Spaces," *Diacritics* 16, no. 1 (1986): 25.

28. Daniel Defert, *Foucault, Space, and the Architects' Politics/Poetics: Documenta X—The Book* (Ostfildern-Ruitz: Cantz Verlag, 1997), 275.

29. Daniel Defert, *Documenta X—The Book*, 275.

30. Francesca da Rimini, personal interview with the author, August 2000.

31. Cramer and Home, "Pornographic Coding."

32. Matteo Pasquinelli, "Warporn! Warpunk! Autonomous Videopoesis in Wartime!" posted on the Internet mailing list Nettime, August 30, 2004, http://www.nettime.org (August 30, 2004).

33. "Jyllands Posten Muhammad Cartoons Controversy" http://en.wikipedia.org/wiki/Jyllands-Posten_Muhammad_cartoons_controversy, and www.cartoonbodycount.com (10 March 2006).

34. See Anne Broache, "Suit Accuses Google of Profiting from Child Porn," CNET News.com, May 5, 2006, http://news.com.com/Suit+accuses+Google+of+profiting+from+child+porn/2100–1030_3–6069014.html (May

13, 2006). See also Nicholas Carr's responses in his Pandora's Search Engine, www.roughtype.com/archives/2006/05/pandoras_naught.php.

35. Chen Jian, "Challenging Conviction of Nudity Chatting: Five Men and Two Women Meet Nakedly Online," it.people.com.cn/GB/1071/43025/3893805.html (March 6, 2006).

36. Huang Li, Jiang Ye, Li Cheng, Li Xue, and Voramon Damrongsinsakul, "In Search of Regulation—Online Nudity Chatting: Evidence from China," paper presented by students for the course Policies and Regulations of New Media, City University of Hong Kong, October 2005, 5–8.

37. Quoted in Mark Forbes, "Navel Gazing Ruled Out as Indonesians Button Up," *Sydney Morning Herald*, February 25, 2006, www.smh.com.au/news/world/navel-gazing-ruled-out-as-indonesians-button-up/2006/02/24/1140670261932.html (March 15, 2006).

38. GAO-03-537, "Child Pornography Is Readily Accessible Over Peer-to-Peer Networks." http://216.239.37.104/search?q=cache:bViQIv32s48J:www.gao.gov/new.items/d03537t.pdf+gao-03-537T&hl=en&ie=UTF-8 (June 15, 2003), 11.

39. GAO, 13.

40. Internet Watch Foundation, www.iwt.org.uk (May 13, 2002).

41. John Perry Barlow, Censorship 2000. Internet mailing list Nettime, www.nettime.org (July 12, 2000).

42. Information gathered from diverse anonymous sources, correspondence between moderators and members of porn sites hosted by Egroups and Visto.

43. Mark McLelland, "No Climax, No Point, No Meaning? Japanese Women's Boy-Love Sites on the Internet," *Journal of Commercial Inquiry* 24, no. 3 (2000): 283–84.

44. The Western Australian Censorship Act of 1996 stipulates that "objectionable" articles are those that "contain child pornography, or depict in an offensive manner crime, violence, torture and pornographic imagery such as necrophilia, sadomasochism, golden showers, and bestiality." (Western Australian Censorship Act, 1996).

45. "Internet Pornography," *Supreme Court Debates*, February 2002: 61.

46. Judith Levine, *Harmful to Minors: The Perils of Protecting Children from Sex* (Minneapolis: University of Minnesota Press, 2002), 15–17.

47. Levine, *Harmful to Minors*, 60.

48. Joan Loviglio, "Librarians Resist Filtering Technology to Block Adult Sites," *Boston Globe*, March 25, 2002.

49. Frederick S. Lane, *Obscene Profits: The Entrepreneurs of Pornography in the Cyber Age* (New York: Routledge, 2000), 235.

CHAPTER TWO

◦—

Post or Perish: The New Media Schooling of the Amateur Pornographer

This chapter presents the works of amateur pornographers engaged in the production and consumption of mediated sex scenes as web-based performances or homemade filmmaking. These skillful amateurs constitute a wave of savvy media practitioners who make products around their candid bodies and sex acts, thus challenging the business goals and performance management of commercial pornography. Their efforts are not to be confused with individuals who pose for porn sites and simulate sex as "glossy amateurs"—bored housewives, horny freshmen, nasty teen virgins, battered Russian migrants, pregnant mommies, crude aunts, or rapist uncles. In most of these cybertypes of commercial porn, amateur roles are scripted, filmed, and edited by producers who direct and pay models to step into their stage setups and play a part in the sex scenes. Real amateurs, on the other hand, are sexually driven consumers as well as media practitioners and producers who make sex scenes to explore personal desires and respond to cultural phantasms as mechanisms of power. They use low-budget cameras to capture moments and then screen the scenes privately or in small groups or upload them to the global web through webcams, live journals, and weblogs (blogs).

Looking at concepts and profiles for amateurs and their ways of having sex, the chapter focuses on their performative schooling in new media. Amateur pornographers thus live the premises of Jon McKenzie's performance theory, developed in his study *Perform or Else: From Discipline to Performance*. They thrive on complex sexual feedback loops, as participants negotiate small-scale business deals and love contracts to steer desire and relationships with partners. They also initiate collaborative work practices that produce the "pornographic contract" between producers and consumers of amateur pornography. The chapter features case studies of independent porn sites, sex/porn bloggers, hyper-sexed porn activists Darrell Hamamoto, Ricky Lee, and Annabel Chong, and new media artists Isaac Leung, Tanya Bezreh, and Barbara DeGenevieve. It also includes an analysis of the HBO TV program *Porn 101: Exxxtra Credit*, a special edition of the magazine-style show *Real Sex* that highlights a group of Boston-based amateur pornographers.

Will the True Amateur Please Stand Up?

Pornography is witnessing a return to one of its original meanings, as a representation of sex acts shared among peer communities. Pornography is an amorphous bundle of sex scenes, as modes of sharing homemade sexually explicit media are being re-appropriated by web users who act out unscripted roles and personal aesthetics. Web users respond with mixed feelings to the manufactured stars and starlets of commercial pornography, knowing that their actual sex bodies occupy a space of learning and experiment. They collaborate in gift economies or Internet piracy as a distinctive culture, making homemade porn, art porn, or activist statements. In an article about gift economies on the Internet, Keith Hart writes that informal gift economies are expanding and are in dialectical relation with dominant capitalist economies, creating a moment of unique ownership:

> Even if the Internet is a creature of capitalism, there have always been strategies for ordinary people to claw back something of the value of what they produce. When such practices are identified as "the informal economy," we can only note that what was taken in the 70s to be an insignificant sector of the total economy is today recognized to be very large in scope at all levels including the global. So it is possible for prac-

tices which are objectively minor to provide a site in which alternatives to the currently dominant economic form are developed.[1]

But who are netporn's true amateurs and how do their practices add up to alternative porn economies and culture? Commercial netporn is cashing in on the burgeoning appeal of amateur pornography, creating lush commodities for consumers to browse and consume. Most Internet porn feeder sites and pay sites today offer huge collections of "amateurs." Still, if we take a closer look at those amateurs, we can see that they follow the compliant scripts of commercial pornography. They seduce clients disguised as "horny college girls, nasty teen virgins, bored housewives, or battered Russian migrants." They act out first-person scenes in dorm rooms, kitchens, streets, and cars, but they do not make autonomous decisions about how to act out amateurism or how to frame and sell it to audiences.

Besides those fake or glossy amateurs, the Internet has also spawned a wide range of independent producers as solo-amateurs or hosts/hostesses of amateur portals. Following Jane Duvall's recommendations on the website Jane's Net Sex Guide, solo-amateur sites are the more personable sites while amateur portals feature different models. Both solo-amateurs and amateur portals offer a person-next-door look to the models, instead of the glossier, airbrushed type of commercial porn. The solo-amateurs include blogging sites like www.candyposes.com, a young feminist porn site offering a mixture of naked photographs and politics. In an entry on June 11, 2006, Candy shares her insecurities about becoming a porn model: "At times I can't believe that I, a self proclaimed über-feminist, chose to participate in such a hobby. Modeling? The poisonous industry that chews girls up and spits them out? How dare I! I know that I'll never be a runway or commercial model, which is really what people mean when they say 'model.' But the fact that I'm participating in something that requires me to rely on how I look is . . . surprising, to say the least." Candy is critical of the industry yet curious to learn a few skills about how to make a public appearance and how to model her naked body. Candy is also known for her rebellious site www.seecandybleed.com, where she depicts and analyzes her menstrual blood—for instance, by painting geometrical shapes on her body.

There are other young feminists such as Toxy of www.toxywonderland
.com, who reveasl herself with melted ice cream all over her face. Others
are the more mature suburban or outdoors exhibitions, such as the South
West Scottish amateur exhibitionist Lynn, who has been posting her
naked pictures for seven years. There are amateurs with big bodies, such
as BBW (Big Beautiful Woman) Ana, and Furry of www.furrygirl.com,
who proudly displays her unwieldy pubic hair and unshaven legs. Absent
in the solo-amateur landscape are women of color or straight men who
pose for women.

The amateur compilations are owned by webmistresses who collaborate with models who act out a variety of body types and genres, such
as busty amateurs (women with large breasts), chained girls (bondage
women), Amazonia mixed wrestling (fights between men and women
where women come out on top), erotic red (women having fun while
menstruating), or East Coast gang-bang boys (married white women
having sex with Black males while their husbands are watching). In the
last site, the models are a group of Black men who "aim to fulfill all of
women's sexual fantasies. Their specialties are: Interracial, Breeding
wives, Girlfriends, Single Ladies, and Cuckold hubbies who want to see
their wives thoroughly serviced." The preview photos show interracial
sex scenes and the site asks interested amateurs to submit images of
their male or female partners.

The website www.bellavendetta.com has a more artistic design and
features models with punk hairstyles, tattoos, piercings, colorful stockings, and punk rock attitudes. This site is a more mature and audacious
sister version of the altporn/indieporn cluster described in chapter 1.
The site www.amateurprize.com does not feature amateur "models" but
is 100 percent real amateur. It asks people from all over the world to
submit their amateur photos and compete for a $50 weekly prize. The
site does not require a membership and anybody can easily post photographs on an unmoderated blog. The photos show mundane bodies and
sex poses; they also receive extensive comments from fellow viewers
and submitters. The amateur bodies are plain, sweet, nonthreatening,
and communicative, promising an image exchange that can lead to significant relationships.

Independent producers make pornography mainly to control the imaging process and to reap the benefits of a lucrative e-commerce. What

they cannot control entirely is the quickly changing "pornographic contracts," or impact of e-commerce and flows of desire between consumers. As shown in the example of www.amateurprize.com, the average consumer of amateur porn ought to exchange images and thus become an amateur pornographer himself/herself. Both producers and consumers are active web users schooled in social networking and sexual representation within digital networks. Their cooperation as shared self-imaging and gift economies have started to traverse the dominant industries to hatch new moments of pleasure and alternative economy. Amateur pornography thus weaves little knots inside the e-commerce clusters, as web users are invested in gifts as widely circulating sexual energies.

Pornography is simultaneously made and consumed by a wide range of web users on p2p file-sharing platforms, video-sharing sites, blogging sites or blog rings, Usenet groups and nudity-chatting (webcam) sites, sex-activist sites, fan communities, and media art. These strands of amateurism are crucial to a future definition of netporn, and its agents live the premises as set forth by Jon McKenzie: The era of performance is characterized by subjects entering a multiplicity of spaces and performance strata. Performance strata are the layers of forces and intensities that give form to matter by organizing small molecular entities into aggregations. The performance strata bundle a variety of cultural, organizational, and technological performances as discursive and embodied working methods. McKenzie explains that the agents of the performance strata harbor multiple forms of normativity, while recognizing cracks, fissures, and "outside" discourses as significant agents.

McKenzie summarizes his thesis as follows: "Performance will be to the twentieth and twenty-first centuries what discipline was to the eighteenth and nineteenth, an onto-historical formation of power and knowledge."[2] Rather than viewing web users as citizens who are ruled by monolithic aggregations of powers, they can be seen as micro-niche communities of performativity and normativity. There is no cohesive voice in these strata, as they thrive on a further dissolution of grand narratives of art, science, and political ideology, a moment in intellectual history labeled by Jean-François Lyotard in 1985 as the postmodern condition. The strata are cultivated and solidified by an attentiveness to the active-performative nature of language and bodily gestures, which are developed as modes of efficiency in corporate-organizational settings, as modes of creativity and competence in technology and art, and generally as a new attitude toward social-sexual networking and cultural vitality. Work ethics, the use of technological languages, and social and intellectual curiosities intermingle and intersect to become strata of power and knowledge.

In these performance strata of the porn economies, agents have distinctive ways of negotiating their pornographic roles and cyber-responsibilities. Whereas nation-state governments and capitalist porn industries are arguably organized by the older "discipline or punish" maxim in which consolidated empires decide to "push down" content onto consumers (or punish consumers who access porn illegally in surveilled places), the performance strata thrive on a different type of consumerism. In the performance strata, web users negotiate and articulate everyday fluctuations of their sexual relationships and pornographic roles. To perform on the web means entering the fields of competency and communication, which include a sharing of porn as personal-social activities and developing mediated work and play practices. Therefore, porn consumers are likely to be McKenzie's performers, web users who access, trade, and make porn outside of the legitimate netporn industries.

We thus encounter a true gestation of this paradigm of skilled amateur pornographers. Larger groups of web users are getting schooled and technologically skilled in methods of sharing and producing products, hence their advanced performativity can be seen as a knot in the system—and a threat to capitalist industries or anti-pornography legislation.

Publish or Perish: Sex Bloggers at the Cocktail Party

In order to grasp the power of bloggers as performative amateurs, we ought to look at the quality of their products and everyday behaviors. Clay Shirky proposes that successful and meaningful performance on the web entails a cocktail-party model of performativity and social networking. The model implies that web users learn how to make small talk and move between parties, relating to ephemeral modes of chitchat or ongoing debate. In this model of performance, web users are dispersed micro-niche agents who feed into organized public culture.

According to Shirky, the cocktail-party model of performance involves acts of sharing products as a labor of love that cannot be easily co-opted by commercial industries. Even though the occasional blog may have a mass following or may aspire to reach the more high-ranking status of *celebrity* that sometimes leads to book publications, "pure" bloggers are amateurs whose journals are linked to those of friends, peers, or people with similar interests. As Shirky writes:

> The vast majority of weblogs are amateur and will stay amateur, because a medium where someone can publish globally for no cost is ideal for those who do it for the love of the thing. Rather than spawning a million micro-publishing empires, weblogs are becoming a vast and diffuse cocktail party, where most address not the masses but a small circle of readers, usually friends and colleagues. This is mass amateurization, and it points to a world where participating in the conversation is its own reward.[3]

In a typical sex or porn blog, ordinary individuals' sexually explicit body images are revealed through daily writing modes and they receive feedback from other web users. Take for instance the portal site www .sexblo.gs with links to dispersed bloggers who post sexually explicit images as part of personal journals or do-it-yourself magazines. The site is announced as a montage, or a putting together of smaller items, including "Art Nudes, Art of Love, Everyday Nakedness, Fleshbot, Geisha Asobi, Sexoteric, Sensual Liberation Army, Sexual Liberation, etc." For example, the site Art Nudes is managed by curator-photographer Michael Barnes, who is a fervent uploader of art photographs of nudes submitted by artists from all over the world. His profile indicates that he is a semi-professional photographer based in Canada who manages the site in collaboration with his friends—photographers based in the United States, the Netherlands, and Portugal. Art Nudes seeks to collect the work of photographers internationally and invites submissions according to certain rules. For instance, Art Nudes refuses to take submissions in the lower categories of "erotic titillation, glamour, or photographs from pay porn sites." The blog started in 2003 and receives about three thousand visitors daily. Looking at the published demographics of the site, one can see that visitors are located primarily in the United States and Europe, yet sporadic visitors come from more exotic locations, including the

Occupied Palestinian Territory, Libyan Arab Jamahiriya, Myanmar, Azerbaijan, Kyrgyzstan, Ethiopia, and the Vatican City State.

One of the activist sites is the Sensual Liberation Army (sensual lib.com) and it has a hardcore sister site, the Sexual Liberation Army. Both sites offer a mixture of pinup photos and links to progressive news sources and political activist sites. The SLA pinups are posted by Pagan Moss, who contributes sexy and authentic female nudes under the slogan "The revolution will be sensualized." The objectives of Moss's revolution are not clear, but her photographs show a unique and eclectic collection of blissful and proud naked females. The SLA also offers stories about current U.S. anti-pornography politics with attention-grabbing headlines, such as "The Anti-Kinsey Report" and "Parents Win Rare Victory in Canceling of Sexy Dolls." The SLA sites copy the design of commercial porn sites but also link to selections of peer bloggers and indie pornographers, such as Furry at www.furrygirl.com.

Important to the history of these oddball bloggers would be the efforts of pioneering webcam pioneers such as Ana Voogt of www.anacam .com and Jennifer Ringley of www.jennicam.com. Their websites documented everyday domestic activities through webcams and included light nudity or sex scenes taking place in the shower or bedroom. The purpose of the webcam was not to focus on sex, but sex was shown to be part of the grind of life. Ringley started the site in 1996 when she was a student, and her acts of exhibitionism appeared at irregular intervals, when she was walking around her house naked, sitting on the couch, or taking a shower. Ringley became a much-reported vanguard webcammer and received plenty of feedback from friends, fellow webcammers, and the more distant masses of web users. When the report of the closure of her site in 2001 appeared on major news sites such as CNN.com, slashdot.com, and the BBC News, under the story "R.I.P. Jennicam," she received the following comments: "I'll miss you. You were like a real friend and lover to me, we spent countless hours together on your couch and in your bed. Marius, England." Marius's comment precedes a snide remark by Alfred: "Shows there is nothing special about some pioneers. This is an age of success for the clearly ordinary person. Alfred, Gibraltar."[4]

In another corner of the cocktail party, artists are brainstorming and planning to make artfully hacked versions of pornographic idols and stars. In 2001, media art curator Anne-Marie Schleiner started a web art project to attract web users to share and modify Japanese dolls, that is, pornographic cartoon characters. She wanted to explore the viral life and aesthetics of these circulating commodities, since she had observed that web users had started to exchange such images. A peculiar doll network emerged through Schleiner's World KiSS Project, which included web users in Japan and internationally. Schleiner asked participants to be creative and feel free to change the sexual orientation of the dolls: "The process of creativity employed by KiSS artists is a form of cultural sampling, hacking, and appropriation, a form of play from which new configurations emerge." The KiSS art consumers are producers of new versions of the dolls. They can hack the image and insert their own gender or queer porn fantasies. Schleiner actually advises them to be creative and disrespect prepackaged notions of sexiness prepared by the industry.[5]

A similar media art project documenting viral aesthetics among web-sharing communities was initiated by Francesca da Rimini in the mid-1990s, when she visited bulletin boards and chat rooms to develop sexual fantasies in collaboration with other web users. Her project resulted in intimately shared fantasy stories of seduction and cybersex, which further resulted in the making of websites and an unpublished book "FleshMeat." The correspondence was carried out in collaboration with other web users on a daily basis. As she writes:

> From the outset I was blown away by the trust and the commitment to the game, the contract, the obligations that my playmates offered me. The gift was theirs, and also mine, it was a field of reciprocal exchange, a free trade zone. I felt free to use the gifts I had been given as source material for both my book *FleshMeat*, and online projects such as *dollspace* and *princess valium*. The contracts I established with my playmates allowed me to use transcripts of our correspondences and online interactions in whichever way I chose, and it was understood that I had an editorial power, but not the right to alter their words. I had no interest in making a direct financial profit from these gifts, it wasn't part of the deal.[6]

In da Rimini's homepage, www.sysx.org/gashgirl, one can see archives of her correspondence with web users willing to enter and perform for her "free trade" zone. In more contemporary story-writing sites, such as literotica.com, people write chain stories in collaboration with other writers. Literotica.com wants to provide an unorthodox and image-free web space. However, these stories are nonetheless published within the customary categories of porn, including "Erotic Couplings—Wild one-on-one consensual sex (17,523 stories); Incest/Taboo—Keeping it in the family (11,191 stories); Group Sex—Orgies, swingers, and others (7,384 stories); and BDSM—Bondage, D/s, and other power games (8,691 stories)."[7] Some of the more prolific authors submit entire novels in a chapter-by-chapter mode, though the editors often reclassify the chapters into the standardized porn encyclopedia. In the category Celebrities we find fantasies about the sex lives of celebrities and pop stars. Writers interweave personal fantasies with stories about sex bombshells like Madonna and Britney Spears and animated heroines and heroes such as Snow White and the X-Men; they speculate about the enigmatic cult detective Hercule Poirot.[8] The site is geared mostly toward amateur writers and readers who are eager to develop stories within an image-free environment. The site is also free of popup advertising and encourages members to engage in free-speech activism. The site stimulates social and intellectual dialogue among users through its requirement that users post feedback to other writers.

In the era of performance strata, these miscellaneous groups of web users are being perhaps paradoxically trained as skilled amateurs. They cultivate significant nodes of competency within the porn industry clusters. However, they also insert personal quirks and meanderings within democratized porn zones, where previously excluded individuals and groups can participate. For instance, women as independent models have come to fruition alongside the development of early webcam technologies and shared acts of chatting and storytelling. The performance status of the porn amateur does not equal the stereotype of a financially lucrative sexbomb or a helpless porn voyeur, but it is a different type of cooperative web agency. Amateur pornography thrives on a new economy of sharing products and maintaining status within micro-niche groups of web users.

Porn/sex bloggers are socially responsible web users who mutually share products while discussing ethical views and controversies. However, it has become apparent that their participation in larger popular networks such MySpace and YouTube is causing public outrage and right-wing protest. These social networking websites offer an interactive network of videos, photos, blogs, user profiles, groups, and internal email systems. They have currently outstripped competitors such as Friendster and LiveJournal to become the most popular English-language social networking websites with extremely high traffic and millions of registered accounts. Media and conservative groups have criticized the sites due to members' posting homemade pornography or pirated commercial pornography. YouTube is a video-sharing site for members to broadcast themselves by uploading homemade videos and excerpts of pirated products. The site has a very smooth, user-friendly interface that allows users to easily upload, download, and watch submitted videos. The sites announce a mass-scale technical revolution, hence the terms of service are conservative and prohibit people "to submit material that is unlawful, obscene, defamatory, libelous, threatening, pornographic, harassing, hateful, racially or ethnically offensive, or encourages conduct that would be considered a criminal offense, give rise to civil liability, violate any law, or is otherwise inappropriate."[9] But many members have disregarded the clause on pornography and use the site to freely exchange excerpts of porn videos. In doing a search on the word *spanking* one can find nearly three hundred movies, which are mostly homemade short films but also including excerpted scenes from popular anime and TV programs. In the category *porn*, however, we can see that aside from a few videos about stars, people have mostly posted witty and creative hacks of mainstream pornography. The shared products reveal viral aesthetics. People mimic each other's products and make slight deviations, as is evidenced in the large collection of porn movies made with Barbie dolls and stuffed animals. Other viral video art is produced on a parody theme song called "The Internet Is for Porn." Finally, oddball contributions appear on the site in the shape of porn rapping, porn confession, and a snippet of documentary footage showing two American girls driving by an adult video store, then bursting out in laughter when passing a road sign that says "Stop the Porn. Be Reborn—Jesus."

Peer-to-Peer Empires and the Unreturnable Gift

Pornography has been an important part of the success story of social networks and p2p file-trading platforms, which now constitute the major gift economies on the Internet. For decades, web users have traded pirated versions of porn and developed collaborative-creative work practices around products. As I have shown before, performing well within a digital network means learning how to plot a course in technological skill development, social networking, and public sexual representation. Performing well also means giving feedback to products and peers, participating in forums, or trading files as "gifts." In May 2002, there were reports that the golden age of online porn trade was in decline, precisely because it had become harder for businesses to convert web users into paying members.[10] Web users find free porn images as teasers on privately managed feeder sites such as www.sublime directory.com (with 10,903 pages of "true" amateur porn) or www .frogsex.com. They also typically trade porn on p2p networks and file-sharing programs such as Napster, Morpheus, Grokster, KaZaA, and BitTorrent. Users access these platforms to share a wide range of pirated products, including vast collections of commercial pornography.

In *Connected, or What It Means to Live in Network Society*, Steven Shaviro theorizes about "the gift" within a liminal or unreal sphere of network society, arguing that network technologies have perfected the creation of luxury and squandering in humans. Using the theories of Georges Bataille, Shaviro sees web users as cultivating an awareness of their role as squandering among excess and the surplus of gifts. Mark Dery equally cites the acting out of excess as a cultural performance: A web-based exhibitionism and voyeurism of excess goes hand in hand with an appearance of its grotesque variations. As he writes:

> Despite the right's unflagging efforts to turn back the clock to the days when people put pantalets on piano legs, we're living in the Age of the Golden Shower, a heyday of unabashed depravity (at least in terms of online scopophilia and virtual sex) that makes de Sade's *120 Days of Sodom* look like *Veggie Tales*. The divine Marquis never imagined aquaphiliacs, a catch-all category that includes guys whose hearts leap up when they behold babes in bathing caps, fanciers of underwater cat-fights, connoisseurs of submarine blowjobs, breath-holding fetishists, fans of simulated drowning, and weirdest of all, people who get off on swimming and showering fully clothed, like Rein, the guy in Amsterdam who likes to take a dip now and then in "business suits, dress shirts, and suit jackets—especially the ones with two vents."[11]

The grotesque epitomizes a self-aware culture of excess and humiliation in the eye of the mainstream moral viewer. Dery mentions the "Breast Expansion Morph" posted by Mr. Licker, which shows a woman kneeling backwards on a beach chair, showing her genitals while looking around and facing the camera. Her breasts extend all the way from her body onto the surrounding lawn, many feet away. In this picture, we are exposed to the strange fantasies of Mr. Licker, a web user who captures and shares images of his woman's morphed body. The fantasy of perfectly altered breasts is a common obsession today, as breast implants have become the most common form of plastic surgery, especially among porn stars. But the breast-expansion morph symbolizes our fascination with imperfect or grotesque breast alteration. The dark soul of Mr. Licker increases the breast size of his woman to such an extent that she is exposed as almost handicapped and unable to move her body. Dery believes that netporn has developed a nasty-performative streak where web users expose their grotesque fantasies with lovers as a ritualized theater of humiliation. Dery relates this tendency to sensational porn sites such as www.thatsfuckedup.com, and he cites the image of a "prone woman, presumably an Iraqi, whose leg is a bloody stump, blown off by a land mine. Under the hem of her skirt, we can see her vagina. . . . 'Nice Puss—bad foot,' reads the wisecracking caption."[12] He relates the politically incorrect joke to the advent of warporn—the sharing of images of war torture and violence as an erotic/pornographic obsession.

Bataille wrote that humans will cultivate excess since they never will find sufficient opportunities to break even within the modern economies of leisure. Hence, they have to resort to intensified gestures or performance modes to channel excess. In *The Accursed Share: Volume 1: Consumption*, Bataille questions how the determination of excess energy circulating in the biosphere is altered by human activity. He juxtaposes secular economy with general economy, postulating that the latter has less-restrictive ways of channeling or utilizing excess energy. Whereas modern economies are founded on a pietistic moral code that condemns idleness and luxury and affirms the value of enterprise, general economy is based on the notion of excessive gifts, which can only be consumed in a different manner. The gift enhances a performed consumerism and leads to a process of self-consciousness, or ritualized enactment of a culture's high point of exuberance, ecstasy, or intensity. The awareness of a culture's "accursed share" is absent in capitalist economies that channel excessive energy by other means, such as warfare. Bataille was interested in the Native American potlatch as a ritual of gift-giving, practiced by the tribes of the Pacific Northwest coast. The potlatch is a way to assert excessive wealth, not in order to gain profit or equal return, but to engage in symbolical alliances. The gift of potlatch is lavish and by its nature cannot be returned in an equal manner. It can only be answered or reciprocated eventually in a performative-symbolical manner.

Gift exchange supplements commodity exchange in that it aims to construct a mechanism of social cohesion rather than economic utility or profit. John Frow's theory of the gift in *Time and Commodity Exchange* borrows insights from Bataille and Jacques Derrida, as well as Annette Weiner's anthropological study on inalienable possessions in Oceania and Aboriginal Australian cultures. Weiner's study of the gift shows that inalienable possessions go beyond a law of reciprocity, as they are the object of most intense desire.[13] In Maori cultures, for instance, women's production of a certain type of cloth becomes uniquely important because it is imbued with a procreative power and requires a specific type of guardianship that turns into rank.[14] Social networking and desire are enhanced by the practice of gift-giving, as material entities are used to influence social-psychological modalities and the spirits of the gods. In traditional societies, acts of prostitution or porn consumption are often hidden away from public culture and would be reserved to secret societies, most often in the male-only domains.

In network society, we are witnessing a reversal of the gender and moral status of these societies as micro-niche consumers participate in the sharing of products and fetishes. The circulation of homemade products or pirated products is almost always tied to intimate private exchanges and desire. In "Can Desire Go On without a Body? Pornographic Exchange and the Death of the Sun," Dougal Phillips proposes a theory of desire based on his case study of the BitTorrent forum Empornium.[15] He defines desire as energy flows in which units of complexities and quantities of sexual energies are invested. These energy flows can survive the "death of the sun" or a material transformation of the body or economies. The data that have been released through porn networks are complex bundles of energies that can no longer be seen as entities distinct from the body: "Networked computers are giving rise to self-perpetuating economies of data, driven in the first instance (currently) by human bodily desire but beginning, it would seem, to take on a 'life' of their own."[16] Phillips observes p2p trading as a near-perfect manifestation of pornography and proposes the idea that the surplus of desire can outlive material transformations.

Investigating p2p porn as an instance of sexual squandering and a sharing of desire, it is interesting to analyze the rhetoric used by the designers of the p2p protocols. As explained on the BitTorrent (BT) homepage, the protocol is viewed by the makers as a free-speech tool, whose implementation is based on an ethos of sharing or cooperative distribution: "With BitTorrent, those who get your file tap into their upload capacity to give the file to others at the same time. Those that provide the most to others get the best treatment in return. ('Give and ye shall receive!')"[17] The protocol works by members "seeding" files that can be accessed by all other members. Each member can access different parts of the file from different seeders and can become a seeder once a complete copy of the file has been downloaded. The BitTorrent protocol enables the simultaneity and multiplicity of downloading and uploading torrents, thus making for a much faster file-sharing experience. For instance, web users can download an entire feature-length porn movie in about thirty minutes, depending on the speed of the Internet connection and how many other members are downloading files at the same time.

In the site user guidelines of Empornium, it is stated that web users who are "leeches," those who download programs without uploading, will be banned from the site: "Seed your posts until at least 2–3 others have the file. At a minimum, torrents must be seeded to at least 1 iteration, meaning at least 1 other person has the complete file. Strategic seeding (seeding to 95% and intentionally stopping) violates this rule."[18] Strategic seeders are frowned upon, while heavy seeders are clearly rewarded by the community by the status of "e-penis" or "e-cock." In one of the most popular BT forums in Hong Kong, www .uwants.com, members purchase movies by using credit points. They lose credits when they have downloaded the torrents, but may win them back by writing feedback on the post. Since writing feedback is an easy way to win back credits, the messages are impersonal and short. It is almost like saying, "Thank you, that is just what I wanted" after buying a product from a shopkeeper. Members write one-liners to quickly thank uploaders, comment on the products, and maintain their credit balance. Needless to say, they will never be able to return the gift of free porn.

The members of the BT forums are industrious workers and squandering humans, as they post products that include self-made descriptions and previews, thumbnails or trailers, or scanned-in movie covers, with web links to the official company website. Some members also volunteer to be administrators of the forums and to monitor other members. They carry out all kinds of duties, including warning and banning members who post illegal content or fake information. They post the BT regulations for each of the forums. They also give ratings to the content and rank some of the products according to the download statistics and their personal tastes.

For instance, on March 31, 2006, one of the thumbs-up sex movies was a Japanese story of the rape of a female reporter when she was interviewing somebody. Other thumbs-up movies had been tapped from major American, European, and Japanese porn empires, including the Peeping Tom videos that are shot illegally with tiny cameras hidden behind the fixtures of hotel rooms, saunas, or toilets. Several episodes of Japanese Peeping Toms are available on the www.uwants.com forum. The episodes show unedited long shots of Japanese women visiting saunas and getting dressed and undressed in locker rooms. Since the women are totally unaware of the presence of the camera, the viewers are invited to follow the intrusive camera-eye. We may disagree with the practice but do get an antidotal view to manufactured pornography—the camera-eye showing a raw or refreshing picture of the erotic, naked body. The women's panties are mostly plain white cotton and the women have bushes of pubic hair. The camera-eye is nasty and unethical in its acquisition of shots, but the bodies and scenery are more resistant than porn, showing women of all ages getting dressed and undressed, zooming in on their relaxed frolicking, or self-absorbed individual soaping and showering, or playing with their skin and bodies.

As of March 2006, it is illegal in Hong Kong to use the BitTorrent software for uploading or downloading such files, though the police are precisely on the outlook for uploaders, those rewarded within the gift economy of BT forums. In November 2005, a Hong Kong court sentenced a man to three months in prison in what was believed to be the first jailing for sharing film files over the BitTorrent network. Chan Nai-Ming was an unemployed thirty-eight-year-old man who called himself "Big Crook" and was jailed for uploading three Hollywood films onto the Internet through BT. Chan was arrested in January 2005 and was charged that April for uploading *Daredevil, Miss Congeniality*, and *Red Planet* without a license by using the BT peer-to-peer file-sharing program.[19] This case initially had a chilling effect on file-sharing groups, but the uploading/downloading activity resumed normal activity within three months. However, secondary schools have started anti-piracy campaigns and Hong Kong's primary ISP, Netvigator.com, has blocked all of its clients' access to BT. Meanwhile, large groups of web users have managed to break through the technical blocks and keep trading files during high-traffic hours, when it would be harder for police to track individual file-sharers. Not only do Hong Kong file-sharers break the law in order to get free products but they are also invested in the new behavioral traits of porn trading. They access materials while carrying out attitudes of excess to maintain their status within the community and help run a powerful exchange of desire.

Not Hard, Not Soft, But Realcore

One result of this trend has been a further splintering and diversification of the established porn categories, a surfacing of porn around less mainstream bodies and desires. Italian porn analyst Sergio Messina has defined the postmodern or dissolved porn as *realcore*. Realcore reaffirms authenticity in a media-saturated society. It also fulfills two of the original missions of the Internet: to connect special interest groups and to encourage do-it-yourself media making. Realcore members mostly behave well, moderate each other's submissions, or stimulate each other within their newly found communities. As Messina explains: "They know each other, masturbate to each other's pictures (often of each other's wives). In some cases, they have been in contact for years. Also, sometimes they meet and swing (if they're swingers) or do fetish stuff, gang bangs, etc."[20] Just like the p2p file-sharers, they are industrious workers who take their growing porn identities and porn collections very seriously. They exchange missing parts of a series to bolster each other's collections and organize massive reposts on special topics that allow them to rearrange their collections.

Realcore fits into the paradigm of gift economies, as people react to each other's movies and photographs by masturbating and offering something in return. They excessively communicate with each other by sending feedback or gifts. For instance, as Messina further explains, "a man may send a couple some women's shoes he's got a kink about. They then post a picture in response featuring the new present and a thank-you note." Realcore website members write to each other about what they would like to see, receive the gift, and send a sign of appreciation. A variation of this practice is the wish list, or a list of presents someone may want, with links to online shops that sell those items. Often there is an online exchange about the gift, such as a picture or a webcam session, in which the object one may have bought for somebody makes a new appearance in cyberspace. People often write messages to each other by holding signs or writing on their naked bodies, thus revealing the actual body as the messenger of the return gift.

Messina became interested in this new type of economy when he found strange collections of pictures on a Usenet group, which included—for example—a picture of a housewife showing off a rubber glove. He then realized people were actually sharing photographs of sexual desires. These fetishes are widely varied and specialized. For instance, on an average day in the spring of 2006, the "breast" group included "breasts, large (331); breasts, natural (340); breasts, saggy, (234); and breasts, small (496)." Saggy breasts have a peculiar type of resonance within this group, even though they are widely frowned upon in the commercial porn industry, which requires its models to artificially augment the aging breast with implants. Within the erotic gay male group, one can find varieties such as "male, anal; male, bodybuilder; male, bodybuilder, moderated; male, chubby; male, hard-on; male, oral; male, oral, cumshots; male, piercing; male, shirt-and-tie; male, tattoos; and male, underwear." This forum includes realcore products like chubby or obese body types and those who have a kink for men in office work attire.

How do people perform in Usenet groups or why do people reveal their tastes and fetishes to each other? First, as we have seen in the example of the video-sharing on YouTube, members mimic each other's products and aesthetics; as realcore models, they perform improvised variations on an ongoing theme. According to Messina, a second characteristic of the performance is to give as much evidence as possible of the authentic sexual interaction (and often bond) between web users. Thus, the photographs and movies give evidence of eye contact between models and producers; they document ongoing conversations and shy away from professional modes of acting. Are they at all influenced by, or do they mimic the roles and gestures of, commercial porn models? Messina does not believe so, as he explains: "Often people are too excited to think about acting. So, as far as I can see, people seem to make their own original movies, and commercial porn genres have little influence on their porn identities. In my experience, I haven't seen one picture or film that tried to make an amateur version of commercial porn. Of course you have some topic images, like the facial cumshot, but the movies are almost always directed in a different way."[21]

As far as the gender status of performers is concerned, heterosexual realcore does reproduce gender stereotypes in that females are mostly shown as center-stage models and males as hidden camera operators or sidekicks. However, these straight amateurs are also testing out bisexual, polysexual, or sadomasochistic modes of performing and viewing. Women often comment erotically on the work of other females. Lesbian and female-to-male (FTM) transsexual models have started to attract comments from straight and gay male viewers. At the same time, lesbian and transgender pornographers are equally exploring aspects of the realcore paradigm.

One of the pioneering porn sites for queer amateur porn was www .ssspread.com, launched in January 2001 by Barbara DeGenevieve, professor at the School of the Art Institute of Chicago, in collaboration with Terry Pirtle.[22] The site was disbanded in January 2004 when the ssspread .com team decided to start producing and distributing porn videos and made *Full Load*. DeGenevieve explains her early ambitions: "We wanted to create a space on the web that would feel comfortable for dykes and transpeople. It would be a membership pay site but without distracting advertisements, where people would be themselves and their bodies represented in porn."[23] The team encouraged queer and transgendered people in the Chicago area to submit porn stories and organized film shoots where people could act out their scenarios. The outcome of this process was uploaded on the site as a weekly slide show.

The site was primarily marketed toward butch-dyke lesbians and FTM transgendered individuals, encouraging them to become producers and consumers of porn and catered to paying members of the web community. The ssspread.com site solicited models who agreed to be showcased on the site, who were paid a nominal amount of money for each film shoot ($75 per person per shoot), and who did not conform to beauty norms. For instance, in the "Road Side Service" slide show posted on October 30, 2003, Chicago-based singer Nomy Lamm acts out a macho-redneck scenario. As a "male trucker," she receives a blowjob from her "transman" partner. She then penetrates the partner anally with a dildo on the car hood, only to finally reveal her "true" phallus in the form of a "real" amputated leg. The members gave feedback to the weekly still images by writing messages on a message board.

DeGenevieve, as a videographer, explains her collaborative process with members who volunteered as models:

> I usually collaborated with the people that I am filming, and I asked them ahead of time to carefully consider what they want to do in the session. Very often, I just left the scene up to them, or they came up with a scenario that we discussed beforehand. I would add something to it or ask them to do something slightly different. But, of course, I myself could never come up with the variety of scenarios that they came up with. A lot of people I shot were young and into punk aesthetics. The environments they lived in are definitely not mainstream, and this became part of the ambience of a shoot. Yesterday, I shot in a model's kitchen. It was a pretty chaotic environment, with dishes in the sink, food remnants on the countertops and floors, and stuff all over the place. There was another shoot a couple months ago in a room where I literally couldn't see the floor for the clothes, CDs, magazines, over-flowing ashtrays, sex toys, pillows. . . . But I find these living spaces really fascinating because these are the places where people really have sex.[24]

Queer porn also differs from regular porn, according to De-Genevieve, in its portrayal of authentic or unusual rather then manufactured bodies, which she sees a sign of rebellion: "The bodies of queer porn are insubordinate, disobedient, unruly, insurgent and anarchistic. . . . Our bodies did not fit a mainstream perception of hot bodies, and therefore our audience was not the typical audience either."[25] The models agreed to showcase their unorthodox bodies and were willing to share them with others. DeGenevieve also observed within her ssspread.com community that most models were eager to embrace gender fluidity as a major aspect of the pornographic act, and thus models were creating complex gender roles as cultural narratives.

Another queer amateur site, nofauxxx.com (*nofauxxx* translates as *nofakes*), looks for concepts of authenticity in the model's ability to disagree with porn's main stereotypes. It is announced as a "woman-owned, subversive, underground porn site dedicated to destroying the stereotypes and hierarchies that exist in mainstream porn, as well as documenting the queer community, fulfilling its need for all-inclusive."[26] Nofauxxx.com also collaborates with the web-based porn distributor Blowfish.com to produce and distribute queer porn videos. Again, these videos are not made with professional models but with amateurs willing to submit ideas and collaborate on photo shoots. On the site's homepage, a casting call asks people to participate in making a new series of porn videos: "Diversity of age, size, gender, ability, sexual expression, and style is essential to the creation of a truly No Fauxxx production, so everybody is encouraged to apply." Heterosexual individuals can also apply but they have to stay away from vanilla themes: "as long as the theme/sexual acts performed maintain a strict distance from what is considered mainstream or straight sexual activity."[27] The intended effect of this kind of porn is not only arousal or documenting the queer body and community but also making general audiences question their own experiences with gender and power.

The second major difference between queer porn and regular porn is that power relations in queer porn are shaped as "play." Models may mimic hetero-normative gender relationships or even scenarios of violence, but they make the viewer aware of their constructed nature. As DeGenevieve writes: "Even when queer porn sets out to simulate violent scenes, even when the acts themselves are very similar to what might happen in straight porn, it is still unmistakably 'a scene.'" She explains that porn play does not aim to be a politically correct media culture, but lays bare perverted power relations or scenes of violence. In this way, queer porn touches on the essence of porn but creates a new type of awareness: "Embracing the need to objectify and be objectified, to fetishise and be fetishised, to play the willing victim as well as the victimizer, opens up a minefield that will be difficult to traverse, but it is a more intellectually provocative and honest terrain from which to understand who we are as complex sexual beings."[28] The complex scenarios are based on real desires and identities, but they are performative, that is, carried out by models who like to show multilayered sexual identities and power roles.

Whether models act out straight or queer identities and sex roles, the discriminating issue is striving for authenticity as a break from porn to show everyday relationships between partners as a knot within the smooth system of e-commerce. There is usually not a thirdhand party involved in the film shoot, as Messina explains: "The sexual scene is authentic when it would have taken place in the same way whether the photographer was there or not. Editing also is crucial: the less cuts you have, the more you can relate to a whole situation rather than the details."[29] The movies belong to an era of do-it-yourself consumer technologies, where people have become used to watching each other's unedited documentary footage. As Messina explains:

> Reality shows, surveillance cams, and webcams are all unedited products, and [are] much sought after in 2006. It is called "low quality versus high temperature content" and came into existence with news footage such as Rodney King, the tsunami disaster, etc. So if you like to shoot a movie of an orgy in a dark room, the only way you can do it is in night vision, and the image will turn out black and green and blurred. But it is real and the blurring is its proof. Darkroom mini-movies are much sought after: glory holes, dark rooms, porno cinemas, parking lots . . . if you're into reality, you can only get it "low-fi" and with real-looking people inside.[30]

Messina sees realcore as diversified and perpetually transforming web groups, whose users view pornographic expression as an everyday behavior rather than an experiment. He says: "It's something that has to do with digital tools. Many people make their own porn because now they can do that easily and discreetly. They see it as an everyday expression, rather than a special experiment. It is still a fringe culture but it's a bit like using Skype software to make Internet phone calls. Today it's a fringe, but tomorrow it might be the actual tool." The amateur clusters differ from commercial netporn in that they are more open to diverse sexual groups, subcultures, minorities, and gestures of rebellion and resistance.[31]

The Revolt of the Asian Porn Wo/Man

Amateur porn includes individuals or groups who may have traditionally been left out of public sexual imaging or been discriminated against within the industries. Take for example Darrell Hamamoto's yellow-porn movement, which he launched in 2003 with the movie *Skin-to-Skin*. This movie was a follow-up to his 1998 activist-intellectual manifesto about pornography. *Yellow Porn* stems from an urge to unleash and represent Asian American male bodies in pornography; the American porn industry has typically ignored them. Asian American men are the "eunuchs" of the American porn industry, where white males are typically featured with Asian girls. Hamamoto's idea of sexual revolt is to challenge the racial divide by producing a new line of Asian American–produced porn: "To engage more specifically in an Asian American porno practice is to take self-determined control of an unfixed, variable, malleable, but thoroughly radicalized human sexuality, shaped and constrained over time by politically oppressive forces."[32] Hamamoto uses the concept of radical jouissance to describe types of pornography able to contain a release of libidinal energy and awareness of sex political struggles.

In an essay and interview by Samantha Culp, Hamamoto explains that he was teaching the course Theoretical Perspectives in Asian American Studies when he asked his primarily Asian American students to discuss the types of bodies they found sexually attractive. He found that all the bodies were white. He saw that response as evidence of how powerful a white-supremacist complex is in the sexual fantasies of U.S. minorities.[33] Culp sees Hamamoto's yellow or golden porn as an astute response to a general lack of representation of ethnic minorities: "The adult world is hyper-saturated with images of the sexy and submissive Asian female, custom-tailored to the fetishes of their primarily white male consumers. And the Little China Dolls and Oriental Blossoms, not to mention their Blonde Cheerleader or Hot Chocolate or Tijuana Spice sisters, are always shown with big strong white guys, or sometimes African-American guys, maybe even Latinos but never with Asian-American dudes." Yellow porn is not only a politically astute discourse about multiculturalism in porn but also an angry outburst about the impact of media on survival and sexual well-being, and therefore an activist argument for DIY media making as a force that can positively alter personal and collective sentiments.

Culp relates Hamamoto's yellow porn to the more down-to-earth "yellow fuck" activism of Ricky Lee of Asian-Man.com. Ricky Lee became the first Asian American porn star on the Internet when, as an amateur pornographer, he started to upload photographs and videos of his multiple sex binges with women of different cultural backgrounds. However, as in traditional commercial gendered porn, the videos are shot with his own face absent or blurred, and a sharp focus on the bodies of his female prey. The site has had a large resonance on the web, specifically with other Asian American males who responded well to his line of sex activism. As he explains to Culp: "I got feedback from the guys who really wanted this, and I realized that it went deeper than porn. They felt they were misrepresented or oppressed, and it made me think about a lot of things. This is a real issue that a lot of Asian-American men face." He deals with the issues at hand through the creation of an alternative porn industry and unique type of dialogue between previously disconnected people.

The status of Asian American bodies in American porn has equally been addressed in the now historical work of Singapore-born porn star Annabel Chong, who agreed to make a gangbang movie for the American porn industry. Her concept was to try to have sex with three hundred men in one day. In doing this, she equally wanted to radiate an image of sexual pride, testing the limits of her body while questioning stereotypes of Asian female submissiveness. At the time of her gangbang preparations, Chong was a student in anthropology at the University of Southern California. In the documentary *Sex: The Annabel Chong Story*, she explains her work as an angry, yet deliberate, gesture to counter sex-negative ideas circulating in higher education classrooms.[34] Chong intended to encourage other people to be more comfortable and capable in sharing their sexual experiences. Her USC teachers were accepting of her ideas, yet it was the commercial porn producer John Bowen who materialized her dream. However, Bowen also made use of her by turning the gangbang video into a commodity for a mostly male consumer market. While she enjoyed being the star of the gangbang action and porn shoot—which had to be interrupted after 251 sessions because of the physical damage she sustained—she never received profit due from the movie *The World's Biggest Gang Bang*, which sold forty thousand copies during its first year of distribution. However, she came to terms with the fact that she had been financially exploited and does not fully regret having joined forces with John Bowen. She explains in another interview that she went home on the evening of the gang bang to finish writing a paper for one of her college classes.

Several years later, Chong's idea of having sex against the clock was taken up by Hong Kong–born artist Isaac Leung, whose nickname "Oriental Whore" grew out of his media art project *The Impossibility of Having Sex with 500 Men in a Month: I'm an Oriental Whore*. Raised in Hong Kong in a family of scientists and named after the Western god of science, Isaac Newton, Leung developed a nerdy identity from an early age. He also cultivated performative web browsing as an artist, while exploring everyday sex encounters with gay men on webcams. In the noncommercial gay webcam sites he visited, sex consumers participate in mutual masturbation sessions that are shown on a split-screen computer window. The pornographic exchange is an intimate media encounter between two people that is free of third-party control by a producer, director, or audiences. The performances themselves resemble the phallic-centric aesthetics of gay porn, focusing mostly on quick masturbation sessions leading to ejaculation and orgasm.

Leung is a very articulate and well-dressed person who lives in Hong Kong. His appearance and ideas show a real sense of wanting to speak to peripheral society. He admits that his artistic interest in sex stems from obsessive fantasizing about the perfect boy and dissatisfaction with his actual sex life. Leung was introduced to cybersex before he had any real sex, using easily accessible gay chat rooms on the web and affordable webcameras and videoconferencing software:

I started to experiment with web cams from a young age onward. I was using existing videoconference software such as NetMeeting, a very

Isaac Leung, video and art installation, The Impossibility of Having Sex with 500 Men in a Month: I'm an Oriental Whore, *Heaven Gallery, Chicago, 2003.*

popular software that splits your screen into two areas and has a chat box at the bottom of the screen. I would say that 90% of the people who use NetMeeting are there to have sex. If you click on an icon, a person shows up on your screen, which you can either ignore or accept for a sex session. But right away you can see yourself and the other person on the screen and based on that visual information, you can accept or ignore his identity. Then you can also start chatting immediately or talk to each other through a microphone.[35]

In his *Oriental Whore* art piece, Leung wanted to analyze his webcam experience as a gay Chinese man in the Western world, his awareness of AIDS, his compulsive sexual desires, and, subsequently, his repression. He disguised himself as an eighteen-year-old Japanese boy and worked daily to interact with gay cruisers (web surfers who openly look for sexual encounters, usually with the same gender) willing to accept his profile. He researched and categorized the cruisers by nationality, age group, weight, and other features. As he explains: "My research methodology worked as follows. I was masturbating and typing with one hand and recording information with the other hand. I was hiding my mouse yet opening other software for copying and pasting the images. I asked everybody about their age, where they came from, their height and their weight, their sexual orientation, and whether they were a 'top' or 'bottom.' These physical features are crucial within the gay community as cruisers are looking for nice bodies and muscular types. Of course there are also people who are attracted to chubby guys but they are kind of segregated."[36]

Leung's website records the daily development of his sex binge and an intricate struggle to carry through with the project to the very end. The diary items in particular reveal a frustrated attempt at materializing an artistic concept: "The project documents the collective experience of orgasm in virtual space. It creates a discourse of sexual politics in the context of post-colonial and interracial sexual relationships by showing my 'oriental' identity through my web camera." Leung did not have a collective experience nor did he make it to the end. He did realize his goals of researching ethnic profiles and the extent to which individuals were lying about their bodies: "People often lied about their dick size, because they say that it is at least nine inches long. That is a real joke in the gay webcam community, as you can see with your own eyes the discrepancy between the actual size and the advertised size."[37]

Other statistics in his research show that a majority of cruisers were married or bisexual men, mostly white, and between the ages of thirty and forty. Leung was emotionally disappointed to find out that so many men were older and that they wanted to be a "daddy" type of personality. He was only rarely meeting people in his own age group. Most men were from European countries such as Holland, Belgium, Germany, and Great Britain. There were also older men from Asian countries, with Hong Kong and Taiwan being the most common ones. He admits that this trend partly reflects the availability of the Internet in those cultures to middle-aged men of a certain social class, which thus became the default parameter of his research.

Most of the chat-room dialogue centered around a persuasion to show genitals, ejaculation, and cum. Leung explains that through the use of a webcam,

> the first thing you show people is your genitals, which is arguably the most private place that you have. It actually takes a long time for people to show their faces on a webcam, you have to actually push them to show their faces. You have to make people comfortable in order to get that result. But some people would get creative and show themselves sucking a remote, or something. . . . I was more interested in seeing the faces and the facial expressions. I was interested in seeing the entire environment around the body such as the bedroom. I was exploring a new kind of voyeurism and exhibitionism.

He writes in his journal about how he started to find the experiment depressing, as he did not find good connections with the participants. Even though he had very successful sexual experiences, they were after all too ephemeral: "In real life I have to work through stuff, dealing with my long-distance relationship and sexual frustrations." Even though he sobered up about finding perfect boys, or successfully dating white boys within the webcam community, Leung continues to want to make statements about his evolving sexual needs.

Back to the Porn Theater: Amateurs on the Big Screen

A parallel development to amateur groups on the web would be people wanting to screen their works in community centers or art house theaters, where the audience is invited to watch and share responses. This development has started to gain attention in the U.S. mass media with TV and film critics expressing both revulsion against and propulsion toward this trend. The pornographic scenes are transported from private video and web activity to larger public screenings in theaters, where they once belonged. In the Boston area, Kim Airs and the art house theater Coolidge Corner Cinema have started to organize annual screenings of amateur porn movies. This event, entitled *You Oughta Be in Pictures*, brings together unedited and more artistically composed porn movies. The producers are amateur porn makers, university students, artists, and queer producers of porn, while the spectators are art house consumers, gay/lesbian groups, general audiences, and voyeurs. The appeal of the event lies exactly in the odd mixture of makers and viewers, the untrained screen performers, and filmmakers, whose unpredictable movies cause exhilarating responses in the audience.

Audiences in these screenings are large and loud, at times shouting out their reactions or laughing hysterically at how the filmmakers conceive of sexual positions and camera angles. In some movies, the scenes fail to be explicit or dynamic at all. For example, a female masturbation scene shows a moving hand on a hidden vagina, where the soundtrack consists of quiet and camera-shy moaning. This is real amateur porn, a bundle of someone's sexual actions and their representation, prompting audiences to consider responses other than their own arousal and masturbation. As one man in the audience of the 2002 screening of *You Oughta Be in Pictures* describes: "I have seen pornography before. I've seen quite a bit of it. But this was unlike any of those experiences. I am not exactly sure what is different about it. But the response that it generated made me feel asexual." Another female respondent emphasizes the importance of humor in the implicit communication between the filmmakers and the viewers. As she writes: "But I think it was the humor part that I really enjoyed. It allows you to step back from all the taboo-ness of sex. There is a give and take in the sense that some filmmakers will poke fun at audience response by deliberately putting extreme images on screen, while audience members will, at points, poke fun at the filmmaker's attempt at sexiness at certain intervals."[39] Amateur porn does not always cater to physical arousal or masturbation but can trigger fulfilling reactions in audiences. Therefore, the screening gives amateur pornographers an opportunity to interact with audiences and to become immersed in changing their standard responses and feedback loops.

In 2003, the producers of the HBO program *Real Sex* decided to cover the growing trend toward amateur porn in art house cinemas in a special entitled *Porn 101: Exxxtra Credit*.[40] A guiding idea in *Porn 101: Exxxtra Credit* was that Boston's amateur pornographers are mostly proud and educated individuals with college degrees, who are in control of the process of representation. The HBO film crew followed the amateur pornographers during their film shoots, at times supporting

their efforts with technical tips and adequate film lighting. *Porn 101:
Exxxtra Credit* shows short excerpts of the amateur movies, at times
adding a separate music track and conducting short interviews with the
amateur filmmakers.

Who are these filmmakers? Mike is a guy with a balloon fetish who
stages an orgy. The audience laughs sincerely at the end of Mike's
movie, after all the balloons have been punctured. The audience gig-
gles and roars throughout the next movie, *Shotzee the Clown*, featuring
a horny clown going at it with a girl who acts as doggie. The next filmmakers highlighted were a loving couple, Nicolette and Leo, who made
a simple bedroom movie with a security camera plugged into their
VCR. Nicolette believes that people are not having good sex and she
wants to show them what good sex is like.

Also included in the special was Tanya Bezreh's spanking musical
The Naughty Garden, which tells a humorous and childlike fantasy tale
of garden flowers, a strawberry, a bee, and a snail. During the audition
of a musical, Tanya, as "strawberry," slips into the back room and gets
spanked by the angry stagehand. The movie goes on to show the spank-
ings as a sexual awakening leading to pleasure and orgasm.

Bezreh is a Boston-based artist who first ran a puppet theater at Harvard University and then helped develop *Brain-Opera* (1996) at Massachusetts Institute of Technology. She then moved to New York City,
where she became a freelance writer for *Artbyte* magazine and contributed to new media exhibits for the Guggenheim Museum and the
Museum of Sex. Bezreh became a web-based artist with her award-
winning website *New Century SchoolBook*, a magazine about electronic
art that turned into a personal photo-diary and striptease. Later, she
used the site to reflect on her sexual growth and crafted a series of lessons to be learned in the digital media environment. As she states:

> Making my web pages (since 1998) was a compulsion and I was also
> mimicking the e-commercial culture's way of selling products. After a
> while, I flipped it around and started to look back at my work and writ-
> ing about how one can learn from compulsions, and the mistakes one
> makes carrying them out. You can click on each of the lessons and go
> back to the webpage that I was developing at the time. For example, I
> was taking a lot of naked pictures of myself, but I was too shy to put them
> on the site without painting blobby clothes onto myself in Photoshop.

So the lessons that link to those images say things like, 'You are a wimp about nudity' and 'You always take your clothes off, but you never put it on the site.' At some point, I had to get over the fear of showing my sexier work, because I was hiding a huge percentage of my artwork. Doing the HBO thing was supposed to help break down the wall.[41]

When Bezreh decided to make the short porn movie for *Real Sex*, she was both the producer and the talent of *The Naughty Garden*. She directed the movie, wrote the plot, and composed the music. There was no money involved in making the movie, even though the HBO crew was following her production team: "They showed up with a 15-person crew and shot us shooting our porn movie. They were actually very friendly and helped us out in many ways. We used our own cameras and they shot their movie in film. We shot about 5 minutes of film and they ended up excerpting about a minute and a half of their footage. They did rush us a little bit and try to make us come to the sexy part a bit faster."

Here the amateur pornographer grabs the opportunity to show her work for a massive TV audience. The deal she negotiated with HBO was specific and respectful of her work; the love contract consisted of her meeting a person named Bruce, with whom she had a special chemistry and rapport, so she selected him to act as cranky stagehand and master spanker in her movie. Amateur pornographer Bezreh is an artist and everyday producer of sex, living sex/love relationships and making porn using digital media technologies and electronic networks.

Tanya Bezreh, screen shot from The Naughty Garden, *2003.*

Tanya Bezreh, screen shot from The Naughty Garden, *2003.*

Conclusion

Amateur pornographers are engaged in cooperative systems of exchange on the web and act out symbolical gestures of excess within the emerging gift economies. As media savvy and porn-friendly web users, they assert their private sexual bodies and fantasies as agents of lust and power within networks. They investigate the role of media in their sex lives and share homemade productions—or share commercial products within illegal zones of trading. What are the most significant lessons for schooling the new media amateurs? First, as was reported in a recent *New York Times* article, women and minority producers are involved in amateur and indie networks, promoting a new sexual visibility and performativity.[42] The producers of realcore porn, queer porn, yellow porn, and art porn have inherited the gender roles and racial stereotyping inherent in commercial porn, yet have been skillful in trying to develop their everyday performing bodies into subversions of the plots.

Second, the commercial porn industry and film cultures in general are responding positively to technical literacies and social networking of new media amateurs. For instance, in 1999, the Danish film company Zentropa Pictures launched its porn-production arm Puzzy Power and launched a manifesto text, *Pornouveau*.[43] The manifesto argued that porn movies must be innovative and must turn people on. Yet, the portrayal of sex has to be as authentic as possible, hence artists should be able to try out diverse forms of energy and sensuality. Sex scenes should be integrated into cinematic narratives and written for the enjoyment of both women and men. Hoping to create positive and inspiring images of human sexuality, *Pornouveau* argued for "the kind of porn that filmmakers themselves would like to watch." In short, rather than believing that porn could be better than real sex, it could at least be a welcome addition to the experience.

Major entertainment industries are capturing the characteristics of performative fringe agencies and porn activism—but will they be able to accommodate the flows of desire of true amateurs? Cultural establishment and porn empires are slowly but surely investigating the influences of netporn on consumers. This is perhaps the beginning of the long-awaited schooling to the traditional pornography industry, and a return to a culture of sharing gifts as moments of sexual pleasure. The aesthetic and social dimensions of these mediated pleasure patterns should be carefully observed and analyzed as case studies in a reclaiming of porn culture and sex education. Instead of applying universal theoretical concepts or outdated obscenity standards, we can study these sexual performers and their acts of communication.

This trend is not yet common among scholars trained in film/media criticism and theory, as it requires a willingness to abandon the ivory tower of speculation, question boundaries between scholarship and physicality, and play and perform in collaboration with subjects who are informed agents of sex. As McKenzie predicts at the end of *Perform or Else: From Discipline to Performance*, there will be no good schools of performance to replace the bad (crusty) ones. There are only pockets of activism that acknowledge a need to perform and to be performed, as interactive technologies are rapidly modifying the way we share knowledge and nurture the body. More abstract and detached claims of academic criticism will all too easily be appropriated and reversed by sex-negative ideology communities and, consequently, by conservative nation-state governments, which globally have started to push and punish porn through radical censorship and surveillance regimes. Amateur

pornographers maintain their sex lives despite the fortified surveillance
of networks. Amateur porn exchange and digital networking will guide
the performance of our sex lives for many more decades to come.

Notes

A previous version of this chapter was published in *Spectator* 24, no. 1 (Spring
2004).

1. Keith Hart, "Regarding the Gift," posted on the Nettime mailing list by
Phil Graham, January 13, 2000 (May 20, 2005).

2. Jon McKenzie, *Perform or Else: From Discipline to Performance* (New
York: Routledge, 2001), 176.

3. Clay Shirky, "Weblogs and the Mass Amateurization of Publishing,"
http://shirky.com/writings/weblogs_publishing.html (November 15, 2005).

4. "R.I.P. Jennicam," readers' comments, BBC News Online, http://news
.bbc.co.uk/1/hi/magazine/3360063.stm (March 17, 2006).

5. Anne-Marie Schleiner, "Open Source Art Experiments: Lucky Kiss,"
posted on the Nettime mailing list, November 26, 2000 (November 15,
2005).

6. Francesca da Rimini, personal interview with the author, unpublished
text, September 15, 2003.

7. Literotica homepage, www.literotica.com (March 17, 2006). A similar
erotic storytelling site is www.mcstories.com/tags/index.html.

8. Literotica homepage, www.literotica.com (March 17, 2006).

9. YouTube Terms of Service, www.youtube.com/t/terms (June 12, 2005).

10. Chris O'Brien, "Boom Times Have Passed for Online Porn," Silicon
valley.com, May 4, 2002 (August 6, 2002).

11. Mark Dery, "Sex Organs Sprout Everywhere: The Sublime and
Grotesque in Web Porn," keynote lecture delivered at Art and Politics of Netporn, Amsterdam, October 2005. Abbreviated version of the lecture available
on Dery's website, http://www.markdery.com/archives/news/index.html
#000048#more (January 8, 2006).

12. Dery, "Sex Organs Sprout Everywhere."

13. John Frow, *Time and Commodity Exchange* (Oxford, UK: Clarendon
Press, 1997), 129.

14. Annette B. Weiner, *Inalienable Possessions: The Paradox of Keeping While
Giving* (Berkeley: University of California Press, 1992), 18.

15. Dougal Phillips, "Can Desire Go On without a Body? Pornographic Exchange and the Death of the Sun," http://culturemachine.tees.as.uk/Interzone/dphillips.html (January 8, 2006).

16. Phillips, "Can Desire Go On without a Body?"

17. BitTorrent homepage, www.bittorrent.com/introduction.html (March 18, 2006).

18. Empornium site rules, http://empornium.us:6969/doc.php?show=rules (March 18, 2006).

19. Lai Ying-Kit, "BitTorrent File-Sharer Jailed for Three Months," *South China Morning Post*, November 7, 2005, http://www.asiamedia.ucla.edu/article.asp?parentid=32956 (May 15, 2006).

20. Sergio Messina, personal interview with author, unpublished text, March 8, 2006.

21. Messina interview.

22. Barbara DeGenevieve, "Hot Bods of Queer Porn," talk presented at Art and Politics of Netporn, Amsterdam, October 2005, posted on Netporn-L mailing list, October 17, 2005 (March 18, 2006).

23. DeGenevieve, "Hot Bods of Queer Porn."

24. DeGenevieve, "Hot Bods of Queer Porn."

25. DeGenevieve, "Hot Bods of Queer Porn."

26. Nofauxxx homepage, www.nofauxxx.com (March 18, 2006).

27. Nofauxxx blog commentary at LiveJournal, http://nofauxxx.livejournal.com (March 20, 2006).

28. DeGenevieve, "Hot Bods of Queer Porn."

29. Messina interview.

30. Messina interview.

31. Messina interview.

32. Darrell Y. Hamamoto, "The Joy Fuck Club: Prolegomenon to an Asian American Porno Practice," *New Political Science* 20, no. 3. A web-based excerpt of this essay can be found at http://www.mastersofthepillow.com/written.html (October 30, 2003).

33. Samantha Culp, "First Porn Son: Asian-man.com and the Golden Porn Revolution," *Wake: Journal of Contemporary Culture* (Spring 2004).

34. *Sex: The Annabel Chong Story*, produced and directed by Lewis Gough (1999, DVD).

35. Isaac Leung, personal interview with author, unpublished text, October 8, 2002.

36. Leung interview.

37. Leung interview.

38. Leung interview.

39. Ewen Syme and Titi Yu, personal interview with the author, unpublished text, January 6, 2002.

40. *Real Sex: Porn 101: Exxxtra Credit* (2003), HBO documentary, directed by Patti Kaplan.

41. Tanya Bezreh, personal interview with author, unpublished text, October, 23 2003. Bezreh, *New Century Schoolbook*, www.newcenturyschoolbook .com (November 7, 2003).

42. Mirey Navarro, "Women Tailor Sex Industry to Their Eyes," *New York Times*, February 20, 2003.

43. *Pornouveau Manifesto*, unpublished text. Distributed by Zentropa Pictures/Puzzy Power, 2002.

⌒

CHAPTER THREE

Porn Arousal and Gender Morphing in the Twilight Zone

This chapter further investigates the role of digital media in rewiring our sexual desires or animal responses to pornography. It gives an overview of clinical experiments in porn arousal studies and then explores porn spaces that challenge or overturn scientifically endorsed concepts of sex and gender. Although we are bombarded with sensational stories about the increasingly harsh effects of porn regimes on our *male* or *female* behaviors, it will be shown that porn websites enable complex and morphing identities of porn browsers. For instance, microniche sites such as gender-fluid models or digitally morphed hypermasculine models are attracting mainstream groups of women and men.

Despite these social changes, journalists have started to report on netporn consumption as one of the worst types of media addiction causing damage to heterosexual relationships. In a plea against pornification, Adrian Turpin writes in his article "Not Tonight Darling, I Am Online"[1] that pornography is now clinically proven to be the crack cocaine of the Internet. He uses statistics from the Internet filter company N2H2 to prove the steady growth of netporn sites. These statistics show that the number of porn sites reached 260 million in 2003—up from 14 million in 1998—and that porn sales hit $2.5 million in 2005, more than double the sales of music downloads.[2]

Turpin describes the effects of the porn boom on users by featuring "Michael," a typical netporn "beast" who is addicted to porn browsing and also has an iffy sexual relationship with his wife. To prove the correlation between his media addiction and sexual neglect, Turpin quotes Anne Layden, codirector of the University of Pennsylvania's Sexual Trauma and Psychopathology Program, who has found that exposure to porn images directly alters brain waves: "Even non–sex addicts will show brain reactions on PET (Positron Emission Tomography) scans while viewing pornography similar to cocaine addicts looking at images of cocaine."[3]

To Turpin, this line of research shows that the human brain is hard-wired to crave pornography. Watching porn is like binge drinking or eating junk food: It releases a chemical in the body that asks for more of the same. Another point of inspiration for Turpin is Pamela Paul's neoconservative book *Pornified: How Pornography Is Transforming Our Lives, Our Relationships and Our Families*. As Turpin explains, Paul is a former liberal who came up with an urgent anti-porn message based on a number of interviews with porn users and their social circles. Paul's book features women complaining about male consumption and men confessing their lack of gusto. Turpin's article ends with a cry of despair about the negative effects of netporn on children, minors, and adults.

However, a wide range of testimonies and porn scholarship would be required in order to actually measure our state of "pornification" as an extreme form of media immersion or unhealthy addiction. Beginning with an overview of empirical studies on the psychophysiological state of gender and porn arousal, these claims of lurid journalism will be questioned in their capacity to capture the digital zeitgeist or to analyze the arousal patterns of netporn browsers. Once again, netporn browsers are seen as those who question mainstream industries and contrived concepts of the pornographic body and sexual desire.

The Scientist's Aroused Subjects

As I have tried to argue elsewhere in this book, different layers of e-commerce and the p2p economy are blending on the Internet. Web users have developed unorthodox responses toward mainstream porn images by interacting with their makers and models, by commenting on their displays, by adding personal comments or profiles, and by discussing cultural politics. Nonetheless, even though we can make a positive argument for the more critical mind of indieporn movements, it is equally important to investigate how these movements experience changing patterns of arousal and orgasm.

The questions as to what kind of porn will arouse people, and what the different arousal levels between men and women are, have long fascinated Western sexologists. Sexologists have tried to measure quantitative responses using advanced technological methods, either by recording changing brainwave responses, or by asking subjects to write down reactions in different kinds of surveys—the SOS (Sexual Opinion Survey), the VRQ (Video Reaction Questionnaire), or the SFQ (Sexual Fantasy Questionnaire). The experiments simulate an intimate home environment and expose subjects to various types of pornography in order to test responses.

In "Selecting Films for Sex Research," a study carried out in the psychophysiology lab of the Kinsey Institute, researchers set out to measure whether men are more biologically wired than women to respond to porn.[4] They reviewed evidence from previous studies that showed that men and women differ in their responses to sexual stimuli. Since those studies were based on exposure to male-centered pornography, which the researchers deemed as gender problematic due to themes of male dominance or the exploitation of women, they were wary of past results. In the 2003 experiment, the researchers included female-friendly porn selections and tested a student group of heterosexual males and females. They found that women responded more positively to a presentation of female-friendly films selected by female researchers, in comparison to more typical mainstream film clips selected by the males. But even though the women reported positively to the female selections, they did not report arousal levels comparable to those of men.

In a 2004 study "A Sex Difference in the Specificity of Sexual Arousal," researchers posited a more rigorous recording of sex difference, showing that sex arousal is "category-specific" in men, whereas women show little category specificity in their porn arousal patterns. Once again, researchers set out to measure different reactions in female and male subjects, this time involving heterosexual, gay, lesbian, and transgender subjects. Their work cited a previous body of work in arousal studies, which showed that female sexuality is generally more flexible than male sexuality, with greater intra-individual variation in preferences, behaviors, attitudes, and responsiveness to cultural influences. The 2004 study retested this thesis, this time digitizing the experiment by using an MP100WS data-acquisition unit and the Acknowledge software. Male genital arousal was assessed with penile plethysmography, using a mercury-in-rubber strain gauge to measure changes in the circumference of the penis as erection developed. Female and male-to-female transsexual genital arousal was assessed via a change in vaginal pulse amplitude (VPA) with a vaginal photoplethysmograph. In addition, subjective arousal or lack of arousal was assessed continuously through self-reporting by using a lever moving through a 180-degree arc.

The researchers acknowledged that their subjects, and women more so than men, were often reluctant to be tested genitally and that their responses may have been influenced by an amount of "refusal" to react. Thus, a second study was carried out that asked subjects to fill out questionnaires. Both psychophysiological data and survey tests yielded similar results—both lesbians and straight women were less category specific in their porn arousal levels. They had lower arousal levels than men and enjoyed a wide variety of porn. The researchers were inconclusive about whether or not these sex differences were inborn or culturally constructed.

The arousal study "EEG Responses to Visual Erotic Stimuli in Men with Normal and Paraphilic Interests"[5] was keen on measuring different arousal levels in different types of males. Males were divided into "normal" vs. "paraphilic" males. The study used EEG (electroencephalography) to capture neurophysiologic measurements of the electrical activity of the brain. These measurements were recorded from electrodes placed on the scalp and/or on the cortex. As the researchers noted, the first EEG study was carried out in 1966 by Lifshitz, who measured the effects on males of artistic depictions of nude women, compared with pictures of ulcerated legs.

The subjects in the 2003 porn arousal study were sixty-two white, right-handed, heterosexual males who were divided into two categories, normal subjects and paraphilic subjects. *Paraphilic* subjects were defined as those interested in scenes of transvestism, fetishism, and sadomasochism and were found in special interest clubs and through announcements in niche magazines. The study worked with EEG analysis because it was based on the hypothesis that "normal" and "paraphilic" subjects get stimuli from different hemispheres of the brain. Whereas the right hemisphere initiates emotion, aggression, and sexual arousal, it does so under regulatory control of the left hemisphere, which includes sexual triggers in the format of verbal cues, rituals, and scenarios. The researchers believed that the left hemisphere could indicate an underlying deviation from normal arousal pattern activity, and wanted to test the presence of paraphilic tendencies in subjects.

The males were asked to fill out an SFQ (Sexual Fantasy Questionnaire) and were then seated in a comfortable chair. They were wired with 1-cm-diameter electrodes on the scalp and around the right eye to measure the EEG responses. They were exposed to slides (projected with an old-school Kodak Carousel), showing a mixture of 57 heteronormative slides, 57 paraphilic slides, and 57 neutral slides (e.g., landscapes and street scenes). The findings of the study overturned the researchers' expectations, as the normal males were aroused by normal stimuli, but the paraphilic males were aroused by both normal and paraphilic stimuli. The researchers had assumed that the paraphilics would have a lack of interest in normal sex scenes but were proven wrong. However, the experiment confirmed that certain parts of the left brain hemisphere were more stimulated in the paraphilic group, parts that the researchers located as the seedbed of fantasies as social scenarios, role-plays, and rituals, as well as the psychology of social shame and awareness. "Normal" heterosexual arousal was primarily located in the right-brain areas.

Taking evidence from this body of empirical arousal studies, one can see that quantitative methods presuppose a difference between "normal" people and "deviants." Similar constructions of deviancy have been used in studies of the arousal patterns of criminals and sex offenders. Take for instance the 1993 study "Sexual Preference Assessment of Sexual Aggressors" carried out in France. This study measured the penile responses of sexual aggressors when exposed to erotic stimuli.[6] The method was phallometry (measuring penile activity), seen as more objective than asking sex offenders for subjective reports about their arousal patterns. The aim of testing sex offenders was to find out if deviant sexual arousal is a crucial factor in the etiology and persist-ence of deviant sexual behavior or if "deviant sexual behavior can be considered the beginning of a behavioral chain that ends in aggres-sion."[7]

In the experiment, the subjects were exposed to audiotapes includ-ing various scenes ranging from consensual to coercive and violent re-lationships. The question was simple: "Will the penis rise when subjects are exposed to scenes of violence?" However, no sufficient evidence was found to prove the correlation between image consumption and behav-ior. Researchers already knew that the sex drive of inmates often col-lapses as they age and experience physiological deterioration. They also already knew that presentenced subjects waiting for a verdict would control their "aggressive" behavior in response to the scientist's ques-tions. In other words, these tests are perhaps invalid for testing the or-dinary sexual arousal patterns of humans, as the material and psycho-logical conditions of the subjects themselves have too much of an effect on their sex drives. But it is also important to note that aside from these obvious pitfalls, the tests rely on outdated concepts of the gendered body and pornographic technologies.

The Sadeian Ghosts: Justine and Juliette

Do these scientific methods for measuring arousal bear any resem-blance to how people get turned on and/or communicate arousal in the *twilight zone* of netporn? My own thesis situates netporn consumers as wanderers who enter porn spaces to access pornography and ritualize social relationships. One way of adopting a wandering attitude toward pornography is by imagining flexible viewing positions in the identifi-cation with models or through an analysis of gender and power rela-tions. In *The Sadeian Woman and the Ideology of Pornography*, Angela Carter writes that the popular and commercially exploited archetypes of pornography hearken back to a world of premodern media, such as the influential writings of the Marquis de Sade. Her book suggests that de Sade's casting of female roles was a hyperbolic gesture of critiquing Catholic mainstream culture. She believes that the Sadeian woman in-vites readers themselves to imagine, reflect, and comment on his acts of gender terrorism: "Nothing exercises such power over the imagination as the nature of sexual relationships. And the pornographer has it in his/her power to become a terrorist of the imagination. A sexual guerilla whose purpose is to overturn our most basic notions of these relations. . . ."[8]

In her book, Carter largely evokes de Sade's painstaking artistry and depiction of helpless young females, typified in the characters of Justine and Juliette. She then argues that Justine and Juliette carry their own seeds of reversal and rebellion. The libertine distortions of the female body lead to their own inner death and destruction. Justine is the naïve and overly friendly female whose presence carries visions of martyrdom as pleasure. Justine is assaulted by the surrounding male vultures who rape her and hurt her feelings. De Sade describes her pain in great detail. As Carter summarizes: "The fluids of her orgasm are the tears that are an implicit invitation to further rape." Juliette is a complementary female archetype, and the driving force in her relations with males is the desire to make money and become rich. Juliette learns how to be their favorite sex bomb. For instance, she is often depicted as being exposed to anal sex, yet she manages to "sell" her anus. Moreover, she sells her anus to libertines as well as the leaders of the Catholic Church. She is not interested in the political views of men when they become her prey. Similar to Justine, she develops her stories alongside their sadistic desires. For instance, she develops a real taste for anal intercourse and becomes increasingly proud and in control of her superb ass and the outrageous, unnatural uses to which she puts it. The libertines become connoisseurs of her excrement, comparing vintages and bouquets just like a wine snob describes a good or bad merlot. As a result, she becomes obscenely rich and lives with opulence. She even gets acquainted with the archbishop and the pope, who worship shit.

De Sade constructs these over-the-top females and males within his sex-crazed literary mind. His depiction of male–female relationships within the sadomasochistic dialectic is blunt and demonstrative but has inspired artistic and critical responses. Several centuries after the death of de Sade, his females have been reborn in the galleries and databases of netporn. Click on any random selection of porn sites and you can get a glimpse of the ghosts of Justine and Juliette. They provide easy prey for their hunters—girls in bondage; girls with tearful faces; girls made ready for gang bangs; girls dressed as maids, servants, or schoolgirls; and girls with mouths wide open to receiving sperm baths.

The depiction of a blissfully receptive female is equally present in alternative and queer porn cultures. For instance, Joanna Angel's persona in the movies *Joanna Angel's Alt.Throttle* and *Neu Wave Hookers* is a tattooed and self-pronounced slut who submits to the desires of a muscular male. The movie opens with extensive shots of Angel's willing submission—she is coached to give him a blowjob appetizer, then prepared for the main dish of vaginal and anal penetration. The scene ends like a typical heterosexual porn scene, with her blissful acceptance of his climactic cum shot.

Do we identify with Angel's bliss as the male or female agency, or the top or bottom of the scene, or can we imagine altering or slightly shifting these positions? The movie *Neu Wave Hookers* already addresses a more complex viewer as it alternates archetypal porn scenes with nonpornographic interludes, like silly dance numbers or off-screen camaraderie between sex workers. For instance, we see a recurring scene of a young sex worker being visited by a retired cab driver in a shabby motel room. The scene is repeated throughout the movie. The old man meets the sex worker and repeats his pathetic lines, but the worker persona is portrayed by different actresses. A simultaneous soundtrack is that of a voice sharing funny stories about her encounters with men. But the movie scene is nauseating rather than funny. She breaks down and confesses her confused state of mind to the old man. She has become exhausted by her line of work and cannot face her ugly client, but she is nevertheless slightly turned on. The viewer is exposed to a film aesthetic that challenges and shakes up his or her set way of viewing and responding to the cliché of the receptive female.

Another pioneering art porn movie that has attacked commercial movie clichés is *I.K.U.: A Japanese Cyber-Porn Adventure*, made in Japan in 2000 by media artist Shu Lea Cheang. *I.K.U.* depicts a futuristic universe where people have become androids. Freed from the chains of computer hardware technology—screens and keyboards, cameras, microphones, external hard drives, plugs and cables—they smoothly insert small chips into their flesh bodies that facilitate the desiring of sex partners. They have sinewy, sexy, and agile flesh bodies just

Shu Lea Cheang, photographs from I.K.U.: A Japanese Cyber-Porn Adventure, *2001.*

like porn stars, which they constantly modify in order to come alive, connect, and have remarkable sex with others.

How do viewers relate to the sexual climaxes suggested in this film? The actual cum shots in *I.K.U.* are almost invisible and can be counted on one hand, thus thwarting the typical porn viewer's conditioned arousal patterns. However, new patterns of pleasure and orgasms are suggested through the beautifully animated scenes. All of *I.K.U.*'s human subjects, whether female or male, own a beautifully designed, colorful, erect penis. This "digital penis" is a device that can be used during sex to help bring the partner to a final head-spinning moment of orgasm. The digital penis does not ejaculate but is a toy that can enter the partner through the vagina and/or anus. The digital penis provides surplus pleasure for the subject, then extracts precious data about the state of orgasm. These elements certainly make for an interesting film; however, from the perspective of the porn viewer, how does one become aroused by images of a digital penis?

The Sex Bomb Who Endlessly Talks

If web users are experiencing any rewiring of the sex brain, this would probably involve brain activity stemming from the crossover regions between *female* and *male* or between *normal* and *deviant* desires. These crossover regions partly emanate from the technologies of digital networks, as people can reach climax in response to porn as visual stimuli (located in the right hemisphere) or by cultivating *female* or *deviant* aspects of sexual performativity. Web users are used to downloading and watching porn (located by clinicians in the right hemisphere) while exchanging chitchat or even while having debates about sexual issues (located in the left hemisphere). For instance, if one looked at the behaviors of sex consumers in adult chat rooms, it would be impossible to demarcate the beginning and end of their arousal in response to an image, as the processing of visual information is always moderated by speech acts.

An amorphous state of arousal and gender fluidity is exemplified in the book *webAffairs*, written by a female artist and scholar under the pseudonym Show-n-Tell. The book records the author's interaction with sexually explicit images in adult chat rooms.[9] The still images in *webAffairs* simulate the sex environment and the book contains large collections of webcam photographs and details of her ongoing correspondence. Show-n-Tell is a sex-curious woman who performs a double role—she watches while responding to the desires of sex-seeking men and women. She narrates the peculiarities of her encounters and analyzes them afterward; both her performative and analytical voices are present in her writing.

The book, described as a sort of documentary, also demystifies the profile of the straight male as a porn beast uninterested in relationships or everyday chat. Men relate to her as a somewhat shy yet warm persona who invents clever strategies to pacify horny males. For example, in the early stages of the project, she asks men to point their cameras away from their bodies and erections into their home spaces, and finds that men love to get this kind of unusual attention. Moreover, the chat rooms are frequently populated with heterosexual couples who both participate in the chat and she tries to relate to both parties. As she writes: "There are many couples that participate in virtual sex together. Still, the woman is the main interest. Sometimes it's the husband who shows his wife to other men, sometimes it's the wife who exposes herself to other men while her husband watches, and sometimes they both perform for an audience of mostly men. I take it upon myself to express interest in the 'forgotten hubby' behind the camera and direct my comments to him."[10] At one point, she has an extensive humorous conversation with an older sexually estranged male and encourages him to get his wife involved. But overall, people in the chat rooms seem eager to show off their lovers, their spouses, their pets, even their children.

Sometimes these adult chatters help each other to work through personal relationship issues. Other times, they invite each other to have sex and conversation in private chat rooms. But even in the private rooms, the performances can be largely nonsexual. Show-n-Tell herself is a married woman who performs sex acts online while her husband sits next to her working away on his own computer. She often discusses her chats and ongoing cyber relationships with him or asks him how far he thinks she can go in her diary of evolving desires.

Is Show-n-Tell a typical female consumer in her ability to be aroused by these chats? Or do the chat logs show that males and females have similar arousal patterns? To what degree are males still "innately wired" to be aroused by visual stimuli? Show-n-Tell's research shows that people develop complex communication patterns that are also determined by laws, as every room has its own rules and some are *polite* or *women-friendly* rooms with stricter rules for males. For instance, polite rooms prohibit men from displaying their genitals and/or inviting a woman

Screen shot of webAffairs, a book by Show-n-Tell, with an
essay by Allucquerre Rosanne Stone (Boston: Eighteen Publications, 2005).

into private rooms. The idea is to make women feel more comfortable
and to boot out any obnoxious men. Since polite rooms have an even
larger percentage of women, men tend to line up for them trying to get
in. Show-n-Tell tries out the polite rooms for a while, but in the end
she finds these women-friendly zones too forced: "I eventually stopped
going to these rooms because it seemed too hypocritical to be participating in an adult room and yet be offended by nudity. Isn't that what
we already do in real life: keep sex apart from the rest of our daily life
and define it as offensive when it is expressed in public?" She prefers to
interact with people's unadulterated performances, regardless of
whether they include sex or not.

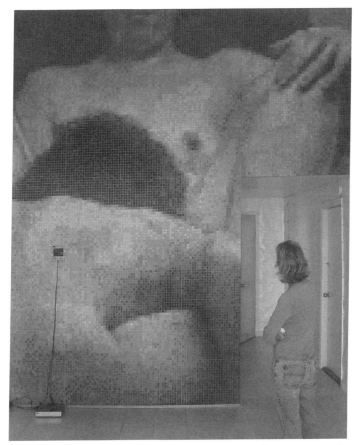

Chantal Zakari and Mike Mandel, Suzy, ceramic and glass mosaic tile mural with video screen embedded, 12' × 13', temporary installation at GASP gallery, Boston, 2005.

Show-n-Tell engages in excessive sexual communication and pornographic exhibitionism and voyeurism. She is committed to acting out complex layers of porn identity. What matters within these layered identities is a consensual sharing of sexual experiments, joys, disappointments, or satisfaction. In light of these identities, would it then remain possible to scientifically measure the arousal levels of these female and male chatters? These subjects are not pacified and exposed to certain porn categories but are personally, physically, and emotionally involved in the act of making and sharing. Moreover, they articulate the sexual flows of everyday relationships as part of the act of porn exchange. Of course, there is an amount of predictability and repetition in the flow, but the arousal levels are integrated into complex types of relationships, which do not stem only from the exposure to images of naked bodies and sex scenes. All of these behaviors are classified as "normal" in the chat rooms as long as chatters show respect for each other.

In these chat rooms, performers mostly have alternating nicknames and alter egos and develop discursive strategies and behavioral traits that are unique to their virtual personas. Thus, it is more important to question whether it is actually viable to maintain established notions of gender and sexual orientation in testing human arousal and attachment to porn. Is the porn browser a male porn beast or a female chatter and wanderer? Can both women and men adopt multilayered types of sexual arousal? We will take a further look at queer porn sites to examine how people construct pornographic identities to carve out these deeply uncharted regions in the sex brain.

Porn Stardom as Hypermasculinities

In the essay "21st Century Schizoid Bear: Masculine Transitions through Net Pornography," Francesco Palmieri writes about the advent of morphing or schizoid identities in amateur gay porn. His essay focuses on self-profiling sites for gay "bears" (big and hairy gay men) and argues that porn spaces have had a tremendous impact on the morphing bodies and identities of gay men.[11] Since bears date each other through web-based communication and peer-to-peer porn sites, creating a porn identity becomes a part of the sex act. As Palmieri further explains by means of a detailed anecdote:

> The word "bear" came through my eyes, my heart, my stomach and my ass, as a total blast. Two tools helped me to perceive myself like that, and both of them have to do with the digitization of relationships and pornography. I was frequenting a transgender club that was owned by a big, hairy, red-bearded man with icy eyes and a psycho-tropic skin smell. I fell in love with him without understanding why. He started to play

with me through a digital camera, taking pictures of my body inside the club. I was very shy because I did not yet accept my body, which was bigger and very different from glittering gay icons. But the fluidity of his camera defined and redefined me; it was a very first step in eroticizing my body. Of course I wanted more and started to experiment taking off more and more clothes. And the more I got naked the more I got excited, feeling hugged and touched and licked and penetrated by the man who was behind the camera. My bearself came alive.

Palmieri needed a peer-to-peer porn model to interpret his lurking desires and to actualize his self-image as a bear. He explains that "bears" were not present in gay scenes in Rome, Italy, and came into popularity with the advent of the Internet. Once again, Palmieri came to understand the political-cultural issues through the lens of netporn and a personal love story:

> I was able to get in touch, forming spaces for socialization that weren't happening in real life inside the Italian g.l.b.t. community. Even though I remembered having erections thinking about female breasts, which I had seen in porno magazines during my childhood, my first sperm production was due to fantasies relating to my teachers, and especially the ones having big bellies, big beards, and lots of hair coming out of their shirts. Starting from these memories, I started searching for mature men websites. Once, while surfing the net, I found an image of a big, big man with a tempest of hair, a cloudy and wild salt and pepper beard, a malicious smile and cut of eyes, a serious epicurean belly, a huge fat sticky cock, two thunder legs and a pair of perfect feet. He was sitting on a rotten couch all naked, legs wide open, showing such a fabulous enormous erection and smoking a joint. The word "Bear" was the title of the picture. Well, I came without touching myself. I then contacted him explaining to him that he had a major [effect on me] in my life. So we agreed that we should have had sex together. Then I booked a plane ticket to San Francisco to meet and have sex with him, fuck deeply with my hidden fears and fantasies and completed this cycle in my life.[12]

The digitizing of online romance made Palmieri understand bear culture and act out his own morphing identity as a young bear. He then started to promote and define a Roman Italian "bearscene" that developed under the name of Epicentro Ursino Romano (www

Warbear photographed by F & M (Fabia Rodi, Marcello Orlando), 2005.

.epicentroursino.com). He became an activist and theorist and named himself "Warbear" to denote a countercultural position, wanting to challenge and think beyond more-acceptable versions of queer identity: "'Warbear' started to become my nickname in the Internet Relay Chats. I was radically different from people who defined their vision of life through the gayscape. 'Warbear' is the hidden fear, the distorted mirror of the invisible power relationships based on a definition of gay identity throughout social roles." Palmieri further explains that he sees himself as a morphing gay subject, eager to deconstruct the more homogenized body images of gay communities. Bears are aesthetically defined as gay men with a different presence—hair, beards, bellies, and blue-collar looks. Their early popularization stems from pornographic magazines such as *Bear* by Brush Creek Media, which promoted the body of the bear. Early cults of bear porn stars were also formed, featuring stars such as Jack Radcliff, Steve Hurley/Tit Pig, and Bill Adams.

Bear pornography first started with mailing lists, which were crucial to circulating information about clubs, parties, contests, and bear porn stars. Bears then started to use chat rooms with links to personal websites. The bear community has meanwhile witnessed a tremendous proliferation of these profiling websites. According to Palmieri, bear porn went through a process of gentrification in which the radical nature of the body image disappeared. Yet, a new revolutionizing of bear formations happened with the advent of websites offering free profiling services, such as www.bearwww.com for Francophone and Anglophone users and www.gayroyal.de for German and Dutch bears. The sites are huge and also host profiles of bears located in non-Western countries such as Ghana and Indonesia.

Presently, these sites host thousands of daily contacts and profiles, and new bears are popping up at every hour. Palmieri sees them as a "huge open opus of Bear life: experiences and self-produced pornography." These picture narratives can be split into two subcategories. On the one hand, sites such as Silverdaddies.com and Bearfront.com are mostly sex-oriented and carry profiles of bears who expose parts of their naked bodies. Sometimes, they only expose isolated body parts because they do not want to be recognized. On the other hand, there are sites featuring bears who want LTRs (long-term relationships) and show their entire bodies in about five pictures, with the last one being a naked picture. In both cases, the more these profiles are uploaded and restyled, the more they are hit and checked as "live immaterial objects." Palmieri writes that beyond these two categories, once can find "endless existential narratives of emotions, intellectualities, loves, exhibitionisms, voyeurisms, sexualities, dreams, hopes, fears, fantasies, crying sadness, and solitude."[13]

Regarding visual aesthetics, a specific type of photographic modeling and framing has emerged due to a number of well-known bear photographers, whose styles are being imitated by DIY bears. According to Palmieri, the semiotic codes of "bearism" reflect Western male stereotyping. Contexts of masculinity are reproduced based on working-class imagery such as truckers' parking and cruising areas, parks and forests, warehouses, police and military backgrounds, and sports backgrounds. Middle-class white-collar imagery is also reproduced in office spaces, backyards, and pools.[14] The bear groups are further divided into splintering micro-identities, including bears, chubs, cubs, daddies, chasers, admirers, couples, and muscle bears. Palmieri's own "punk" profile as

"Warbear" on www.bearwww.com/warbearhc shows two pictures of his face with a long beard, one sideways showing a nose ring and one frontal looking the viewer sternly in the eye, and two pictures of himself intensely embracing a tattooed guy in a toilet. The text reads as follows: "Warbear seeks celtic/caucasian but he is open to other ethnics and hybrids. Long beards—especially sp and white, daddybears, polarbears, maturebears, graybears, silverbears, whitebears, pappabears, Santa clauses, big old bubbas, bearded good 'ol boys, cinnamon bears." Warbear, as mentioned earlier and described in his profile, is from Rome and speaks four languages. His other interests include "altered states of consciousness, urban anthropology, queer culture and gender studies, countercultures and radical thought, literature sociology, body manipulation, electronic music, independent publishing, new media studies, experimental graphix."[15] In a profile created for the mainstream social networking website MySpace, Palmieri mentions that he was actually banned from the site on three occasions because of his attempts at using his pornographic self-profiling as "Warbear."[16]

Palmieri's profile is connected to other masculinities apart from basic "bearism," for instance, those of morphing bulls, bearabs (Arab bears), and transbears (female-to-male transsexual bears). In reference to the surfacing of web-based Arab bear communities, Palmieri writes that Arab bears assert their ethnic identities and present themselves as "big fat, hairy, moustached, dark-skinned, lascivious men, mostly naked or dressed up in typical Arab clothes and set in typically Eastern or Palestinian settings."[17] The Arab bear stereotype began in Germany and grew out of an exoticization of Arab masculinity among German bears, a trend which has meanwhile resulted in www.hairyturks.com, a site primarily for gay Turks and Turkish migrants living in northern Europe.

The dating websites www.kelma.org and www.citebeur.com are for Arab gay minorities living in France called "beurs." *Beur* is a word used in reference to the second and third generations of migrants who arrived in Paris in the 1960s. It's also a play on "Le Petit Beurre de Lu," a brand of sweet golden cookies with a hue similar to the skin color of people from the Maghreb, a region of northwest Africa comprising the coastlands and the Atlas Mountains of Morocco, Algeria, and Tunisia. The beurs of Kelma.org organize regularly as "BBB" (Blanc Black

Beurs) in gatherings, soirees, and couscous parties. They highlight elements of ethnic pride or difference in their erotic/pornographic self-profiling. As explained by Kelma founder Fouad Zeraoui, the site aims to create a zone for those who were typically excluded from white gay masculinity. The use of macho hypermasculinity may be unfriendly toward women but is seen as necessary in establishing a culture of pride and pleasure. The Kelma "dossiers" have an extensive collection of articles and interviews about the complexities of gay beurism, covering topics of racism in the suburbs, homosexuality in Islam and Arab home countries, homophobia and violence among Arab migrants, homophobia in hip-hop music, and so on. As indicated in the articles and interviews on www.kelma.org, the beurs are frequently confronted with racism from white French society. Their use of pornographic profiling is also a controversial statement within the Maghreb community itself, hence contributing to the complex "schizoid" identities of contemporary masculinity.[18]

Connecting strands to gay netporn sites are the North American "morphing bulls." Morphing bulls grew out of the Yahoo! group "Bulls Empire," owned by Bull Neck. Bull Neck defines bull identity as a virile response to the gentrification of bear culture, as bulls embody "extra brute strength, a large bulky body and an attitude of smug aggression." They have short haircuts and get rid of facial or body hair, distinguishing them from bears. Some examples of typical bulls include power lifters, football offensive linemen, and off-season bodybuilders. These types are said to combine the best elements of beefiness, power, and actively expressed aggression.[19] Bull bodies are fetishized and inflated through hyperbolic imagination, and the images are manipulated by means of digital imaging techniques. Bull bodies are redrawn to include extra layers of muscle and huge erections. Morphing bulls look as if they are have reached the end of the masculine human form and are about to explode. As seen in the work of GB Morph on the site www.GBmorphs.com, artfully morphed hypermuscular gay men pose in single pinups or in acts of embracing and kissing. The site also links to various collections of muscle drawings and animations made by artists such as AP Bear from www.apbear.com and Jeff Muscle from www.jeffsmusclestudio.com, as well as Japanese manga-style art.

Finally, as Palmieri mentions in his essay, there is also a strand of "transbear" culture wherein female-to-male transsexuals adopt the bear look. In the absence of what is commonly recognized as a biological penis, the transbears are gender-twisters who develop beards, a butch presence, and the performance of "straight" masculinity. Palmieri explains that an alliance or sex between male bears and transbears could be seen as a "pornographic sublime," as a powerful encounter creating desire, yet also outrage and disturbance. Even though he admits to having a physical block with regard to a potential relationship with women or transmen, he supports the idea of an alliance on his visionary-activist grounds.

Transgendered Porn Stars and the Variety Fuck

Clinical experiments in porn arousal strive to assert a biologically determined binary order. As in the 2004 study "A Sex Difference in the Specificity of Sexual Arousal," women are shown to have reactions to porn selections that are different from those of men. But how can we assess the agencies of our morphing genders and modes of desire? The web has meanwhile also seen the emergence of FTM porn stars who attract male and female viewers who are testing out new arousal patterns. "You have seen chicks with dicks, now come see a dude with a pussy," proclaims Buckangel of www.buckangel.com. Buck wants to "change the face of porn" by constructing a profile that merges hypermasculinity and hyperfemininity—a tattooed and muscular torso, large moustache, and retro-style sunglasses, along with a decidedly slutty "cunt" pride. Buck was born as a woman and later became a man who enjoys raunchy sex. He emphasizes his authentic female genitals but adds layers of masculinity. He is a "man with a cunt" and declares that "two holes are better than one." Buck enjoys sexual actions that involve both of his openings.

We see a further mixing of female and male attributes in his ability to "variety fuck" his sex partners: "See Buck fuck guys, gals and she-males." We can see it in a range of photos: Buck sucking cock; Buck smoking a cigar while looking at a dildo going into his vagina; Buck kissing a woman's breast; and Buck being penetrated in the vagina by a man. Buck is really getting it on in every possible way and shows a flex-

Buckangel, Buckangel Entertainment, Leather 1, 2005.

ibility and willingness to arouse both biological and transgendered females and males, so long as they can also get aroused by his performance of roughneck masculinity.

The porn website NoFauxxx.com equally wants to stimulate gender
fluidity in members. It offers "cute pin-up girls, hot boys, chubby
chicks, gorgeous BBW babes, steaming hot couples, punk, goth, hippy,
natural, pierced, tattooed, shaved and unshaven models, sexy trans-
gender/transsexual models (FTM & MTF), erotica, straight, gay, lesbian, and bi-sexual models, black models, Asian models, soft-core,

Buckangel, Buckangel Entertainment, Fire 2, 2005.

hard-core, and realistic SM and bondage." One could argue that this site mimics the portal model and atomized databases of commercial porn, but the site actually wants to deconstruct the notion of male or female gender in its producers and consumers. As we can read in its policies for models: "NoFauxxx has no 'boy' and 'girl' categories, and for a reason. We believe that, for many people, genitals have nothing to do with gender or gender expression. We do have many trans and gender queer models, and we ask that you respect them by referring to them by their preferred pronouns ('he,' 'she,' or 'ze' are the most common, and it will be specified in the model's bio), if you're blessed with the chance to interact with them on our message boards or through other means. If there are any reports of abuse or disrespect to any model for any reason, action will be taken to remove you from the message boards, and if necessary, the site."[20] Through these statements, the site asks its members to question their culturally conditioned notions of distinctive female and male sexuality.

Feminism and Netporn:
The Cross-Voyeur and Hybrid-Hybrid Professor

Porn spectators are active navigators whose identities change as they adapt their gaze to the varying displays of gender. They can also be seen as "cross-voyeurs" who peruse selections beyond the boundaries of their niche sites and communities. Porn spectators visit their favorite spaces while checking out activities in neighboring zones. They buy products made by specific producers or micro-niche communities but end up eyeing and/or participating in porn sex cultures.

For instance, one could think about the popular "dickgirl" figure in Japanese *hentai* porn. These images depict girls with a penis attached to their bodies, presenting an uncanny yet beautifully fitting new organ. These images have joined the ranks of Japanese *hentai* and anime cultures, which generally define the cutting edge of porn in an assault on femininity and s/m dialectics. For instance, a free preview tour for a *hentai* porn site introduces the sci-fi story "The Naked Earth," which shows a cult of android Amazons engaged in fierce combat with violent monsters. After some women have been strangled, raped, and murdered by the tentacled monsters, and we see their corpses bleeding from between the thighs, one Amazon urges the headmistress to make an exit. The headmistress replies: "Escape is not an option, my child!" as the page scrolls over to membership sign-up information for the porn website.

However, in the upper-left corner of the Naked Earth site, a popup sales window displays a dickgirl rhythmically sucking her soft, elongated penis. The dickgirl here is a soft and humorous infantile-feminine figure. She happily sucks her fantastically engineered and *soft* genital for voyeuristic audiences.[21] In a 2006 presentation at Hong Kong University, as part of the conference Film Scene: Cinema, the Arts, and Social

Change, I showed a collection of photographs of dickgirls and asked the audience to write down their comments. I asked people to specifically think about whom they thought these images were made for. The response from female and male audience members was quite varied:

"To my eyes it seems quite grotesque and a quite castrated image— Between a nice pretty face and breasts we have an ugly big penis instead of pussy."

"Men give women the cocks they want to have."

"The thing about porn is that, like any market addiction, it leads to the next product, the next possibility. When you get tired of it, or played it out, things that you rejected before become like 'hmmm.'"

"I don't find it grotesque but powerful, a woman with a dick."

"Surprising how exciting it is (26yo man). Brilliant."

"I would think it's more disturbing to men than to women as women are into cocks, instruments of power."

"Kind of funny, awkward."

"To free oneself from physical and mental limitations."

"Shocking, disturbing, weird, and ugly."

"Transsexuality has everything to do with satisfying he/she. It especially works in countries like Thailand—to gain more business perhaps?"

"Notion of shame in these images, not sure why. I don't find these erotic at all (look at big dicks in old erotic woodcuts)."[22]

The original dickgirl was invented by a *hentai* artist to suit himself and his peers, but it has now become a major fetish on the web and has reached other connected web users. Even though the images are more instinctively understood and appreciated by niche consumers of *hentai* sites, they may be reinterpreted or appropriated by other groups of web users. For instance, queer communities looking for transgender constructions of the female body can appropriate dickgirl as their own. One well-known example of such "cross-voyeurism" would be the Japanese softcore animation *yaoi/shounen-ai*, which portrays gay sex scenes or "boy love" for female consumers. Their "lesbian" counterparts are called *yuri/shoujo-ai* and can be seen as a new type of "soft" arousal for males.

Both lesbian and gay images made for "cross-voyeurs" are a refreshing change from the sexist and violent premises of most *hentai*. As Philip Mak explains in his *shoujo-ai* database, people like *shoujo-ai* in order to adopt "feminine" feelings of affectionate desire: "For some of those who have a soft spot for warm-and-fuzzy-feeling romantic stories, it is the appeal of seeing a nice girl-girl relationship, which, while not rare, is also not as common in anime fan fiction as some of us would like. . . . Others get bored with predictable everyday situations in anime fan fiction, where the roles in relationships are clear cut: the man's job is to defend, provide food and shelter and be manly, while the woman's job is to support the man, keep the food and shelter straight, and be demure. In a lesbian relationship, these roles are not clear cut at all; the relationship becomes exciting and unpredictable again."[23] Mak believes that these lesbian bodies and relationships may attract male viewers who want to see a shift in bipolar gender relations.

Thus, new types of user interactivity are articulated by web users who have developed morphing identities as producers and consumers of pornography. Marije Janssen uses feminist theories of performativity to analyze mechanisms of profiling and user interactivity in altporn sites such as SuicideGirls.[24] Janssen specifically explores strategies of subversive feminine mimicry as proposed by the French feminist Luce Irigaray. Irigaray postulates a distinctive masculine or feminine morphology in gender discourses, but she also believes that we can denaturalize these morphologies. Thus new modes of "femininity" can be drawn within dominant discourses and image regimes. As one cannot formulate a language of power outside of these dominant discourses, it is important for women to enact and mimic their roles within them. As in the Sadean portrayal of femininity, females deliberately assume and perform submissive roles, thus converting a form of subordination into affirmation, and thus they can begin to thwart these roles. For instance, in Eon McKai's movie *Neu Wave Hookers*, the young sex workers deliberately act out clichés. The porn numbers in the movie are very traditional, yet the nonpornographic scenes make viewers aware of the constructed nature of the sex bomb. For instance, the porn stars have very typical facial expression of bliss and satisfaction when they are being ejaculated upon, but they show power and humor when they are shot behind the scenes.

Judith Butler has criticized the position of Irigaray and theorized the possibility of gender morphing, or the use of performativity in "innumerable" sexes. Butler uses the concept of *masquerade* to argue that people can take on different identities by adopting gender codes. Janssen suggests that this theory holds special value in the online world, where people are more likely to take on parallel or alternate identities, whether real or virtual, by easily replacing one profile with another, or by avoiding contact in real life. Specifically, she looks at feminist interpretations of the psychoanalysis of Jacques Lacan, who reviewed the role of the phallus in relation to male and female identity. According to Lacan, the phallus is the primary signifier of the subject, as opposed to the biological penis. It is a signifier that can be detached from the male body and can be adopted by women. Women can steal the phallus and reconstruct identitities, but they can only function that way once affirmed by males and masculine culture. Butler places this kind of masquerade outside the framework of binary gender roles and male affirmation. For her, masquerade is seen as a way to denaturalize authentic forms of desire/arousal and to foresee endless possibilities of gender. In addition to these theories of performativity, a newer wave of cyberfeminists sees the networked body as a pragmatic interface. Rosi Braidotti argues that people can use mediated spaces and identities to reverse the patriarchal order and try out mimetic strategies of gender. Unlike Butler, Braidotti is more skeptical about the concept of the transferable phallus and of our ability to adopt an endless variety of gender codes. One cannot revolutionize gender so easily even though one can more easily play with its codes using new technologies. A real change of gender identification would take time and require hard work, pain, and effort.

By adopting cyberfeminist theories of gender, one could articulate porn users as people who adopt artificial codes of (hyper)masculinity or femininity, even though they do not aim at transgendered identification. Fifteen years ago, Donna Haraway predicted a trend toward morphing femininity. According to Haraway, women would be able to fight oppression by transcending biological determinism and making new alliances with technological data and changing animal behaviors.[25]

These types of hybridization with porn data also have an impact on the profile of the Internet researcher. Marinka Copier has questioned scientific paradigms in media studies and discusses *boundary-work*, a term used in science and technology studies to discuss the formation of artificial boundaries between "scientific" and "nonscientific" knowledge.[26] Whereas boundary-essentialists favor a strict definition and application of science, constructivists argue that separations of science and nonscience are social conventions. As Copier explains: "Essentialists do boundary-work, constructivists watch it get done by people in society." Copier favors the researcher as someone who merges with data and constructs certain boundaries in order to carry out observation and analysis. She refers to the example of fan scholarship in media studies, where scholars have long acknowledged the possibility of being a devoted fan of media and poignant researcher at the same time. This type of scholarship allows researchers to explore particular sites but also still partitions them from the rest of the community. With this adapted profile, researchers can test subjects as they invest in pornography to create identities and reflect on them. Science then becomes more involved, with honest exploration and discussion with subjects, whose arousal reflects their status as pornographic beings and networks in an age of digital media.

Notes

1. Adrian Turpin, "Not Tonight Darling, I Am Online," *Financial Times*, April 31, 2006, http://www.ft.com.
2. In the blog Onanism 2.0, Nicholas Carr has a dialogue with Seth Finkelstein about the validity of Turpin's statistics. They are deemed unreliable as they were issued by the N2H2 censorware company as part of a global publication relations campaign. See http://sethf.com.ifothoughts/blogf/archives/000424.html and http://roughtype.com/archives/2006/03/onanism_20.php.
3. Turpin, "Not Tonight Darling, I Am Online."
4. Erick Janssen, Deanna Carpenter, and Cynthia A. Graham, "Selecting Films for Sex Research: Gender Differences in Erotic Film Preference," *Archives of Sexual Behavior* 32, no. 3 (June 2003): 243–51.
5. Rogeria Waismann, Peter B. C. Fenwick, Glenn D. Wilson, Terry D. Hewett, and John Lumsden, "EEG Responses to Visual Erotic Stimuli in Men with Normal and Paraphilic Interests," *Archives of Sexual Behavior* 32, no. 2 (April 2003): 135–44.
6. Louis Georges Castonguy, Jean Proulx, Jocelyn Aubut, Andre MacKibben, and Michael Campbell, "Sexual Preference Assessment of Sexual Aggressors: Predictors of Penile Response Magnitude," *Archives of Sexual Behavior* 22, no. 4 (August 1993): 325–34.
7. Castonguy et al., "Sexual Preference Assessment of Sexual Aggressors," 326.

8. Angela Carter, *The Sadeian Woman and the Ideology of Pornography* (New York: Penguin Books, 1979), 21–22.

9. Show-n-Tell, *webAffairs*, with an essay by Allucquere Rosanne Stone (Boston: Eighteen Publications, 2005).

10. Show-n-Tell, *webAffairs*, 51.

11. He refers to Les Wright's definition of the "bear" in *The Bear Book: Readings in the History and Evolution of a Gay Male Subculture*, parts 1 and 2.

12. Warbear, interview with author, unpublished text, November 17, 2005.

13. Francesco Palmieri, "21st Century Schizoid Bear: Masculine Transitions through Net Pornography," unpublished text.

14. Palmieri, "21st Century Schizoid Bear."

15. Warbear profile on http://www.bearwww.com/warbearhc (May 15, 2006).

16. Warbear profile on www.myspace.com/warbear (May 15, 2006).

17. Palmieri, "21st Century Schizoid Bear."

18. Malek Boutih interview, "L'homophobie en banlieue" (Homophobia in the Suburbs), http://www.kelma.org/PAGES/DOCUMENTS/malek_boutih.php (April 15, 2006).

19. Bull Neck's description of bulls on groups.yahoo.com/group/bullempire (April 15, 2006).

20. Nofauxxx, mission statement, http://www.nofauxxx.com/tour/mission.htm (June 15, 2006).

21. Naked Earth website, http://www.nakedearthcomix.com (February 21, 2003).

22. Responses to an author's survey handed out to participants of the conference The Film Scene: The Cinema, The Arts, and Social Change, Hong Kong University, April 21–22, 2006.

23. The Philip Mak Shoujou-ai archive, http://www.shoujoai.com (April 21, 2006).

24. Marije Janssen, "We Are So Much More Than Our Naked Boobies: The Use of Sexual Agency by Young Feminists in Online Pornographic Communities," master's thesis, University of Utrecht, Spring 2006.

25. Donna Haraway, "A Cyborg Manifesto: Science, Technology, and Socialist-Feminism in the Late Twentieth Century," in *Simians, Cyborgs, and Women: The Reinvention of Nature* (New York: Routledge, 1991), 149–81.

26. Marinka Copier, "The Other Game Researcher," in *Level Up! The Proceedings of the Digital Games Research Conference at Utrecht University*, ed. Marinka Copier and Joost Raessens (Utrecht: Universitiet Utrecht, 2003), 404–20.

CHAPTER FOUR

~

Eros in Times of War:
From Cross-Cultural Teasings to
the Titillation of Torture

In *Escape Velocity: Cyberculture at the End of the Century*, Mark Dery un-ravels the desire to have sex with remote bodies within the 1990s cy-berculture and the growing inclination to share one's sex drive with data and machines, which he frames as a Western masculine obsession with new technologies. The circulation of mainstream and amateur (realcore) pornography in digital networks has enabled people to artic-ulate and represent a meticulously morphed body and share sexual im-ages through p2p connectivity. But these strands of people's porn are not completely divorced from a naïve dematerialization of the body and an acting out of geopolitical conflicts. Hence, the most vibrant histo-ries of amateur porn are welded into people's use of images of violence or political fundamentalism that revel in the ecstasies of war. Web users "go to war" while exchanging porn images or while fantasizing eroti-cized visions of death and violence. In this chapter, netporn criticism revisits Klaus Theweleit's model of visual culture analysis of war culture in *Male Fantasies, Volumes I & II*, to search for visual-performative ex-pressions of war bodies and fetishes in contemporary porn cultures. As we know from the Abu Ghraib warporn torture controversies, soldiers are wired citizens who have entered the network to document and share databases of visual icons as primal desires.

Looking at the resonance of these images to further examine porn arousal, erotic expressions are shown to stir hatred, violence, and interracial conflicts within commercial domains and p2p routes of web traffic. Finally, the chapter responds to a perception of a spiraling of ruthless violence and racism in netporn by examining the value of contemporary art, resistance strategies of the sexual-creative body, the art of sadomasochism, and warpunks. I do not mean to argue that war art is redeeming in comparison with war pornography, but it is the case that artists can show us how to access, manipulate, and share images of sex and violence in a more critical, more sensual, and less cowardly manner.

"Steelhard Goes to War" Porn

Klaus Theweleit's mammoth study of the war psyche of Nazi soldiers compiles evidence from a wide variety of sources, including autobiographical documents and fragments of popular culture, including soldiers' diaries, propaganda, cartoons, and movie posters. His major mantra is austere and bleak, as he points to the cultural organization of a steelhard male body, primarily characterized by a desire to be freed from all that can be identified with warmth and love, fluidity and sensuality. He evokes the mythic-collective psychosis of fascism as an organization of the armored male self in a world constantly threatening its disintegration. Thus, we can see a visual-performative enactment of fanatical discipline, such as the military goose step or Nazi salute. We find solidity in bodies, uniforms, and leather jackboots, all of which become a most effective shield in protecting the body. The body becomes a war tank that is able to plow through the landscape of myriad bombardments: material disintegration; eruptions of battles and bombings; oppressive mental shocks and pains; ideological corruption within the ranks; global political madness; anarchism and resistance; and, last not but least, presence of the enemy.

Theweleit identifies fascism as a solidity of the body and a rigorous belief in gender difference, or the assertion of a machine-like strength and control over bodily processes, erupting bodies, and enemy bodies associated with femininity. As explained in Jessica Benjamin and Anson Rabinbach's foreword to *Male Fantasies*:

Two basic types of bodies exemplify the corporal metaphysics at the heart of fascist perception. On the one side, there is the soft, fluid, and ultimately liquid female body which is a quintessentially negative "Other" lurking inside the male body. It is the subversive source of pleasure or pain which must be expurgated or sealed off. On the other, there is the hard, organized, phallic body devoid of all internal viscera which finds its apotheosis in the machine. This body-machine is the acknowledged utopia of the fascist warrior. The new man is a man whose physique has been mechanized, his psyche eliminated.[1]

These antithetical bodies are reflected in Nazi propaganda and popular artworks, in the construction of male and female archetypes, and in male testimonies of fears about the perpetually engulfing *others*. The fear and revulsion of the feminine manifests itself in incessant invocations and metaphors of approaching fluids and floods, dirt, streams, lava, dying bodies, diseases, and emissions of all sorts. It produces a collective-psychic neurosis that disciplines, controls, and contains fears, sexual desires, and the flows of violence. According to Theweleit, the soldier psyche cultivates a mental determination to be whole and remain whole.

One way in which Nazi soldiers engaged in sexualized bodily rituals was by carrying out ritualized acts of torture, such as public whippings. Camp commanders forced prisoners to publicly display their vulnerability and violated their naked bodies. We can see this in one of the scenes of Liliana Cavani's movie *Night Porter* (1974) in which Dirk Bogarde as Maximilian Theo Aldorfer, a former Nazi SS officer, meets with Charlotte Rampling as Lucia Atherton, a concentration camp survivor. The two accidentally meet after World War II in a Vienna hotel and fall back into their broken lives' memories of the past, acting them out in an erotically sadomasochistic relationship. In one of these scenes, Aldorfer is seen staring at the prisoners and filming them as they are forced to walk around as naked masses. But he meets again with Lucia after the war in order to exorcise his fascist past and have a meaningful love experience, which is not possible in his political climate where all his actions are watched and his affair with the Jewish other leads to his murder by fellow ex-Nazis.

As we can read in Theweleit's testimonies, most commanders pretended to be emotionally untouched by their prisoners, even though they were indeed manipulating them within acts of voyeurism and exhibitionism. Some commanders carried out the task of whipping prisoners while others were watching the spectacle. Theweleit details an account of the ritualized whipping of a homosexual camp prisoner which provides the tormentor's release: "Ritual flogging seems to me to be most sexual, the most obviously phallic of all forms of torture; one which forces the victim to participate in a form of negative coitus. The rhythm of the strokes offers a fair imitation of coital thrusts; the screams of the victim rise along the lines of the excitability curve, climax, and then slacken."[2] The whippings of the prisoner had a specific duration to satisfy the voyeuristic tormentor, who then also "switched" to become the main performer in the spectacle: "Its primary product is the totality of the experience of the tormentor, his absolute physical omnipotence. Torture not only involves the public display of the victim, but also of the tormentor; it is he and not the victim, whose actions function as deterrent."[3] But even though the tormentor became a phallic agent in this drawn-out scene of abuse, he did not show off his arousal but carefully contained the danger of losing himself.

According to Theweleit, the tormentors followed the script of protecting the armored self. They did not stream with joy at whipping helpless victims, as they were buffering their bodies and exorcising their expression of emotion and desire. Theweleit attacks fascist masculinity by referring to Wilhelm Reich's study of sexuality and orgasm, which formulates a "streaming" body linking the sexual human being to the external cosmos and striving toward orgasm. It is a cultivation of an "oceanic" feeling that allows individuals to break boundaries between the self and the cosmos, or the self and others. Reich wrote in the 1930s that the concept of orgasm was in danger in his modern society. In many older cultures, a spiritual acknowledgment of desire was practiced within animistic types of religion. Reich also criticized the psychoanalytic theories of Sigmund Freud, who constructed a modern-industrial male and female ego. Reich challenged the gender binaries of Freud and resurrected a primitivist theory of pleasure and orgasm. Sexual inclinations do not develop in our identification with our parents, or with our symbolic Mothers and Fathers, but stem from libidinal feelings and emotions triggered by natural environments and the cosmos.

But even though soldiers became war machines, they still secretly engaged in acts of erotic pleasure and transgressions. As Thor Kunkel's controversial research and novel *Endstufe* (Final Stage) brought to light, Nazi soldiers cultivated forms of leisure that included the production of secret collections of pornographic home movies. Some of these movies were shot in 1941 and have become known as the Sachsenwald films, including the pastoral movie *Desire in the Woods* and the movie *The Trapper*.[4] Officially, pornography was forbidden under the Nazis, but in reality these films were screened privately for the amusement of senior Nazi figures. Kunkel also believes that they were traded in African countries in exchange for commodities. But despite the new evidence about private transgressions and the existence of Nazi porn, the public face of fascism presented an untouchable body, a body without sex drive. Thus, the soldiers publicly volunteered their lyrical-emotive evocation of the body as the enemy, a catalyst of total chaos, leaking fluids, and anarchist thoughts. The artful mythologizing of engulfing enemy-bodies coincided with the mythologizing of dead war victims as the soldiers' "war trophies."

In order to analyze the nascent love affair between soldiers' representations of war and pornography, it is also useful to look into the history of photography and mass media as they started to impact practices of public violence. Vicky Goldberg argues that the public representation of images of violence generally has coincided with a process toward dematerialization and the disappearance of actual deaths from the public sphere. In earlier centuries, material death was experienced as a nearby reality, as corpses tended to be buried in nearby pits and graveyards, and decomposed bodies and bones turned up when new trenches were being dug. Moreover, criminals were executed in public squares until the mid-nineteenth century, and their bodies were often displayed at length so that the flesh was slowly decaying in front of people's eyes. But as life expectancy increased by small increments, people found ways to dispel the everyday immediacies of death, or reinvented death as abstract romantic myths and dramatic fictions. Graveyards were moved into suburban neighborhoods and into the countryside; moral-religious portrayals and spiritual citations of the sufferings and death of Christ and saints were replaced by a secular spectacle culture—the idea of death transformed with our need to create distance and promote fictionalization.

Goldberg believes that the nineteenth-century transformation of death was slightly out of sync with its disappearance from immediate public culture. It was as if documentary photography took a leap of faith: "Yet there they are doing a slightly out-of-step minuet across time: as the dead leave the realm of transcendence to become beautiful dreamers and tame objects, as executions retreat behind prison walls, as the mortal coil gets shuffled off in isolation wards and eventually in far-away nursing homes, the new reproductive media offer more realistic or exaggerated visions of how we die."[5] Goldberg further documents how photographers embraced and beautified death by taking tranquil deathbed pictures, in keeping with the new idea of the afterlife as a comfortable bourgeois existence. In the mid-nineteenth century, photographers even created a strand of spirit photography, where they claimed to be able to tap into the afterlife by photographing the dead body. As Goldberg summarized: "A desperate yearning for mastery buttresses our combined fascination, fear, and avoidance of scenes of death."[6] Along came the fascination with visualizations of dead bodies in accidents and natural disasters: railroad crashes, shipwrecks, explosions, floods, and epidemics in developing countries.

Just like the Nazi evocation of decaying enemies as red floods, we witness an upsurge of extreme violence and blood in fictional disaster films and war movies. In 1955, Geoffrey Gorer first labeled the fascination with blood and violence as pornography in his essay "The Pornography of Death." He argues that natural death becomes smothered in prudery, while violent death plays an ever-growing part in the fantasy representations offered to mass audiences as a kind of arousing image culture or pornography.[7] This tendency has been set in motion by photographers and the mass media for more than a century, but has reached new heights in the contemporary war era, as soldiers in battle have become photographers who display their culminating snapshots of death and violence on the Internet.

Severed Heads and Ears: Fictions or Facts?

What is a war trophy? When soldiers kill, they collect body parts of the dead or photograph them for personal memories, or they show them around to friends. As Tom Engelhardt writes in his essay, "War Porn and Iraq," from the late nineteenth century on, war trophy photos began to appear; for instance, photographs of Europeans holding Chinese heads after the Boxer Rebellion was crushed by a European-American-Japanese expeditionary force. Japanese soldiers brought back entire photo albums from their expeditionary campaigns on the Chinese mainland in the 1930s, with snapshots again of Chinese heads being removed.[8] During the Vietnam War, there were accounts of soldiers taking ears, fingers, and even heads. Sometimes actual body parts were strung together to make a necklace. Often these trophies were meant to be kept for private records, but they then leaked into public culture. The struggle with enemies as inferior, irrational, inhuman beings increasingly became something to be recorded and shared to establish a sense of target and closure. Engelhardt remembers seeing one of these war trophies in the late 1960s in an alternative newspaper. The photograph displayed a grinning American soldier holding up a severed Vietnamese head in a trophy-hunting pose. Engelhardt's online essay links to photo galleries of contemporary war trophies. Digital tools and networks have provided the trophy photo with new power and radiance in the ongoing Iraqi war as they help soldiers bring closure to traumatizing encounters with enemies.

In late April 2004, the U.S. television newsmagazine 60 Minutes further reported on a story that had been broken in an article by Seymour Hersh in the New Yorker revealing regular torture by the American military of Iraqi inmates. The story included photographs made by American soldiers in the Abu Ghraib prison depicting the torture and sexual abuse of Iraqi prisoners, and resulted in a substantial political scandal.[9] In follow-up articles, Hersh showed that the torture and abuse were part of a larger Pentagon operation that encouraged the physical coercion and sexual humiliation of Iraqi prisoners in an effort to generate more intelligence about the growing insurgency in Iraq. After the scandal was revealed to the public and the prison itself came under attack by insurgents, the U.S. Department of Defense made efforts to remove seventeen soldiers and officers from duty. Between May 2004 and September 2005, seven soldiers were convicted in court martials, sentenced to federal prison, and dishonorably discharged from service. The two ringleaders of the spectacle, Specialist Charles Graner and his former fiancée, Private Lynndie England, were sentenced to ten years and three years in prison, respectively, in trials ending on January 14, 2005, and September 26, 2005.

When the Abu Ghraib abuse photos were revealed to the public, several critics used the word *warporn* to denote the soldier's eroticized and self-conscious sadistic representations of prisoners. Warporn refers to a blurring of abuse and war mythologies as Sadean fictions. The distribution of war torture images on the Internet contributed to its transformation into *warporn*. Remote viewers were watching these images of abuse, not as war documents, nor as porn scenes evoking arousal, but as a new representation of a liminal scene. Warporn was always depicting a scene in between fact and fiction and transforming collectively with our wandering gaze and consciousness. The torture techniques were fed on sadomasochism—and s/m practitioners no doubt have equally snooped around online to look at the torture photos—but warporn itself is neither torture nor s/m. As a representation of liminal reality, warporn images are eroticized political documents and can indeed cause intricate chains of political violence, outrage, and revenge. The Abu Ghraib photographs were shot and distributed by soldiers as a new kind of homemade pornography. When the images started circulating on the web, they were eagerly reposted in private databases, primarily as a kind of rehashing of the grand patriotic scenario of U.S. imperialism facilitated by the ease of digital media distribution. The images easily floated beyond the initial in-crowd to become a public mythologizing of violence, sexual humiliation, and racial hatred.

As Hersh explains, these acts did not only point to the questionable behavior of the soldiers, but they were actually ordered by the Pentagon. For both patriots and antiwar campaigners, the images became a way for people to celebrate or fear the depths of U.S. imperialism and violence in porn culture. The members of the U.S. extreme right admitted that these tortures were horrendous and criminal acts, but they did not point to the corruption of leadership. The soldiers themselves were seen as an anomaly within the system, as perverts and as spoiled by sadomasochistic porn, specifically porn of the gay kind. The officials maintain that Abu Ghraib was an aberrant military act, a temporary loss of masculinity and control leadership.[10] The left-wing authorities showed disapproval and also lamented the fact that the boundaries between war and porn were slipping in network society.

Warporn was seen as a dangerous media development aiding the cause of U.S. military rule. They were more politically correct than the right wing—they did not point their fingers at gay porn or s/m porn, but at porn as the eternally exploitative misogynistic enemy of progressive culture. The anomaly in their case was the fact that there were female soldiers, Private Lynndie England and Specialist Sabrina Harman, who were clearly and proudly part of the sadist binge on Iraqi male nudity. Finally, the photographs initiated a sequence of mediated hate wars and physical violence between pro-war/anti-Islam factions and Islam fundamentalist groups and leaders. From within the soldiers' private domains, the images leaked and trafficked inside the belly of the beast. Abu Ghraib soldiers swapped images of prisoners as their personal homemade trophies, but journalists and the wider masses saw them as warporn. The images insulted and aroused people and were followed by political countermoves, such as the public beheading of Nick Berg, a U.S. contractor in Iraq. Berg was seeking telecommunications work in Iraq when he was abducted and beheaded in May 2004 by Islamic militants. The decapitation, the first of a series of such killings of foreign hostages in Iraq, received worldwide attention because it was filmed and the footage was subsequently released on the Internet, reportedly from a Malaysian homepage by the Islamic organization al-Ansar. The U.S. Central Intelligence Agency (CIA) claimed that it was one of the primary insurgents, the Jordanian-born head of al-Qaeda in Iraq, Abu Musab al-Zarqawi, who had personally beheaded Berg. His killers indeed claimed that his death was carried out to avenge abuses of Iraqi prisoners by U.S. soldiers at Abu Ghraib prison.

And what was to be the next move? Tom Engelhardt wrote a postscript to his article about trophy-culture: "On June 9, soon after I wrote that article, I got my wish. The U.S. military killed Abu Musab al-Zarqawi, took a photo of his dead head, blew it up to enormous proportions, and displayed it in a frame at a press conference. From the way it was framed, the head could have been connected to a body or not. Presumably this was meant to be not only proof of his death, but a kind of revenge for al-Zarqawi's beheading of Americans. The image would fit perfectly in a collection of war trophy photos."[11] As one of the last episodes of the exchange of warporn, it becomes clear that such strategies of performative mimicry fuel the racial hatred and on-going warfare. There is neither sensuality nor consensus between the players of s/m in warporn; their session is sad and out of control. Per-haps these sessions will be with us for many more decades, as they were set in motion many decades ago and long before the Abu Ghraib tor-tures or September 11 attacks.

Theweleit argues that Nazi rituals of violence are assisted by the construction of steelhard masculinity. Can we see in the Abu Ghraib photographs a resurfacing of the divide between steelhard soldiers and the other masses? How has contemporary war culture evolved from Theweleit's thesis and its reverberations in the public sphere? Some commentators emphasized the recurrence of antithetical bodies, or the continuing fear of revenge of the other body. Max Gordon, a Black male and self-confessed porn addict, argues that the warporn actions are the epitome of a historical American fascination with the public torture of others. He mentions Hilton Als's essay in *Without Sanctuary: Lynching Photographs in America*. This well-known photography project and website details a history of public lynchings, including the murder in 1916 of Jesse Washington, a Black man from Waco, Texas, who was castrated, mutilated, and burned alive in front of a crowd that in-cluded women and children. A postcard was sent around with his im-age on the back and the message: "This is the barbecue we had last night." Afterward, Washington's corpse hung on public display in front of a blacksmith's shop.[12] Washington's corpse indeed mirrors the photographs of tortured and dead Iraqis as trophies accompanied by cynical captions. The easy distribution of such documents points to an ongoing dematerialization of our understanding of death, yet such dis-tribution rekindles fears. It evokes sentiments of fiery patriotism and lethargy. Gordon understands that these sentiments are indeed caused by the hybridization of war documentation and pornography. He gives a full and precise testimony:

> The prison photographs represent the perfect hybrid of two of our great-est current cultural addictions—reality television and violent porn. No one seemed to understand where the photographs came from, and yet Internet porn use and its related addictions are at an all-time high, de-picting ever harsher and more realistic forms of abuse and sexual cruelty.

The line between simulated and actual rape becomes more blurred each day. The most shocking realization about the photographs at Abu Ghraib is that they weren't shocking at all.

The Internet, its "virtual" torture chambers, and the children and adults who are exploited there are all part of an unspoken American shadow—an illuminated screen in the privacy of our homes, paid for with a credit card and accessed late at night with a secret password. Collectively, we were disturbed by Abu Ghraib, and yet alone we were hungry for these images, desperate to understand how "they" (the depraved few who we were told betrayed our country) could do it, and left wondering if any of "they" is in us.

The question was never how could we commit the atrocious acts seen in the photographs, but rather how could we not—given our unexplored relationship to sex and racial violence, and our unwillingness to examine the role [sex] has played as entertainment and a stress reliever, since the slave trade.[13]

In 2005, the Abu Ghraib photographs and videos were officially made available on the Internet through the Abu Ghraib Files, a comprehensive collection of carefully annotated galleries, compiled by Mark Benjamin and Michael Scherer for Salon.com.[14] The files contain 279 photographs and 19 videos from the Army's internal investigation record. As we can see when browsing through these files, the gender dynamic between soldiers and victims has shifted, as the abuse of Iraqi women and men was carried out and recorded by American men and women. But the prisoners as suspected insurgents were nevertheless tortured by means of feminization. They were often forced to wear women's underwear on their heads. As one prisoner testified to the CID (Criminal Investigation Command) investigators: "[T]he American police, the guy who wears glasses, he put red woman's underwear over my head. And then he tied me to the window that is in the cell with my hands behind my back until I lost consciousness." In another photograph, Specialist Sabrina Harman herself poses for a photo with the same red women's underwear on outside of her uniform. She is the tormentor but shows off a private moment of mimicry of the prisoner's forced "feminization." The report found that there was ample

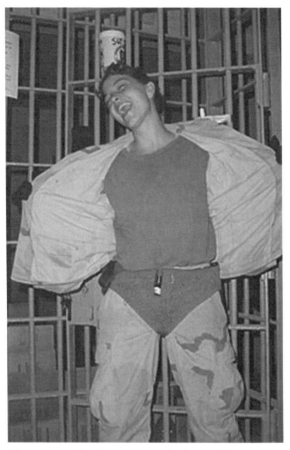

Photo reprinted with permission of Salon Media Group. Salon's full report on the Abu Ghraib files can be found on the Salon.com website.

evidence of prisoners being forced to wear women's underwear and concluded that this may have been part of the military intelligence tactic called "ego down," adding that the method constitutes abuse and sexual humiliation.

There is an infamous photograph showing Private Lynndie England holding the leash of a detainee, a photo that was taken by her fiancé, Charles Graner. England is shot in Graner's arms with a big smile on her face, perhaps as one of the first-ever glowing female patriotic war-

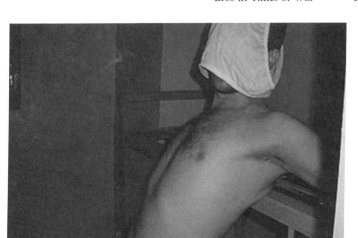

Photo reprinted with permission of Salon Media Group. Salon's full report on the Abu Ghraib files can be found on the Salon.com website.

machines. In one of the most famous cases of abuse, seven detainees and suspected rioters were "verbally abused, stripped, slapped, punched, jumped on, forced into a human pyramid, forced to simulate masturbation, and forced to simulate oral sex, several Army reports concluded." England told the Army's CID investigators that she had visited the military intelligence wing in the early morning hours of that abuse case, because it was her birthday and she wanted to see her friends. She said that Graner and Frederick told her that they were bringing in seven prisoners from a riot at Ganci. The prisoners were brought in with handcuffs and bags on their heads and wearing civilian clothes. She said that she initially watched the ordeal from a higher vantage point. Everyone else was downstairs pushing the prisoners into each other and the wall, until they all ended up in a dog pile. Later on in the session, England went down and took part in preparing the dog pile. She is photographed smiling and pointing at the naked detainees with a cigarette in her mouth. She is also photographed arm in arm with her boyfriend in front of the dog pile. Throughout this session, Graner is photographed as the master-executor, wearing green rubber gloves to distinguish himself from the dogs. His facial expression is tense, while England shows a beautiful, shy female smile showing off the detainees as her (almost) personal trophies.

Photo reprinted with permission of Salon Media Group. Salon's full report on the Abu Ghraib files can be found on the Salon.com website.

As shown before, the Abu Ghraib photographs were not an isolated incident in the making of warporn. Warporn documents have continued to be produced and distributed until the present day. In April 2006, the media revealed that Florida resident Chris Wilson was sentenced to five years of probation for running the popular website www.nowthats fuckedup.com (NTFU), which included photographs of war dead taken by U.S. troops. Wilson gave soldiers free access to porn in exchange for posting pictures from both the Afghanistan and Iraq wars. In a September 2005 interview with George Zornick in *The Nation*, Wilson claims there were about 150,000 registered users on the site, 45,000 of whom were military personnel. Zornick describes the development of the web-

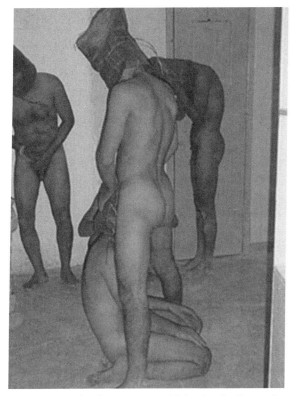

Photo reprinted with permission of Salon Media Group. Salon's full report on the Abu Ghraib files can be found on the Salon.com website.

site. The postings by U.S. troops began as "benign images of troops leaning against their tanks, but graphic combat images also began to appear." Most of the time the photos were accompanied by "sadistic glee," cynical comments, or "pathological wisecrack" captions.

> [There are] close-up shots of Iraqi insurgents and civilians with heads blown off, or with intestines spilling from open wounds. Sometimes photographs of mangled body parts are displayed. . . . A series of photos showing two men slumped over in a pickup truck, with nothing visible above their shoulders except a red mass of brain matter and bone, was described as "an Iraqi driver and passenger that tried to run a checkpoint

during the first part of OIF." The post goes on to say that "the bad thing about shooting them is that we have to clean it up." Another post, labeled "dead shopkeeper in Iraq," does not explain how the subject of the photo ended up with a large bullet hole in his back but offers the quip "I guess he had some unsatisfied customers."[15]

The military personnel used the NTFU site as a venue to showcase their war images and trophies. The site was an outlet for soldiers in reconstructing daily struggles as closure and victory over enemy bodies. As stated by an anonymous soldier in an interview with Mark Glaser: "To answer your question about posting the gory pictures on this site: What about the beheadings filmed and then put on worldwide news? I have seen video of insurgents shooting American soldiers in plain day and thanking God for what they have done. I wouldn't be too concerned what I am doing on a private Web site. I'm more concerned of what my fellow soldiers and I are experiencing in combat."[16] As of September 20, 2005, there were 244 graphic battlefield images and videos available to members. When Wilson was finally arrested in April 2005, U.S. military officials refused to state that the combat photos posted on a porn site were troubling. The county's sheriff officials stated that the arrest was made because of the site's sexually explicit content, not the pictures of war dead.

Wilson's lawyer, Lawrence Walter, thus laid out an argument in defense of Internet pornography—an argument that was previously used by the ACLU in order to strike down COPA.[17] Walter defines cyberspace as a global and multicultural universe, and argues that it would be a mistake to apply the moral norms and legal justice of the most restrictive country. He also points out that NTFU is not an isolated site in offering a combination of porn and pictures of accidents, political violence, and war casualties. He mentions the brother site www.ogrish .com, which on July 8, 2006 had a post entitled "Baghdad's Morgue Receives Increasing Number of Bodies." It is a video with a sample of ten murder victims as they are collected from the morgue.[18]

Zornick concludes that these images and sites should not be censored but rather should be made available and analyzed: "If there is any redeeming value to such a clearinghouse for images of destruction and death, it would rest in the site's ability to offer an unflinching look at the obscenity of war—and war's impact on the psyches of the soldiers called to fight it." The very complicated question of how web users and political parties should further react to these images brings us to a discussion of the gridlock arguments made by bloggers, artists, and intellectuals for open sexuality and freedom of speech.

Fight with the Pen or the Sword?

The mass media coverage of the Abu Ghraib torture worsened ethnic relations and racial hatred between the United States and Iraq, and between Islamic and Western cultures all around the globe. The publication of the Abu Ghraib photographs alerted the world to the military tactics and media monopoly of the U.S. government. The assaulted parties were invited to take revenge. A significant episode in the growing global crisis was the hateful teasing in the *Jyllands-Posten* Muhammad cartoons. The controversies started on September 30, 2005, after twelve editorial cartoons depicting the Islamic prophet Muhammad were published in the Danish newspaper *Jyllands-Posten*. The newspaper believed that the publication of caricatures made by Danish artists was a contribution to debates about Islam and self-censorship. But the images caused a bloody cycle of protest and violence, besides the discussions of freedom of speech. Danish Muslim organizations spread knowledge of *Jyllands-Posten*'s publication and held public protests. As the controversy grew, examples of the cartoons were reprinted in newspapers in more than fifty other countries, which led to both peaceful and violent protests as well as deadly rioting, particularly in the Muslim world.[19] As the riots broke out, several individuals collaborated on compiling levelheaded daily news and testimonies on the Wikipedia website. Many other websites sprang to life that consolidated reactions of hatred, fear, and violence. People commented once again on being endlessly aroused by the aesthetics of war and warporn in a widening spiral of violence.

One of the most sensitive images was that of Muhammad with a bomb in his turban, with a lit fuse and the Islamic creed written on the bomb. I believe that this image harkens back to the male fantasy syndrome described by Theweleit. The stereotype of the Arab religious leader as an explosive alpha male or suicide bomber reveals fears about the perpetual engulfing Islamic enemies and their violent material disintegration. The cartoon artist explains that he made that image because he was angered by the dangers of totalitarian religious practices of Islam. A second recurrence of male fantasies can be seen in the Western racist's subtle ways of feminizing the enemy. One cartoonist depicts abstract stick figures wearing headscarves, while their faces are a crescent moon and star, showing the flag of Islam. The caption says, "Prophet, daft and dumb, keeping women under thumb." In another cartoon, Muhammad has a saber in his hand and is ready to go the war. Yet he is flanked on either side by two women in black veils or burkas. The veil hides the women and reveals their eyes, where the eyes of Muhammad are covered with a black tag. We can see in this drawing a blindfolded Muhammad and we can see in his eyes the reflection of his embattled female slave escorts. Even though these cartoons were made to assert the artist's right to free speech and to discuss the sexual abuse of women in Islam, they once again revealed a fictionalization of the feminized others. The male insurgent blends into his female as an ever injured, repressed, and traumatized force: better watch out for that!

Some television news broadcasts opted out of showing the cartoons on air. Alternately, numerous websites decided to repost the *Jyllands-Posten* Muhammad cartoons. On one level, these sites asserted freedom of speech and tried to help the plight of assaulted Danish artists, yet they threw more bombs into the debates. Many of these cartoon galleries have meanwhile been compiled by Michelle Malkin in a cartoon blogburst, which linked to about a hundred bloggers who reposted the cartoon.[20] Malkin was interested in the reposting as online free speech activism, as she writes in a message: "Ok. Let's do it. If you've posted some or all of the forbidden Mohammed cartoons on your blog in support of Denmark and the Jyllands-Posten, send a track back or e-mail me your link. It'll actually be a very useful road map for the enormous number of Internet users around the world who are trying to find the cartoons." But it remained a small effort for web users to find the cartoons, and the blogburst mostly consolidated creative outbursts of racism and hate speech.

The photo "Piss Muhammad" is an example where we see the image of Muhammad with a bomb in his turban, drenched in a haze of red-colored urine. This image of the explosive enemy drenched in red fluids or a red flood is a penultimate male fantasy. It was made by blogger Sobekpundit, who sticks out his tongue to the dandy photographers of the Western art world: "What do you think [this is] edgy? As in, I'll be super-trendy amongst Manhattan super-liberals who drooled all over themselves for Andres Serrano's Piss Christ?"[21] Another blogger "Face of Mohammed" conducts a poll to find out how many people and cultures actually support freedom of speech, and he generates a map of the world based on his test results. His cartoon "Clash Map" shows the United States and European countries supporting free speech, whereas large parts of Africa and the Middle East oppose free speech or respond to it with violence. As a matter of fact, the very center of the globe (on his flat map) is a red area erupting with lava, fanaticism, blood, and violence. It is as if the red masses are once again encroaching upon our territories, our freedom of speech, our more enlightened bodies.

In the same blog, the "Face of Mohammed" blogger contrasts an image of an enlightened male with a pen with that of a violent male with a sword. The violent male's head depicts a bomb, as if at any time he could explode in your face and destroy whatever elevated idea you happened to be writing down.[22] But as a case in point, isn't the "Face of Mohammed" blog site itself just another example of couch-potato extremism expressing death and destruction of the enemy? The most blatant anti-Islamic site was produced under the authoritative domain name www.danishmuhammedcartoons.com. It is another hate-speech site with satirical depictions of Islam. The site promotes a Lego game for ages six and older, made in Denmark, which is "Halal, and not suitable for girls." It shows Muhammad having intercourse with a woman. The caption says that Muhammad has twenty-three wives including the six-year-old Aisha. The website contains many materials about Islam, including photographs and videos of public executions of criminals in Islamic countries.

When the Jyllands-Posten first solicited the Muhammad cartoonists, many refused to partake in the project and cited the bloody murder of Dutch filmmaker Theo Van Gogh by the Islamic fundamentalist Mohammed Bouyeri in 2004. Van Gogh was a well-known independent filmmaker and symbol of Western free-speech culture. Not unlike the Dutch far-right politician Pim Fortuyn, who was murdered in Rotterdam in May 2002, Van Gogh also had a history of Islam-bashing as a way of outing the hypocrisies and tensions of the Dutch welfare state. He was an anti-immigration ideologue who questioned the welfare state's models of globalization and multiculturalism. The short film *Submission* equally contained a critique of the Islamic fundamentalist subjugation of women. The story is told by a young female who complains to Allah about her abuse by males within the family. The film was shown on the Dutch public broadcasting network (VPRO) on August 29, 2004. The film also portrays a Muslim woman as having been beaten and raped by a relative. One of the images in the movie is that of a woman in a long white dress with knife wounds and words of the Koran carved into her back.

Theo Van Gogh's murder was equally carried out in ritual-spectacular fashion but not recorded on video. Mohammed Bouyeri shot Van Gogh on his way to work until he fell off his bike. Bouyeri then slashed his throat and stuck a note in his chest with the knife, a death threat to the next person on his list, Ayaan Hirsi Ali. The death note also contained a hateful condemnation of the Western world and foresaw its auto-destruction: "I know for sure that you, Oh America, will perish. I know that you, Oh Europe, will perish."

Hirsi Ali is a well-known Dutch politician and renegade Muslim of Somali origin who had helped Van Gogh write the script for *Submission*. The murder caused her to go into hiding and caused outbursts of violence in the Netherlands and Belgium—anti-Muslim violence, anti-Semitic violence, and anti-welfare-state violence. The image that accompanied the newspaper coverage of Van Gogh's murder was the naked female body of *Submission* (there was a lack of footage of Van Gogh remains.) Van Gogh wanted to redeem the Islamic female body, but Islamic parties did not want to debate with him. They perceived the image as an invitation to destruction and revenge. It became erotic flesh leading to the spectacular slaughter of Van Gogh's own body, his image-machinery, and his voice. As in the Muhammad cartoons depicting abused females, the identity of the enemy-male (Van Gogh) blended with the images of female trouble (Hirsi Ali and the female body in the film). Before he could be applauded in his eagerness to help the female other, he was simply silenced through the most extremist of practices.

The Ficto-Analysis of Warporn Imagery

Many other types of war documents and testimonies have meanwhile been posted on the web, and they are being accessed or analyzed by web users for different reasons. However, even though we may think of them as documentary evidence, these soldiers are creators of mythologies who fictionalize, fantasize, dream, and terrorize when narrating their experiences. As in Theweleit's methodology, these documents are waiting to be dissected by scholars who can tackle the zone between fantasy and documentary. For instance, the United States' National Endowment for the Arts (NEA) has recently sponsored the giant project Operation Homecoming, in which distinguished American writers are working with soldiers at twenty-five military installations to record their experiences. The NEA has managed to collect about a thousand pages of writing, and a selection of these will be published in an open government archive. A preview of the stories was published in the *New Yorker* on June 12, 2006, while audio recordings and images were made available at the *New Yorker* website.

When going through the previews of Operation Homecoming, we can witness the blurring of fact and fiction—but these stories and myths are very different from those presented by the mass media. There are some testimonies of soldiers utterly traumatized by killings, dead bodies, and death—dead Iraqis and dead fellow Americans. Death does not lead to closure but is a powerful ever-present force that drags you down. Sergeant Tina Beller explains her encounter with death during one of her first battles: "The Iraqi behind me kept nudging me in the doorway, but my legs were glued to the ground." Or death is like constant stress and a deep feeling of lethargy and heaviness, as Captain Kelly writes: "Things have hardened into routine, like an old artery that has carried the same, tired blood along the same, tired path for years. Pump, return, pump, return, wake, eat, sleep, wake, back and forth, boom! Rocket attack. Pump, return, pump, return. . . . We've worn a trail through the gravel with our boots plodding back and forth from the hangar."[23] The lurid images of torture as s/m are in contrast with the many accounts of the culmination of stress as everyday experiences with death.

As Vicky Goldberg suggested in "Death Takes a Holiday, Sort Of," the daily bodily experiences of death in modern societies have been hijacked and turned into porn by the mass media. Captain Kelly writes that there is a huge discrepancy between her experiences in Iraq and those of us who are absent. How can we respond to this line in her diary? Is there any way that we can read it and be more present? Can we make our own war media and pornographic media to share a deeper understanding of cross-cultural violence?

Videopoesis: Grinning Monkeys and War Punks

What does it mean when the bloodstained and viral aesthetics of warporn become a type of media hype and sexually inclined entertainment? Female and male soldiers and Western and Islamic image makers have entered the connective network and posted their homemade photos as a visual-performative grammar of victory, hatred, and revenge. What can we do when these images force us into the role of a detached viewer? In August 2004, a few months after the Abu Ghraib abuse scandal, Pasquinelli wrote the essay "Warporn! Warpunk! Autonomous Videopoesis in Wartime." His essay begins with the confession that we react to these images like grinning monkeys, that is, as human beings excited and aroused by the magnitude and novelty of the spectacle. We also react with indignation, disgust, protest, and outrage. For instance, in May 2004, former vice president Al Gore showed his deep emotional anger and outrage during a speech about the war in Iraq and the Iraqi prisoner abuse allegations. We cannot hide our fascination. But, more honestly, we share a fascination besides indignation. Like grinning monkeys, we sense in those images the death instinct or paralysis of the soldiers and surrounding war culture. We see their complex experiences transforming in front of our hungry eyes as a blatant and aestheticized torture of others. Do we have no choice but to consume these images? According to Pasquinelli, we have to try think beyond the "techno-crisis" at hand and analyze a "video-clash" between civilizations. He points out cultural differences between Western and Islamic religious cultures in the reception of mass media. As he summarizes, American corporate media are organized around videocracy, a power principle that mixes news with hypertrophic advertising and infotainment, whereas Islamic power regimes are iconoclastic or "video-clastic" and forbid the centralizing role of images:

Alongside the techno-conflict between horizontal and vertical media, two secular cultures of image face each other on the international media-scape. The United States embodies the last stage of videocracy, an oligarchic technocracy based on hypertrophic advertising and infotainment, and the colonization of the worldwide imagery through Hollywood and CNN. Twentieth-century ideologies such as Nazism and Stalinism were intimately linked to the fetishism of the idea-image (as all of western thought is heir to Platonic idealism).[24]

Islamic cultures, on the contrary, are traditionally iconoclastic: It is forbidden to represent images of God and the Prophet, and usually of any living creature whatsoever.[25] The Western impetus to produce mythic images of victory and victims would then be answered by violent acts and aesthetics of image destruction. Pasquinelli suggests that we forget about the mechanisms of videocracy and use a different aesthetic to start analyzing the fascination with war imagery in which we got trapped. More particularly, he proposes *videopoesis*, a new agency coming out of the clash between videocracy and videoclasm. Centrally produced and manipulated war footage, such as CNN's infotainment shows, have caused a surplus of excitement, anger, and energy in couch-potato viewers around the world—and videopoesis means a meditation on and reworking of this productivity and the death instinct, rather than casting it aside through feelings of guilt or indignation. As he writes, videopoesis should speak, at the same time, to the belly and to the brain of the monkeys.

> In such a clash between videocracy and videoclasm, a third actor, the global movement, tries to open a breach and develop therein an autonomous videopoesis. The making of an alternative imagery is not only based on self-organizing independent media, but also on winning back the dimension of myth and the body.[26]

Pasquinelli believes that independent media makers and artists can be warpunks or find aesthetic strategies for distributing alternative images of war and eroticism. We cannot ignore the attraction of war or porn, but we can be less cowardly and distant from media to win back the dimension of the body by creating alternative performative acts and

imagery. As autonomous media makers, we can moderate our media addiction and create our own ecstasies of love and war.

Pasquinelli cites the work of Chris Korda, who made a video-
montage of September 11, in which he mixed images of the burning
towers, fanatic soccer fans, and masturbation scenes, to criticize our fascination with war porn. Pasquinelli analyzes this work as a warpunk: "I
like to watch video porn scenes of oral sex and masturbation mixed with
those of football and baseball games, together with well-known NY911
images. The phallic imagery reaches the climax: the Pentagon is hit by
an ejaculation, multiple erections are turned into the NY911 skyline,
and the Twin Towers become the object of an architectural fellatio. This
video is the projection of the lowest instincts of American society, of the
common ground that binds spectacle, war, pornography and sport. It is
an orgy of images that shows to the West its real background."[27]

Warpunks should confront Western media addiction with a coun-
tersquadron, throwing libidinal bombs and radical images into the
heart of its videocracy. An art collage in response to Abu Ghraib was
presented by David Boardman at the 2005 Art and Politics of Netporn
conference. He describes his photo collage "My Favorite Abu Ghraib
Links" as "schizophrenic video about Abu Ghraib jail tortures, a porn
movie that mixes the photographs of Abu Ghraib tortures with images
of radical sadism."[28] He uses a high-speed-frame sequence so that the
eye's perception blends together the two types of photographs. He ends
the photo collage with still images from *Apocalypse Now*, in which we
see rowdy soldiers get aroused by female performers. As if this type of
male gaze has gone totally berserk in the contemporary era, he cites
J. G. Ballard's question: "Perhaps violence, like pornography, is some
kind of an evolutionary stand-by system, some last resort device for
throwing a wild joker into the game?"

Adam Zaretsky responded to the Abu Ghraib tortures by issuing the
satirical USSMEAC (the United States Sado-Masochistic Ethical Advisory Commission) report. In his report, he issues a call for the American s/m community to be the performative role models for the U.S.
military leaders. The report contains an extensive registration form
where submissive people can sign up and register for a nickname and a
password and then choose from a very detailed list of interrogation
techniques. The submissive people can then become heads of the pro-

gram and can defend new ethical values, including consent and respect. When I ask him why is he writing this satirical report as a body artist, he replies that body artists are used to thinking about the aesthetics and politics of the body as self-imposed alterations:

> There are those who fear body invasion of their supposed "integrity of human-ness" and those who identify with the (or their) body in transition, i.e. mutated, mutilated and manipulated. But who can better advise the general public on a preferable course of action than those with actual experience of self-imposed irretractable body or identity alterity? Intelligent debate on the ethics and aesthetics of future war and peace issues should include subcultural practitioners. Being able to speak from creative experience, as body artists we are some of the few experts available for safe, sane and consensual variants on the architecture of future world domination analysis. My TransWar movement "USSMEAC" focuses on the voices of s/m's public practitioners. Our slogan is: "Our analingus is underutilized." We practice in a humane way which grants us a free and independent moral compass to express fertile transgressions and pregnant pauses, opinions and suggestions. Our direct orders contradict current propaganda regimes through our humor or omnipotence from the outside in. USSMEAC hopes to promote debate that may influence the direction of what we see as an impending world war based on pain and war against eroticism and play.

Body Art and S/M Performance: The Servant Who Came on Top

A second strategy to combat Western media addiction is to create a new aesthetics of the body in its relation to its cravings for sex and pornography. This brings us to the question of affect and sensuality, or how we can develop love and political solidarity among people when sharing sexual images and discourses of violence. For instance, Tobias Van Veen argues for independent erotic/pornographic media zones where people can trust, affect, and touch each other—and also reach out to a larger audience. Pointing to Hakim Bey's idea of temporary autonomous zones, Van Veen believes that "we must seek [to] touch. On the agenda of an open affect of hospitality . . . is an engagement with affirmative desire."[29] Left-wing groups have to reacquaint themselves with a positive philosophy of desire and technology, reinventing strategies of affect and sensualism.

Van Veen perceives in right-wing propaganda a resurfacing of the steelhard body: "The Right embraces affect as its inverse: a hate politics of the foreign other (the immigrant, a race, etc.), of the nonbeliever, of sexuality (hatred of the other's body, of one's own body). The state embraces affect through discipline, conformity, and work."[30] Nonconformist formulations of desire can be found in the work of contemporary artists who use the sexual body to comment on media conditioning and a global politics of crisis. Included in this exercise are new philosophies of sensuality within the art of sadomasochism. In talking to people who are engaged in s/m practices, they explain that s/m players try to find and understand each other's physical signals so that they can complement each other in a request for play or perversion. Even though Nazi and American soldiers engage in s/m rituals with prisoners, their concepts of the body are radically different from those of the more routine s/m players.

As explained by Theweleit, Nazi culture emphasizes an antithetical relationship between masters and slaves, where s/m masters and slaves find each other in a search for complementarity. As explained by s/m practitioner Sergio Messina, "In a session, both partners work together to achieve a common state, both mental and physical."[31] In this sense, s/m sex acts differ from regular vanilla sex acts in that partners are not trying to be in competition with each other. Moreover, sex emanates from different zones and prompts the body and brain to distinguish the act, as "genital intercourse or penis and vagina are not the center of operations, the places where sex is. They become means among other means, to achieve that state of complementarity."[32]

The dominant should be flexible and work very hard trying to understand the needs and desires of the submissive. As Messina writes:

As far as the dominant side, in my view the real servant is always the Top. The scene is always about the sub's limits, fears, kinks, etc. Empathy (especially from a Dom) is essential. You have to know what's going on in a sub's body and mind in order to take a session somewhere. Moreover, empathy is an important tool. Complementarity needs empathy, and empathy brings unity—physical and mental. For example: I don't feel the sting of the whip on my body, but I have to know exactly how much it hurts, where to strike, for how long. . . . You understand this through empathy, observation and extreme attention on the other persons. In a way, you need to feel what they feel and know where he/she's at. You could call this shifting boundaries. . . . So part of the art is balance. It's a very thin balance to understand exactly how another person feels and then appear to ignore it; to be the sole ruler of a scene, sometimes ruthless, but also center the session on some kink/taboo of the sub. For example: to whip where it hurts and caress someone at the same time, giving coherence and complete meaning to both acts; in a way it means to rejoin opposites, to be able to mix water and oil, to create a storm and then safely navigate home."[33]

When I ask Messina about his reactions to Klaus Theweleit's thesis and to the Abu Ghraib photographs, he gives a sketch of his feeling of masculinity:

S/m sex practices make me feel less like a male. One of the reasons I really like to belong to a sexual minority is that I think much less like a male now. You could say less dick/pussy, more brains. It seems to me that this more mental way of perceiving and practicing sex is more feminine. I certainly feel very different from straight people, and s/m gives me the confidence to question typical straight stereotypes, attitudes, and behaviors (simple questions such as "is this thing I'm doing useful and meaningful?"). Being the strong hand by common agreement also allows me to be the gentle one, to be as sweet and passionate as Romeo. Except that Juliet is tied up so that she can only move her eyelids. A bound, helpless Juliet: how can you not be sweet Romeo?[34]

When I ask him how he reacts to the sharing of bodily fluids, he writes: "Intensely well. One way to become one is to mix fluids. I agree that this fear of fluids might have to do with the fear of the power of women's sexuality (which is more [powerful] than the male's). But the way I see it, in s/m this power is not antagonistic to the man's (as it is in vanilla sex) but it's more power for the One. So the more powerful a sub is, the more power we can use. The Dom doesn't curtail this power but channels it. So if the idea is to mix, to become one, the two-way fluids exchange seems essential, and symbolic—almost like a Communion (and the term seems very right)."[35]

Conclusion

Theweleit's *Male Fantasies* shows how Nazi war propaganda and pop culture helped soldiers to mythologize an asexual war machine and how they used technology as a process of dematerializing the body. Despite the evidence about private sex games and desires, there is a public denial of contact with other bodies or enemy bodies. In recent times, we have seen an upsurge of web-based representations of war activities and dead or tortured bodies as war pornography. War pornography is caught up in a dematerialization of violence and death, a transformation into endless lurid representations in media evoking our fears and fantasies about enemy bodies. Warporn lingers between a documentation of reality and a popular s/m fantasy. Hordes of people have accessed these documents within a liminal space, but few actually know how to properly respond. As Max Gordon admits in his testimony as a porn addict, war pornography is not a shocking phenomenon but an emblematic zone of web culture.

This chapter outlines how the growing conflict between Euro-American and Islamic cultures and media regimes has caused mediated and networked warfare. People can no longer safely reveal and distribute hostile, satirical, or humiliating images of the other without getting caught in the larger spiral of violence. But rather than suggesting that there could be an end to the circulation of stirring images, the chapter suggests that we learn how to develop performative responses in a different manner. The work of media activists shows a critical analysis of porn and war media and an embracing of alternative porn to establish a new kind of affect. Besides media artists, there are s/m practitioners and body artists who develop acts of consensual eroticism, and sensualism as a fascination with death, to represent a new way of thinking through the "pain–pleasure" regimes of contemporary pornography.

Notes

1. Klaus Theweleit, *Male Fantasies*, vol. 2 (Minneapolis: University of Minnesota Press, 1987), foreword by Anson Rabinbach and Jessica Benjamin, 19.

2. Theweleit, *Male Fantasies*, vol. 2, 303.

3. Theweleit, *Male Fantasies*, vol. 2, 304.

4. Thor Kunkel, *Endstufe* (Frankfurt: Eichborn, 2004). For an overview of the controversy surrounding his book, see Luke Harding, "Porn und Drang," *Guardian*, February 12, 2004, at http://arts.guardian.co.uk/features/story/0,11710,1146258,00.html (July 7, 2006). Kunkel's evidence about the existence of Nazi porn is in part based on interviews with people who had been involved as actresses and distributors of these films.

5. Vicki Goldberg, "Death Takes a Holiday, Sort Of," in her *Light Matters: Writings on Photography* (New York: Aperture, 2005), 212.

6. Goldberg, *Light Matters*, 221.

7. Geoffrey Gorer, "The Pornography of Death," *Encounter* 5, no. 4 (October 1955), cited in Goldberg, *Light Matters*, 235.

8. Tom Engelhardt and David Swanson, "War Porn and Iraq," Lewrockwell .com blog, http://www.lewrockwell.com/engelhardt/engelhardt197.html (July 15, 2006).

9. Seymour M. Hersh, "Torture at Abu Ghraib," *The New Yorker*, April 5, 2004, www.newyorker.com/fact/content/?040510fa_fact (July 15, 2006).

10. For examples of these right- and left-wing responses against pornification see Frank Rich, "It Was the Porn That Made Them Do It," *New York Times*, May 30, 2004; Katharine Viner, "The Sexual Sadism of Our Culture, in Peace and in War," *Guardian*, June 1, 2004; Linda Burnham, "Sexual Domination in Uniform: An American Value," published May 22, 2004 on www .counterpunch.org (January 25, 2005); and Susan Sontag, "Regarding the Torture of Others," *New York Times*, May 23, 2004.

11. Engelhardt and Swanson, "War Porn and Iraq."

12. Max Gordon, "Abu Ghraib: Postcards from the Edge," October 14, 2004, Open Democracy website, http://www.opendemocracy.net/media-abu_ghraib/article_2146.jsp (July 15, 2006). *Without Sanctuary: Lynching Photography* is located at www.withoutsanctuary.org (July 15, 2005).

13. Gordon, "Abu Ghraib: Postcards from the Edge."

14. Abu Ghraib Files introduction. http://www.salon.com/news/abu_ghraib/2006/03/14/introduction/ (July 19, 2006).

15. George Zornick, "The Porn of War," *The Nation*, September 22, 2005, http://www.thenation.com/doc/20051010/the_porn_of_war (July 19, 2006).

16. Mark Glaser, "Porn Site Offers Soldiers Free Access in Exchange for Photos of Dead Iraqis," September 20, 2005, http://www.ojr.org/ojr/stories/050920glaser (July 15, 2006).

The Geneva Convention includes Protocol I, added in 1977 but not ratified by the United States, Iraq, or Afghanistan. It mentions that all parties in a conflict must respect victims' remains, though it doesn't mention the photographing of dead bodies. This could well be a judgment call, and the celebratory and derogatory comments added on NTFU make the case more clear.

17. The conflict between these concepts of space is further clarified in this book's chapter 1, "Netporn Browsing in Small Places and Other Spaces."

18. See http://www.ogrish.com/index2.html (July 20, 2006).

19. See http://en.wikipedia.org/wiki/Jyllands-Posten_Muhammad_cartoons_controversy (July 22, 2006).

20. See http://michellemalkin.com/archives/004446.htm (July 24, 2006).

21. See http://sobekpundit.blogspot.com/2006/02/ladies-and-gentlemen-i-give-you.html (July 24, 2006).

22. See www.face-of-muhammed.blogspot.com (July 24, 2006).

23. "Dispatches from Iraq, Soldiers' Stories," *The New Yorker*, June 12, 2006.

24. Matteo Pasquinelli, "Warporn! Warpunk! Autonomous Videopoesis in Wartime," *Bad Subjects: Reviews 2004*, http://bad.eserver.org/reviews/2004/pasquinelliwarpunk.html (August 15, 2005).

25. Babak Rahim writes in "Social Death and War: U.S. Media Representations of Sacrifice" that the Iraq War was presented by the news in 2003 by the use of cinematographic techniques to reduce the horror of war to a consumable and entertaining phenomenon. The focus of CNN, MSNBC, ABC, and Fox News was on the real and graphic animation of U.S. military technology and the three-dimensional imagery of the battlefields, rather than war events. The article was published in *Bad Subjects*, no. 63, April 2003, http://bad.eserver.org/issues/2003/63/rahimi.html (August 15, 2006).

26. Pasquinelli, "Warporn! Warpunk!"

27. Pasquinelli, "Warporn! Warpunk!" Chris Korda's video can be viewed at www.churchofeuthanasia.org (August 25, 2006).

28. David Boardman, *My Favorite Abu Ghraib Links* can be viewed at www.netzfunk.org/index.php?task=viewabu&=en (July 18, 2006).

29. Tobias Van Veen, "Affective Tactics: Intensifying a Politics of Perception," *Bad Subjects*, no. 63, April 2003, http://bad.eserver.org/issues/2003/63/vanveen.html.

30. Van Veen, "Affective Tactics: Intensifying a Politics of Perception."

31. Sergio Messina, personal interview with the author, unpublished text, 2006.

32. Messina interview.

33. Messina interview.

34. Messina interview.

35. Messina interview.

CHAPTER FIVE

Post-Revolutionary Glimpses and Radical Silence: Netporn in Hong Kong and Mainland China

They aren't revolting against anything. For them, it's a thrill—a chance to become something other. . . . For Félix Guattari, such moments are "soft subversions" and "imperceptible revolutions" . . . a revolution on a smaller scale that is all the more effective because it isn't completely noticed by the majority. It is radically silent.

—Don Anderson[1]

Preliminary Notes on Netporn Research in Hong Kong

This chapter contextualizes an emerging world of mediated pornographic identities and online micro-revolutions in Hong Kong and greater China. Since Hong Kong and China have not developed an equivalent of Western-style Internet porn, it is interesting to see how web users enact and consume it differently, how nation-state governments are regulating the silent online transgressions, and how people self-censor and hide their mediated love lives. As I have explained in previous chapters, Internet pornography exceeds the objectives of streamlined commercial industries, as it belongs to alternative domains where people share hacked images or homemade porn. Besides the blossoming of indie and amateur image regimes, web users are building porn culture and porn discourses around their image consumption. For instance, the blog revolution (blogolution) has invaded China and Hong Kong, as people use the web to write sex diaries, poetry, and fictional stories or to share information about their swinging and alt-sex adventures, their multiple virtual marriages and divorce, and their public appearances as nostalgic Lolitas or other anime characters. These are examples of the Chinese people's porn, as sexual vanguards-to-be or horny mob cultures who manage to partially ignore commercial industries.

I wrote this chapter after having lived and worked in Hong Kong for one year. Since I do not speak Cantonese, it has been hard for me to get access to any information about people's porn and mediated sex lives or to share honest insights about hypersexual lifestyles and dealings with the law. Of course, it is never a smooth process to cull this kind of information, but I am a foreigner or *gwailo* in this city where people mostly do not take pride in sexual self-revelation. And so I started a difficult journey into the reticent dirty mind of Hong Kong. I decided to use my skills as an Internet researcher and my status as a foreigner. Being the wrong person to speak for or about Chinese people, I was the right person to observe and ask questions. I also wanted to get a taste of Hong Kong sexuality and hoped I was not merely walking the beaten path of white male lust for willing Asian beauties.

I tried to look deeply inside the *visual culture* and porn discourses of Hong Kong's netporn spaces, where people build sex lives and experience a profound shifting of the boundaries between the facts and the fictions of life. These spaces are not totally imperceptible since they are accessible to visitors on the web, but people are quick to hide or change their embodied identities. The boundaries between dream lives and actual facts are lost. The *twilight zone* is a 24/7 space where daytime meets the night, and where subjects splinter into multiple selves as they develop alter egos and meet with others. I would suggest that these spaces are not "unreal" spaces but "fuzzy" spaces where people try out new kinds of engagements between selves and others. Moreover, these collective dreamlands increasingly have impact on politics and legislation. The twilight zone of netporn is slowly but surely breaking into public culture. To enter these fuzzy spaces in order to do research, one has to equally create a participatory identity and engage in other people's fantasies. Even if the netporn researcher eventually has to wake up from his/her ethnographic journeys to write a chapter or produce another type of document, it really is necessary to approach people within their multiple identities—and to share their high hopes and anxieties. And most importantly, it is important for the researcher to try out these play zones as areas of vitality and muddy honesty, rather than looking for "clean subject matter."

I have plunged into those discourses to reveal traces of colonial history and racial stereotyping, as well as sex revolts. But it will take Chinese voices to nurture this small gesture into more detailed and rigorous (and hopefully wet) scholarship. More specifically, scholars and activists will need to speak of people's pornography and sexual freedom while waging a fierce, uphill battle against biases, institutionalized hypocrisy, and censorship. It will be an unwieldy yet nutritious topic of study, as it epitomizes tensions among traditional Chinese culture, online sexual libertines associated with the West, and the ruthless and politically corrupt private sex markets.

Who are the people who are looking for sex and porn in other spaces? The first zone where Hong Kong creates online sexual identities is in and around p2p file-sharing platforms. For instance, Hong Kong high-school and university students use the very popular BitTorrent software to illegally exchange music, software, and porn files. Their habits of computer-mediated porn consumption can be seen as a new type of sexual engagement with others and their machine toys. For instance, my interviewee and fervent porn downloader "Harvey06" is a twenty-four-year-old university student. He thinks of himself as a typical user who downloads several porn movies on a daily basis, even though he may not watch all of them. Because of his frequent BT transactions, he has received the status of "Superalien." He enjoys having this status as it allows him to visit special restricted sections of the Adult Video zone and view VIP videos such as the Hong Kong "Peeping Tom" videos that people have shot with their mobile phones and uploaded on the web. Since these "Peeping Tom" videos are illegal in Hong Kong, they are delegated to a special section by the BT administrators and are only accessible to the more active members of the community.

In order for people to use the BT software, they have to hide their IP addresses and port settings, since the Internet service providers

(ISPs) and universities in Hong Kong have restricted access to this software. Harvey06 is not afraid of breaking the law, as he believes that people should have unrestricted access to those movies that cannot be found in Hong Kong's legal DVD markets. He uses BT mostly to download Japanese "high-quality" productions, which means to him that the image is of high-resolution quality, that models have good body shapes, that the stories are good, and that there are no tags on the genitals. He thinks badly of the official Hong Kong porn industry, as it lacks all those assets of Japanese porn. In his opinion, the movies have bad actresses with less attractive bodies and they have low production values. He is also a fan of Japanese porn with fantasy scenes showing girls dressed in uniforms—schoolgirl uniforms, air hostess uniforms, or office lady uniforms. He specifically admires the fact that Japan's uniform porn is shot in actual settings, as if the scenes take place on a real airplane or inside a subway; other examples are the scenes with bad boys inside a classroom. He dislikes Hong Kong pornography because it tends to take place mostly inside the bedroom.

When I ask him if he ever tries to share or discuss the sex scenes from his videos with his girlfriend, he wants to protect these scenes as his fantasies. He replies, "I don't think it is possible to ask girls because they are men's fantasies." They give him space to relax and to imagine what he cannot do in real life. He does not believe that women would be able to understand or participate in these fantasies and thinks that they would likely have a negative view about his downloading habits. When I ask him how he feels about the tightening anti-copyright and anti-pornography legislation in Hong Kong, he states that he firmly believes that the climate is actually very open and free. At least he says he is determined to go on and would like to see a more relaxed type of legislation.

But it is not only the (mostly male) downloaders who are constructing and protecting their fantasy zones. Similar developments are taking place in other sections of society and in women's communities. For instance, Hong Kong is a city where, on Sunday afternoons, thousands of domestic workers from the Philippines and Indonesia gather in Victoria Park and in other public spaces, buildings, squares, and bridges around Central district. Domestic workers tend to live with their host families but are expected to leave the house on Sundays. They gather in the already swamped public spaces of Hong Kong to share food and drinks and to chat and listen to music. The workers like to publicly display their love for each other and sometimes their lesbian relationships. They are actually mostly lacking in social and sexual relationships with Chinese men and women. A research project about their use of Internet cafés in Central has revealed that they feel like an inferior class to the Chinese and would prefer to chat with lovers from the homeland or from other countries besides Hong Kong (American lovers are indeed still popular).[2] They use Internet cafés on their free Sundays to chat with people and create virtual identities to live out romantic dates and fantasies. Audiovisual documents and porn discourses are shared, not just as a way of finding romance or getting laid, but also with a desire to develop societies different from those that rule the sharper and more well-defined world outside.

Hong Kong's History as a Sub

Before starting my analysis of the twilight zone, I will introduce some basic historical facts about Hong Kong's sexual identity. Despite prevailing rumors and sex surveys showing that people in Hong Kong have a less-than-average sex life, Dr. Man Lune Ng writes an uplifting essay about Hong Kong's sexuality in the *International Encyclopedia of Sexuality*: "Hong Kong is a very special place as far as sexuality is concerned. One finds it very sexually open if one reads the newspapers, watches the illegal videotapes or disks that are easily available in street shops, listens to sexual discussions on the radio and television, experiences how easy it is to find casual or commercial sex and follows up [on] the lifestyle of some of the movie stars and social celebrities."[3] But he warns us that there are undercurrents of severe moralism in this fancy metropolis and that the voices for social conservatism are loud and clear. Moreover, a clear sexuality split is found in Hong Kong people, as the Chinese and Western mind-sets often fight and crash vigorously with each other.

Hong Kong is a highly consumerist metropolis, a vast network of commercial interests and supersonic cultural exchanges, but Hong Kong has never been truly independent as a political entity. Hong Kong's sexual identity cannot be thought of outside its history of colonization and the specific power relations it has carved out for its peoples. As with other places and spaces, its identity is specifically tied to its history. Hong Kong was colonized in 1841 by the British and was used as such to become a vibrant capitalist enclave and free port on the edge of China. In 1984, the British and Chinese governments agreed that Hong Kong would return to Chinese sovereignty on June 30, 1997. The agreement also specified the premises of Hong Kong's autonomy from the mainland China government and the Chinese Communist Party, and stated that the territory would retain its social, economic, and legal system as a special administrative region of China under a unique "One Country, Two Systems" arrangement.

The agreement guarantees freedoms of speech, press, assembly, association, travel, and religious belief, and the right to strike. However, the chief executive and some members of the legislature are still appointed by Beijing.[4] In other words, Hong Kong has been transitioning from one type of political ruler to another, both of whom are associated with both authoritarian leadership and puritanical values. Hong Kong, as a result, is not a vibrantly happy or radical sex or culture zone, but a super-workaholic place obsessed with commerce and survival and fighting hard for a minimum of political autonomy from the mainland.

Historically Hong Kong has functioned as a space of exoticism, mystery, and romance for British, Australian, and American expat visitors or members of the nomadic business class. We can see a vivid depiction of the expat desire to taste the flesh of Hong Kong in the Hollywood movie *The World of Suzie Wong* (1960). A bohemian and handsome American painter arrives in the city to take a break from the grind of life, not just for a holiday, but to explore the city and the lifestyle of an artist. He takes a cheap hotel room in the Nam Kok Hotel in the Chinese neighborhood of Wan Chai, surrounded by snake charmers and a sprawl of shops covered in slabs of dried meat. At first, he avoids the sex services offered at the Nam Kok Hotel, eventually falling into a tempestuous affair with one of the workers, Suzie Wong. Rather innocently, he invites her to be a model for his paintings, but then answers her begging requests to be her lover, falls in love, and explores her exotic nature.

He appears in Wan Chai not only as a delirious bo-bo (bourgeois bohemian) but as a mythical figure who bursts into a world of difference to transform everything. As Gina Marchetti explains in *Romance and* the "Yellow Peril": Race, Sex and Discursive Strategies in Hollywood Fiction, our American hero is not a stuffy and overly racist expat, but a modern type of American man. He is ready to transgress racial boundaries and have a more refined relationship. As the story unfolds, however, the colonial mold of the city gets to him. Suzie's sexiness and Chinese-ness are seen through his painterly eyes and fantasies. For instance, he likes to see her in a traditional silky outfit, the cheongsam, and gets angry when she appears to him in modern Western outfit. Or, as Marchetti explains, Suzie is a sexy and mysterious heroine who is emotionally troubled and needs a foreign investor to find her Chinese identity: "If the 'Orient' is seen reflected in these heroines, then it, too, metaphorically is presented as divided, contradictory, self-deceiving, childlike, and in need of the strong, paternal hand embodied by these American heroes."[5] Suzie displays an infantile, hyperemotional, and needy disposition. Hong Kong's visitors have stigmatized her in this state of "feminization," where they can take a taste of her, frame her as an exotic subject, and look down on her, or, in the best case, fall in love and help her gain autonomy.

Michael Berry theorizes a second moment of traumatic memory besides that of colonization. In his analysis, new sexual identities and anxieties have been formed in connection with the 1997 handover, which coincided with people's fears of being relegated to the People's Republic of China (PRC). As he writes: "After a long, brutal century of violence, war and political purges, as China approached the fin de siècle, it seems that memories of the brutal past stained not only her collective memory, but also, her future."[6] In the wake of the Tiananmen Square massacre on June 4, 1989, the 1997 handover of Hong Kong inspired visions of impending violence. The massacre had a profound impact upon the city of Hong Kong and its psyche, as it occurred between the 1984 signing of the Joint Declaration and the 1997 handover. Berry writes that Hong Kong thus started life with its anticipated Chinese atrocities. For instance, panicked residents, including a large percentage of Hong Kong lawyers, doctors, pharmacists, accountants, and property surveyors, vowed to leave before the transfer of sovereignty, not only to places like the United States, Canada, and Australia, but also to less obvious places like the tiny Central American country of Belize.

The historical moments of decolonization and handover came with trepidation deeply rooted in a complex historical matrix of violence and atrocity, in memories of the Chinese civil war, the Sino-Japanese War, and the purges and violent political movements carried out under the Communist regime. The lurking newly dominant PRC caused a chill and a corresponding process of desexualization. Hong Kong lost its sexual identity as a land of femmes fatales, sex adventures, and smooth colonial pleasures.[7] The PRC replaced the horny expat with a eunuch who bans sexy fashions like *cheongsam* and encourages clothes like the *zhongshan* tunic that blurs the boundaries of the sexes and encourages "equality of the sexes," as in Mao's famous saying "Women hold up half the sky." Berry thus contextualizes the 1997 handover as a new traumatic and nonsexy page in Hong Kong's history. The PRC is not a new colonial ruler who decides to have his way with her, but a triumphant dictator who perhaps commands an even more troublesome return to the mythic mother- or fatherland.

However, as Dr. Ng and other scholars have pointed out, Hong Kong is equally influenced by Chinese sex principles that preceded its history of colonization and subsequent handover to the Chinese government. There is an original Chinese Taoist-Confucian premise with a documented history of more than five thousand years, which holds a natural and utilitarian view of sex and postulates an interaction of two cosmic forces. Yin and yang are thought to be universal and essential for the existence, change, and growth of all matter. Both the reproductive and pleasurable aspects of sex are given high consideration, and the teachings are centered on the different pleasures of the female and male. Sex within marriage must serve the purpose of procreation, but outside of marriage, a wide range of sexual behaviors is acceptable or at least tolerated.[8]

Sexpert Hsi Lai explains that one of the principles for male revitalization is called "Gazing at the Green Dragon" and is supposed to create intense sexual energy (*ching*) by transferring energy from body to the brain. The male is supposed to watch his female having sex with another male, either by gazing directly at them or by peeping into the bedroom through a secret hole. The male is supposed to stick around his female to give her support in the process and allow her to indulge to the fullest extent with the Green Dragon, the other male. This Taoist exercise sets up an encounter between a heterosexual couple and an outsider and suggests specific types of games for each of the parties to experience revitalization. More specifically, the Jade Dragon male "holds the base of his penis tightly with his left hand so as to trap the blood within the penis shaft, he applies muscular contractions to the glans penis, doing so thirty-six times slowly and in succession, while intently watching the White Tigress (female) perform with the Green Dragon."[9] Even though we may be suspicious of the deeply ingrained gender binaries of Taoism, these rituals are perhaps less suffocating than the idea of endless love through marriage.

Continuing with the wisdom from precolonial Chinese history, a more stringent neo-Confucian premise was introduced in the Song dynasty (A.D. 960–1279) by groups of scholars who proposed fundamentalist norms and practices, denouncing sexual intimacy, pleasure, and all types of physical enjoyment. The danger of sexual pleasure to bodily health and to spiritual pursuit was emphasized through a sexual domination of females, who now had to be guarded at all costs. Dr. Ng writes that Hong Kong's Chinese society in general today is still primarily characterized by a dominant role of men over women. In this, Hong Kong has been equally influenced by fundamentalist Christian ideas on the denunciation of sexual pleasure, the love–marriage–sex trilogy, and the exclusively monogamous marital system. Even though Christians represent less than 10 percent of the Hong Kong population, the Christian ethos has become increasingly influential in modern times. As Dr. Ng writes: "They feed the Christian doctrine to the youngsters whether or not they will ultimately be converted Christians. Many of the elite students become the ruling or influential class in Hong Kong and help to spread the Christian premise consciously or subconsciously."

However, there are also signs that Hong Kong people are getting progressively dissatisfied with the monogamous marital system. The annual number of marriages is declining, while divorce cases are on a rapid increase. In recent years, the large number of males who engage in extramarital affairs or take mistresses in mainland China has caused a number of serious marital tragedies and social concerns. As we will see later, the twilight zone of Hong Kong is encouraging males and females to mend or alter their broken sex lives.

As for lesbian, gay, and transgender rights and activism in Hong Kong, it has to be noted that consensual sexual conduct between males aged twenty-one years old or older was only decriminalized in 1991. Decriminalization has been slow but has permitted the coming out of lesbians and gays in Hong Kong, with the opening of homosexual and lesbian bars and the founding of a number of new homosexual societies. There are basic rights for FTM and MTF transgendered people, as it has become possible for transgendered people to get medical services and recommendations for surgical procedures. However, discrimination and harassment in everyday life, at work, on the streets, and by the police force is tremendous. Unlike the social fabric and public culture of the third sex in Thailand, or the public visibility of transgendered people in Singapore's or Japan's halfway districts, the Hong Kong streets are mostly devoid of transsexuals, except those we can glimpse in one of the sex bars in the small sex district of Wan Chai.

Apart from, or related to, Hong Kong's sex identity and history, the city is also the ultimate "rush city" where workaholic urbanites walk around as if on a cocaine high, among a wealth of loud commercials and extremely noisy phone conversations and always riding the immaculate public transportation systems. Hong Kong moves elegantly with supersonic speed and a tense face, but her journeys still bump into a lack of material space—cranky city mobs live and work in too-tiny spaces, surrounded by monotonous high-rise architecture. I would have to say that it would be nearly impossible for Hong Kong not to fall into the twilight zone, as there is simply a lack of physical-material space for people to date and have sex. People live together in very tiny domestic spaces built high into the sky, but they also live in many other spaces, temporary sex spaces like love hotels or the web. In many Hong Kong families, the children may live with the family until the age of marriage, which can be a downright oppressive or inconvenient situation for the sex drive. People are tied to the strictures of the state, the city, and the family, and hence are extra prone to be attracted to lead other lives within the smooth, imperceptible, or more radical-revolutionary places for romance, perversion, and relief.

Cyber Awakenings and Big Brother Voyeur:
People's Republic of China

Recent academic studies and newspaper stories show that the PRC party-state encourages the spread of the Internet while it believes that it can monitor and censor those aspects of activity that it sees as destabilizing, dangerous, and unhealthy. The PRC indirectly regulates the Internet by directly regulating intermediary actors/owners of cybercafés, ISPs, Internet content providers (ICPs), and everyday citizens. For instance, the Guangdong public security department has agreed with local telecommunications companies to pay a reward of up to 2,500 yuan (US$309) to people who report on any type of netporn traffic. For each of the reported websites, the provincial department will pay the first informant 1,000 yuan to 2,500 yuan in thirty days after police confirm the information and close the case.

Gudrun Wacker outlines the Chinese government's provisions that were included in a draft of regulations in the year 2000 to govern telecommunications and the publication of news and electronic information on the Internet. First of all, there are *forbidden contents* that are banned from distribution or electronic publication, including

> information that (1) Contradicts the principles defined in the constitution [of the PRC]; (2) Endangers national security, discloses state secrets, subverts the government, or destroys the unity of the country; (3) Damages the honor and the interests of the State; (4) Instigates ethnic hatred or ethnic discrimination, or destroys the unity of [China's] nationalities; (5) Has negative effects on the state's policy on religion or propagates evil cults or feudal superstition; (6) Disseminates rumors, disturbs social order, and undermines social stability; (7) Spreads lewdness, pornography, gambling, violence, murder; (8) Offends or defames other people, infringes upon the rights and interests of other people; and (9) Other contents that are forbidden by law or administrative regulations.[10]

These regulations are not new, as contents banned on the Internet are nearly identical with those prohibited in other media. Hence, Internet and electronic information services are basically treated like any other forms of publication.

Secondly, there are *restrictions on the distribution of news*, which include regulations that prohibit the distribution of news through the

Internet, unless this news has either been published on the Internet by the official state-owned media or the news departments of state institutions themselves, or has already been published by authorized media in another form. As Wacker concludes, the PRC is trying to kill two birds with one stone. The government officials have a political or ideological purpose of containing and directing the proliferation of news material into relatively manageable channels. They also aim at securing the economic interests of the official media vis-à-vis pure Internet portals operating in Chinese, such as Sina, Netease, and Sohu, which have become very popular due to their early web presence and timely and attractively presented news services. The PRC also recently requested the American companies Google and Yahoo! to submit data about potential forbidden content of their web users and to create censored versions of the search engines for China. Google and Yahoo! submitted to the PRC's request in order not to lose their business in China.

Wacker believes that censorship not only entails the physical ability of the state to surveil and punish people, or to find some kind of a compromise between authoritarian dictatorship and capitalism, but also infringes on how web users have internalized these complexities when trying to build trust, vitality, and sexual desire in relationships with fellow users and the technology. Even if the PRC seems to be currently more concerned with tracking political dissidents than Internet pornographers or sex seekers, the official and complete ban on pornography and sexual communication has more than paralyzed the public's sex drive. There is a simultaneous incentive to stimulate the younger generation's urge toward cyberculture and sex and to quash attempts at sexual liberation and punish the emblematic figures of the revolution.

As seen in the online newspaper for Asian sex politics, the *Asian Sex Gazette*, China and Hong Kong are going through a blogolution. The China Internet Network Information Center estimated there were 94 million Internet users and about 4 million bloggers in China in 2004, which is the second-largest Internet population in the world. For example, blogger Qin Dai has created a buzz in the online community by revealing her romance writings and snapshots of her naked buttocks and back. Qin Dai has compared herself frivolously to Franz Kafka, but this statement caused hostile comments from her online critics. How can she be like Kafka? Her opponent Annie Rose was angered and wrote that readers would appreciate the great works of writers rather than their nudity.[11] Blogger Mu Mu became popular by posting pictures of her naked body while refusing to reveal her face. She made people speculate about the motives behind her pornographic discourses.[12] Blogger Lost Sparrow is compiling an encyclopedia of lovemaking noises and how they may sound different in different parts of China.

These female sex bloggers are just the latest of a lurking sweet sexual revolt that is sweeping through China with the gradual implementation of the Internet. Bloggers have gained an unusual type of power in public discussions of sexual relations and fantasies.[13] The popularity of bloggers also increases tremendously when they get picked up and courted by the mass media, but the PRC's ministry of information has already implemented legislation aimed at curtailing bloggers. In March 2006, the PRC went a step further and introduced a new law that banned the sending of pornographic cell phone messages, with penalties including a fifteen-day detention for Chinese citizens and deportation for foreigners.[14]

In July 2005, the *Asian Sex Gazette* published a report about China's "great Internet pornography trial" in which eleven defendants were charged and sent to prison. Five of those Internet pornographers were university students who had been invited by Fujian resident Wang Rong to help administer an online bulletin board system (bbs) called 99bbs.com. They all lived in different parts of the country and knew each other mostly through their nicknames on the bbs. The site 99bbs.com started as a general-interest forum and then offered pornographic content to 75,000 fee-paying members in a separate porn section. The website was hosted on an overseas server but nevertheless fell under Chinese jurisdiction. Except for the main administrator Wang Rong, the defendants did not get paid for their services in administering the board and they used it as a social network to write personal stories, to share files, and for personal communication.

Wang was absent from the trial; he was said to be hiding in the United States. The other defendants were sentenced to between three and twelve years in jail and 10,000 to 50,000 yuan in fines. The female administrator Zhao Yong was sentenced to twelve years. In an interview posted on the *Sex Gazette*, she writes that she used the website to post her writings and journals "to become immersed in the Internet and to make friends." It was an honor for her to be promoted by Wang to be the site administrator (these admin posts were labeled "teacher director" and "school principal") and was promised a fee of 500 yuan by Wang to pay for her Internet bill, but she never received the money. China's great Internet trial was an attempt of the government not to eradicate porn distribution but to undermine the very vitality of a new social network. The values of this Chinese network were different from those of official mainstream society controlled by the PRC. It announced a sex/porn revolution in a twilight zone: It included the sharing of sexual ideas and communication by both women and men and gave its people access to pornography.

The news about China's Internet trials and the internment of these young people involved in sexually explicit social networks no doubt has a strong effect on web communities in China and neighboring countries. Taiwanese sex activist Josephine Ho explains that Chinese societies are experiencing a tightening of the social sphere. Her analysis of Internet censorship in Taiwan shows that this is not only the result of monopolizing state control but also is an effect of the ways in which state power is transferred horizontally to various supra-state international organizations or downward to various local or grassroots citizen groups. The groups that have been most eager to introduce censorship legislation in Taiwan are conservative child-protection NGOs, who collaborate with the state to accomplish a network of exchanges, resulting in an expansion of state power and criminalization of social-sexual minorities.

As Ho argues: "Instead of state power being weakened, as most global governance theorists argue, state power has been expanding to ever more social spheres and gaining strength in relation to newly constructed subjects for rule, and in relation to new spheres where the regulation/surveillance of marginalized populations and their activities carry insurmountable weight, where bodies and everyday life serve as prime targets."[15] She further explains that Taiwan's awakening queer and cyberqueer climate has suffered from continuous slanderous media coverage of either gay or sex-related happenings, and from a series of new laws, litigations, and rules banning all sex-related information, contacts, and inquiries on the Internet. Taiwan has a sex-phobic atmosphere that, for example, led to the seizure and confiscation of gay pictorial publications in 2003 and to the indictment and sentencing of the one and only gay bookstore in Taiwan in the following year.

Coming into existence since 1995, Taiwan's sex-phobic atmosphere has been influenced by the anti-prostitution "Law to Suppress Sexual Transaction Involving Children and Juveniles." The law was originally meant to prevent the sale of young aboriginal girls in city brothels in the mid-1980s, but was then reoriented in the 1990s to halt the increasing voluntary entry of urban youth into the sex industry. In order to block the channels through which youths may learn about possible job opportunities in the sex trade, the law was amended in 1999 to include all Internet-related transactions, and it now explicitly states that "those who use advertisement, publication, radio, television, electronic signal and internet, or other media to publish or broadcast messages that induce, broker, imply, or by other means cause one to be involved in sexual transactions shall be punished with imprisonment of no more than five years and alternatively coupled with a fine of no more than one million NT [New Taiwan] dollars."[16] (One U.S. dollar is about thirty NT dollars.) Those who now potentially fall victim to the law are all sexually active web users and those in the sexually active sexual subcultures and minorities who depend on the Internet for information, communication, and contact. The moral panic around Internet sex and porn has grown after more than 2,500 cases were sent to court, among them web users who were playing in clearly marked sexuality chat rooms or bbs. To conclude, the Taiwanese law does not successfully target commercial profit-making porn but instead goes after noncommercial sexual self-expression and interaction on the Internet.

Despite a tightening and monitoring of all types of innocent Internet uses, porn users willy-nilly are part of a brave vanguard of cyberculture and desire as they fabricate ever-more-sophisticated types of software to share products and banned information. Chase, Mulvenon, and Hachigian explain that despite the PRC's attempts to exert efficient control, p2p technology's impact on commercial computing and the free flow of political information in China has been breathtaking.[17] The researchers did case studies in 2001–2002, when people began to more frequently use the new unbrokered p2p architectures to distribute pirated and censored materials. For instance, the bbs Freenet China was managed by a small and dedicated group of computer specialists who held free speech as its highest principle. Even though the website was blocked on the mainland, people kept installing and using the software by circulating it on email. Other U.S.-based Chinese activists and computer specialists launched Dynaweb, a software application that could be used to look at banned websites and download banned documents. While mainland users are more technically equipped to access activist cyberculture, the government has already responded by extensively promoting self-policing and self-censorship, by making selective physical arrests, and by using the p2p networks themselves for spreading propaganda and disinformation. The researchers conclude that "the future picture of p2p as a tool of political change in China is decidedly mixed, as the advocates of innovative technical measures to advocate openness will be blocked by technical, political, bureaucratic, and economic countermeasures in Beijing."

Immaculate Girls and Their Law-Abiding Avatars

As stated before, the values of these networks are very different from those of traditional Chinese culture. But young people's romantic interests and sexual relationships are to a great extent influenced by their online alter egos and by sexual profiles developed in illegal p2p file-sharing communities. If p2p porn forums are heavily dominated by men, women equally develop fantasy characters and digital romance around pop culture, such as Japanese erotic animation. Going back to Jon McKenzie's theoretical premise of "perform or else," both male and female groups are learning how to be technologically skilled networkers, and they cannot separate these activities from their need for sex, love, and/or pornography. Moreover, they also take their mediated role-play and communication patterns into real life when they go out on dates, or when they dress up as cosplayers (costume players) to act out their favorite characters.

The first area where people in Hong Kong act out new types of relationships and networks around originally Japanese cartoon characters is through the culture of cosplayers and Lolitas, or people who physically embody cartoon characters by wearing costumes and by interacting in gatherings as their characters. The cosplayers and Lolitas are a heavily female-dominated subculture. This goes back to the Japanese popular wave of *Shojo*, which refers to Japanese products (books, comics, and movies) marketed toward young women. Sharalyn Orbaugh identifies the *Shojo* archetype as a "female child" or "a state of being that is socially unanchored, free of responsibility and self-absorbed—the opposite of the ideal Japanese adult." She believes that *Shojo* characters can be used as a tool for the critique of contemporary society.[18] In *Busty Battlin' Babes: The Evolution of Shojo in 1990s Visual Culture*, Orbaugh explains that Japanese critics have reacted strongly and emotionally to this culture, which they see as a representation of the feminization of their nation. They identify with the self-absorbed preadolescent girl yet also criticize the fact that the culture is becoming "girl." They interpret the feminization and the wild growth of cute products as a sign of weakness or downfall, relating it to the Japanese knack for consumerism, endless consumption and distribution of commodities, and signs and images from other cultures. Whereas women and sex in the male-oriented *Shonen* products tended to have "raunchy and silly" connotations, *Shojo* offered complex love stories and same-sex narrative such as the *Yaoi* or "boy love" tales. Hence, girls want to look at gay boys and experience cross-gender identification through anime culture, just as boys and men have become massively interested in the girl-like *Shojo* products. Orbaugh points out that the industry has reacted to this trend by creating female characters that combine elements of innocence and action-driven woman-warriors.

In taking a glimpse at cosplayers' gatherings in Hong Kong, what kind of performative statement do women make within an urban landscape dominated by consumerism? First, the Hong Kong Lolita scene is a girl-dominated culture for young adults mostly aged between fourteen and twenty-four. They insist on being a misinterpreted and misunderstood subculture. They are not just a subbranch of cosplayers but their own performative breed. Hong Kong Lolitas originate in Japan's fashion style of cuteness and eighteenth-century European court clothing, and firmly distinguish themselves from Nabokov's "American" Lolita who lusts for sex and older men. Hong Kong Lolitas are less female–male hybrids and have a rather uptight and old-fashioned girlish appearance, belonging to an older and colonial era, where girls were kept under the tight rule of family authorities. They mimic an extreme state of purity as they do not wish to be fashionable in a modern sense. They share their own old-fashioned (and even dowdy) sense of fashion; they are going against the grain of time by desiring less originality and young, sexualized femininity, by sewing their own clothes and wearing bloomers in public. Except for her fashionable 1990s platform shoes, a Lolita looks like an almost lifeless Victorian porcelain doll and wears the clothes of bygone eras—voluminous lace-filled, knee-length dresses, with bloomers underneath, white stockings, and a bonnet on the head. Hong Kong Lolitas are duller and more traditional than Japanese ones. They have no punk or high-fashion ambitions and very little originality in assembling their retro outfits.

They insist on belonging to one of three types: Sweet Love Lolita, who dresses in pink; Gothic Lolita in black lace; and Classical Lolita in white. Pink Lolita could be seen as a sign of difference but is equally begging to be included in Hong Kong's mainstream fashion. She simply mirrors and intensifies children's and young women's almost sick fascination with pink. Hong Kong Lolita fashion has a slight inferiority complex in comparison with Japan Lolita fashion. It is also a fad that has been reported to be on the decline.

Lolitas get together in city gatherings such as high-tea parties where they eat sandwiches using forks and knives, while they also pose for curious Hong Kong photographers and journalists. Lolitas crave a kind of improper attention. Lolita ChiChi told me in an interview that Hong Kong photographers try to take photographs from underneath their dresses, which seems a very unlikely scenario in the public spaces where they meet. There is an interdependency between Lolitas and the media, the one seeking attention and the other making use of them to create fashion trends. Unlike Japanese critics, Hong Kong journalists and the public have not officially recognized in them a growing state of infantilization, feminization, and consumerism, but they do complain about the Lolitas' unstable psychology. The RTHK television documentary *Pretty Bizarre* broadcast interviews with Lolitas and the general public and largely corroborated its naïve-sensational and negative view of the subculture. RTHK interviewed several people about Lolitas and edited together their mostly negative reactions of outrage, bias, and aversion toward these psychologically disturbed or oversexed young female members of the community.[19]

Even though Lolitas dress up and gather in public settings, most of their discussions and transactions happen in the online world and at blogging sites such as www.lolionline.net, where they look at each other's photo albums and share experiences and pictures on blogs. The main reason they cite for developing their fantasy characters is the need to wear a mask. Cynthia explains: "I think that it doesn't change my personality, but it makes me more comfortable and makes me want to be in front of the camera more. It is more like a little mask that you wear in front of people. For instance, I smile a lot less usually but when I am in my character I smile a lot more. It is also how people interpret me."[20] Cynthia's smile is not the fake one, but rather a dream and escape from everyday life and boredom—or from tremendous pressure at school and work and from family and friends.

Huang Li and Voramon Damrongsinsakul carried out a case study of the popular Chinese-speaking site Animation Garden. It was founded in 2002 and has about 80,000 members, 38 percent of whom are male, 26 percent female, and 36 percent whose gender is not specified. The members are mostly located in China, Hong Kong, and Taiwan, but the site is also used by overseas Chinese people. One of the most important characteristics is that Animation Garden has a lot of laws.[21] Rather than wishing for a society without laws, the society seems obsessed with making and remaking laws, specifically in the area of marriage and divorce settlements. Every member has to have an Animation Garden ID, even though a new law was recently passed allowing members to have two IDs and to alternate the genders of each of the IDs.

The society also wants to keep its members healthy and smart as it organizes plenty of online sports events and anime or singing competitions for people to manifest their talents, and gives members an opportunity to belong to other types of organizations and clubs. For instance, in August 2007 there is to be a Summer Lover competition in which people post their virtual images as a specific animation character. They have to apply to become a contestant in the competition and everyone gets to cast one vote. Since the demand to participate is too high, the administrators have to set special rules. For instance, this year's competition is strictly reserved for men to embody a male character. In a car-racing competition, the members are encouraged to post an image of a cool car, but the competition also requires that they post the image as fast as possible. In an Olympic Games competition, members are awarded points according to the speed with which they post messages.

Animation Garden members are keen on having a good economic system and exchange items for virtual money called *huabi*, which is one of the current nicknames of the Chinese currency, renminbi. Animation Garden has areas for people's sharing or exchanging of Japanese anime products. They used to do this by depositing *huabi* into each other's accounts managed by a virtual bank or by sending actual money to each other in the mail. However, with the increasing use of the Bit-Torrent file-sharing software, the banks have gone out of business and people use the BT software to engage in virtual trading.

The very popular discussion forum Nongfu Mountain is the most fashionable area and differs from the other forums in that the topics go far beyond anime. It consists of a reading room where people post their articles, such as discussions of animation, poetry, or fiction. There is no limitation on the genres of writing, but the articles are rated by administrators, who post the best ones in a special "essence" section. Nongfu Mountain is also the mountain that people climb to declare love and engage in online marriage. As a matter of fact, they organize online wedding ceremonies under the wedding laws of the community. The new couple is awarded a certificate that is displayed on the site. The members of Nongfu Mountain belong to couples and families, and they create online communities with wives, husbands, sons, daughters, uncles, and so on. When members are newbies to the community and start socializing, they can adapt halfway roles rather than full ones. For instance, Sasha is a Hong Kong high-school student who has been using the site for six months and currently has "a little husband." Another woman, Krairi, is an animation fan from Shanghai who has about ten younger brothers. She also just married her new husband, both in virtual and in real life. In order for him to marry her online, he had to divorce his former online wife, after which he and Krairi had a grand online wedding for the Nongfu Mountain community. Little V from Taiwan is a pioneer of the Nongfu Mountain community, as well as the very first member to get married and later to get a divorce. At the time of her interview, she was still very upset about her divorce and not willing to talk about it.

Even though about 36 percent of the members do not specify their gender and use nicknames, the wedding ceremony and certificate are reserved for heterosexual couples only. Even though there have been discussions on the theme of lesbian and gay marriage, lesbian girl lovers and gay boy lovers can thus far only engage in relationships without getting married. However, members actually use their online characters to engage in their marriage, although those genders may diverge from gender subjectivity in real life. Oftentimes people who are married online are already married in real life. On top of that, they can be married a third time by means of their second online ID. Since online marriage has become a growing trend among youngsters, the legislators have had to invent new and more relaxed rules for divorce settlements. For instance, either one of the married parties can file for a divorce if the other one fails to be online for more than one month or if a partner is found to be cheating. Moreover, if one party desires to have a relationship in real life, the other party who does not want to do so can automatically file for a divorce. The judges of Animation Garden are very open-minded and actually give advice to members who are going through marriage or divorce problems.

When I ask Hua Ling why she believes the Chinese government is not censoring these open-sex societies, she answers that they are mostly interested in censoring political topics and pornography. She believes that people have creative ways of circumventing government laws by using porn sites that are hosted on servers outside China. She explains that administrators usually immediately remove politically sensitive topics from Animation Garden, but not the making of nontraditional relationships. These relationships do not have any sexually explicit images inside Animation Garden, but, of course, people develop sexual communication and porn sharing in private chats and through the use of webcams.

Flashing Asians and Trembling Caucasians

Hong Kong is characterized as a reticent city where people do not easily reveal their sexual inclinations; they also do not walk around wearing flamboyant subcultural clothes, piercings, or tattoos. Though the impact of liberal-minded and forthcoming sex experts and subcultures no doubt have had their effects on the city, signs of an inner carnival are carefully hidden and lips mostly remain sealed. There is a Chinese saying that thwarts the efforts of the researcher looking for confessions: Western people like to talk about sex while Chinese people just like to do it. There is a Chinese joke that says, in Chinese culture, for every actor there are about six people watching and about one hundred people talking about it. This Chinese joke holds for the rest of the world, as findings have been confirmed by Internet researchers—only a small percentage of members within a web group are actively participating in the community, while a much larger percentage are passively observing the transactions. I am interested in finding people's "other spaces," whether they are active or passive agents, but I see their agency as having an impact on everyday minds and bodies, on cultural behavior, and on legislation. Passive porn users may have a strong desire to hide behind curtains when living out fantasies, but their fantasies are part of the equation when it comes to analyzing cultural politics.

I started work on a case study of Hong Kong dating and swinger networks on the web, more specifically the Hong Kong zone of a very popular American adult networking site, Adult Friend Finder (AFF), and its spin-off site for alternative sex encounters at www.alt.com. These two sites are very popular in Hong Kong and have attracted both Chinese-speaking and English-speaking populations, though not in equal numbers. The sex-seeking on www.adultfriendfinder.com is largely dominated by white English-speaking males, both the horny mobs who want to score and the liberal-minded swingers looking for more sophisticated types of company. The site has about 60,000 males, most of whom are heterosexuals looking for women but only a small percentage of whom would be active participants. The site has only about 3,000 female sex-seekers, hence it automatically routes the attention economy in favor of the female. This means that if one enters this site as a female, one automatically gets an enormous amount of traffic, which is overwhelming and perhaps good for the ego, but requires one to be slightly dismissive and critical of one's suitors. AFF's small queer community has about 2,000 males looking for men and about 1,000 females looking for women, and also attracts lots of men and women who identify as "bi." Other than that, the site is also used by transgendered/transsexual people or crossdressers who are looking for male and female or other transgender sex partners. Every time a member is contacted by another member, there is an announcement in the private email account. On the actual AFF site you can get a message or a wink from interested members. A member can reply to messages and winks in any number of easy or more laborious ways and can invite people to become part of a friend network, which allows you to see people's photo albums and read their blogs. The site is very user-friendly and neatly organized and explains to members how to construct a photo album, how to maintain a weblog, and how to upload homemade videos.

Apart from catering to a wide variety of sexual orientations, AFF tries to set people up with various types of encounters, from dates with picky singles or divorcees looking for a long-term relationship, to meetings with people who want a one-night stand—either alone or as a group for an orgy or a gang bang. AFF is a social networking site that gives very restricted access to standard members and constantly interrupts correspondence with sign-up information about silver and golden memberships. The spin-off site for alternative sexuality, www.alt.com, has a much smaller population than AFF but its members are more flamboyant and eager to show off their kinks and desires. One of the crossdressers is a forty-two-year-old married Chinese man looking to seduce another man who would role-play his teacher. He insists on dressing up in schoolgirls' uniform. His photo gallery is artistically refined and has a very feminine touch, revealing doll-like and youthful girls superimposed on a very colorful and flowery backdrop.

In response to the crossdresser and all others who contacted me, I created the profile of Lizzy Kinsey, a forty-year-old bisexual woman. Lizzy is much like myself but with an added note of fantasy. I made her a "switch" for the alternative s/m community, which means that she could take the position of either dominant or submissive or switch from one to the other during a session. I also made her the imagined granddaughter of Alfred Kinsey, the pioneering American sexologist whom I admire and have occasionally tried to impersonate in crossdressing performance-art pieces. I assumed that very few people in the Adult Friend Finder world of Hong Kong would get the reference to Kinsey and considered my surname to be my little secret. I primarily just wanted to appear and interact as a mysterious bisexual woman. In actuality, I was investigating the intertwined engines of sexual longing and intellectual pursuit. I really did not clearly plan to go out on sex dates with my suitors but did feel a desire for sex.

The alter-ego profile hides the real identity but has to be close to the real identity, otherwise one has to concoct a number of lies that would be hard to maintain and would certainly backfire in the long term. For instance, one time, Lizzy got winked at by a ninety-one-year-old male, which immensely aroused her curiosity and eagerness to have some kind of encounter with this guy. But when she asked him about his true age, he told her he was actually fifty-one years old, which at that point was too young for her. Like many women, she did not enjoy being confronted with a straightforward liar.

I was also afraid to get turned on too much to carry out my experiment and therefore posted a generic and short message: "Dreamers: I am looking for males or females, just open-minded kinds of beauties. People with suggestions, sweet ideas & fantasies. Want to see me first?" This message was very vague and lukewarm but many people contacted me. I interacted with some people and sent them a picture of naked Lizzy—actually, my naked body, but wearing my blue wig and sunglasses so that people would not be able to recognize the real me. It is a very common practice on AFF for people to send pornographic pictures of their naked bodies and genitals, while covering their eyes or faces so that they would not be recognized. I believe that the habit of sending a pornographic picture stems from the impetus to play and respond to signals within the system and hide or protect the actual, more holistic, personality. From an outsider's point of view, it may seem that people are vulgar or desperate to reduce their identities to exhibitionistic images of their naked or sexually engaged bodies, but it is also a safe and fun strategy for masking the real-world self and for pleasing the anonymous groups of voyeurs who do not wish to interact.

I took photographs of myself with a simple digital camera that had a self-timer and sent them off to certain people. I do not think of myself as a very beautiful-looking person, but I did manage to get shots that I thought were satisfying and I also did get very nice responses. It seemed that most men, women, and couples on AFF are happy to look at an average-looking forty-year-old woman. In some of the photographs, I had a message written on my stomach that said, "Are You Ready?" I was inspired by the realcore web photographs (discussed in chapter 2) in which people send each other images of themselves holding written signs or with messages written on their bodies, which is something that really turns me on. But even without sending out pornographic photographs of myself, people were horny and happy to get in touch with Lizzy and told her that she had a great profile. They sent her their own photographs and generic profiles, hoping we would correspond in detail later or just have sex. Oftentimes people like to take on clichéd alter-ego names like "EndlessFun," "HK juicy lover," "Black Stud," or "HK_puppy_dog" and often just attach an image of the erect penis to their email. The message sounds something like: "Hi there, I like what you have written in your profile and would very much like to get to know you and share secrets and adventures with you, as well as wanting to meet you and share some exciting times with you, if you are interested. Am English, 31 living in Hong Kong, so you can contact me at anytime and we can talk and meet at any time. Hoping to hear from you." Or "Dear lizzy_kinsey: How are u. Oh! I feel you are so nice & so sexy! You Attract me very much! Let me give u excitement and happiness! See u! G." But the same message is indeed sent to a large number of females, and it is unlikely that this man would really "like" my profile, as it is equally as generic and nonmeaningful as his.

Some of the members shared more extensive personal letters or messages in poetry and rhymes, like the proudly Caucasian Irish man who sends out his generic poem:

> Hi to you on AFFind,
> I'd like to play and to be kind.
> I'll take my time and await your reply,
> Whatever your wish I will comply.
> I'm mature and nice in a pleasant way,
> I hope we can meet some way some day.
> I'm fit and well built and very strong,
> A well endowed weapon, don't get me wrong.
> I'm as white as expected from the West.
> From Ireland I hail where the men are the best.
> We have a humour most would desire,
> And a passion so wild it's full of fire.

> I like the pleasures of the bed;
> Giving a lady plenty of required head.
> Making her cum more than once;
> Me feeling good is an added bunce!
> Promises will not be made to break,
> What you see is your call and to take.
> I will abide by the rules your make,
> I'm very real and not a fake.
> So if you are interested drop me a line,
> If you don't reply; that'll have to be fine.
> We all have a right to choose our wish,
> I writing to your; hoping you'll be my dish!

A considerable number of inquiries came from travelers who were visiting Hong Kong for a few days and wanted to have a one-night stand. Others were local expats and Chinese men, or couples and women, who wanted to meet with Lizzy, go to dinner with her, make her dinner, give her a massage, give her massive amounts of foreplay, sleep with her, or go to a play-party with her, command her to be their slave, their mistress, their teacher, or their fellow switch. I was quite overwhelmed by these responses and did not know how to handle them. I also found myself unable to distinguish between people or to remember to whom I replied or not. I was really enjoying checking out profiles but not as seriously horny or ready to go out as I could have been. I could not find the signs of a true call or actual chemistry, even though I had experienced true love and desire in previous cybersex encounters.

To be honest, I started out the case study with an enormous amount of anxiety. First, I was worried about the sex-binge study ruining my private life and relationship. But I soon learned that this primary fear was widely shared by many other "friend finders" (the name of the service as it appears on one's credit card bill), who are, more often than not, married or attached people who use the site to develop discreet extramarital or other affairs. People were very responsive to the fact that I could not just reveal my entire personality to them, but I also became very wary of people who were cheating so strategically and abundantly on their partners. Some of the swingers are actually married or attached couples who play the games of sex openly and together, but others clearly want to hook up behind the backs of their partners. Alternately, people do use AFF to go out as an "AFF couple" and look for a third partner or another couple to join them.

Adult Friend Finder is the sex zone where people perfect the split between a public (often heterosexual married or attached) persona and a privately queer, outgoing, adventurous personality. Even though I am also attached and living with a partner while playing on the AFF site, I am not used to cheating on him, and I share most of my poly-amorous and s/m desires with him (though surely I keep some of my little secrets from him). But the second reason why I am unwilling to completely hide my Lizzy Kinsey persona is that I am a sex researcher who wants to reveal, share, and analyze information.

That is also the reason why I told those members whom I got to know a bit more seriously that I was doing a mixture of research and sex search, and this hybrid profile of the sex (re)searcher seemed to be well understood. People were not worried about meeting with me as sex (re)searcher, but I was still worried about meeting them. I was worried about driving my partner crazy and about getting into trouble at work. I was worried that this research would be of a terrible quality and would lead to a kind of manic-depressive, self-absorbed scholarship. Moreover, I felt guilty about making sex appointments with people that I then would cancel at the last minute. Finally, I decided I had to keep going. My worried self as it is, is definitely part of who I am.

I am unlike most others on AFF, whose pornographic self-images or sexually liberated discourses are deliberately out of sync with their public personas, and in many cases need to remain completely separate. The AFF twilight zone to many of its members may seem like a close-up of their private bedroom, but it is a world more properly described as an upside-down room directly over their private bedroom. The friend finders want you to know exactly what they do or look for inside their upside-down bedroom, but they are quite adamant on hiding what they are and do in the real bedroom. This type of double identity suits the AFF sex zone very well.

It is also a type of "imperceptible liberation" that arguably suits the Chinese mentality of Hong Kong. Unlike sensual cultures or the oozing sexuality of places like Barcelona and Naples, or the hubs of bubbling and seedy eccentrics like New York City and Amsterdam, Hong Kong's public spaces are cold and well behaved, or at least hesitant.

One of my fellow AFF friend finders, Damon Lust, believes that it could be partly the result of the history of colonization, the centuries of rule by the (cold and uptight, or racist) British minority who controlled Hong Kong's public spaces, held power over the Chinese, and infantilized them. Unlike the hipsters and queer suburbs in cities like Amsterdam and Melbourne, Hong Kong's people are conservatively well dressed and meticulously groomed, and their overall sense of fashion does not radiate a rebellious, spunky, or queer appearance. Public displays of people's inner happiness or affection for each other are not uncommon, but they are very short-lived and inaccessible to the culture at large.

The city of Hong Kong has built imperceptible pleasure holes into its densely packed consumerist public spaces, its up/downmarket home spaces and housing estates. Hong Kong has a good number of *love hotels* where people gather by the hour(s) for commercial sex sessions, for dates requiring sex, or just to live out swingers' affairs. Damon Lust tells me that his dates with couples take place in hotels in the neighborhoods of Tsim Sha Tsui, Mong Kok, and Jordan, either in a lavish hotel like the Shangri-La or in the cheaper love hotels on Nathan Road. If an AFF couple invites an extra person, the male typically pays for the hotel bill or the expenses are shared. He says that there are rarely any quibbles over the bill. I ask him why this is the case: "The expenses are reasonable and everybody is happy because it is a sex party. Sex parties are the premise for good management of the community. Everybody is so happy that transactions are very smooth."

As I have pointed out before, there is a split in the sex psyche of Hong Kong as a result of its colonial history and ongoing tense relations between Chinese and white people. Damon Lust tells me that there is a lot of traffic between Caucasian males and Asian females on AFF. Lizzy Kinsey also noticed that Caucasian men often have to make special excuses for wanting to go out with a white woman. As Sexy Subbie wrote me in an extensive message on alt.com: "I am now over the yellow fever stage. I love Caucasian women, the conversation, the sense of humour and the lack of child-like behavior that we see so often here."

But the AFF site also has a fair number of sexually aggressive Asian females who know how to control the hormonal rages of white men and use them to their own benefit. One may argue, though, the racial dynamic on AFF replicates the Orientalist "White Knight" fantasy shown in Hollywood movies like *The World of Suzie Wong*. In actuality, Asian women are a precious property on AFF and they are chased by hordes of white men. They use this power dynamic in their favor and develop demanding or aggressive know-it-all personalities. Take for example the Hong Kong twins, Ning and Nin, who are in their early thirties and who are quite demanding in their search for Caucasians only: "We welcome overseas applicants, Caucasians only." Their profile opens with the following warning: "For those who have short concentration span: All emails without a recent face pic and cock size will be banned immediately." The profile further explains that Ning has a 34D bra size and her nipples (of course) are delicious. She is 5'2" and has the smoothest white skin. She hates being spanked! Nin is the naughty younger sister, thirty years old. She is 5'6" and has small tits, keen nipples, and a nice tan. She loves being spanked during doggy.

Ning and Nin both love young hot white guys between the ages of twenty-five and thirty-eight. These guys must be athletic and very tall, but not young at heart, and no saggy asses either. Rock-hard average cocks: 7 inches. Not too thick as they both have tight pussies. They will update their profile accordingly if they want to venture into huge black cocks or 9-inchers. They ask men to not shave their balls as they love them natural. Hairy chest and soft lips are a must as they like to be kissed for hours.

Ning is a very smart and articulate writer who posts daily humorous messages on her blog entitled "Save the Double Asses." She likes to explain the difference between Ning and Nin. Ning's buttocks look like a pear and Nin's like a peach. Ning and Nin are funny. They take photographs of themselves parodying a porn image that they found on the web, with both of them sucking a penis. They say that the penises that come their way are different from porn images, as they are huge and real. They are proud AFF swingers and do not want to be mistaken for hookers.

A Korean woman on AFF says that she needs to see an erection shot before taking people into consideration. She is married with a very successful business partner but is sexually unsatisfied in her marriage. She describes herself as a very difficult and arrogant lady but secretly wants to try everything and is very open to anything. She also wants to hear about your experiences with Korean girls in detail.

Then there are the softer Asian females who write out their honest emotions and advice about AFF pursuits in a blog. Winnie Cheung is a twenty-six-year-old IT administrator who uses her blog to educate males about female sexuality by revealing specific details of encounters that have turned her on. For instance, she talks in detail about different massage styles males have used on her. She is biased against younger men and believes that they are too anxious to go into action.

AFF males are perhaps a less boisterous or less articulate presence than their proactive female counterparts. Damon Lust says:

> There is a Chinese revolution of sorts going on this site, but it is a female revolution. The Chinese men do not seem that interested, even though many of them have affairs by visiting sex workers or take on mistresses from mainland China. The *gwailo* population like myself takes advantage of this situation as there are a high number of sex starved Chinese women who are relatively easy to get. But there is some kind of revolution in that these women are starting to take control of this situation and take pleasure in it, by talking about it and showing it off. They have more lovers than you think they do. And of course the Internet has made it is much easier for these women to participate. You'd be surprised to see how many respectable women are actually out there.

When Damon had just signed up as an AFF member, he tried to meet with one of the sexually forward women who wrote him that "she was in a gangbang mood." However since he did not have any pictures of himself at that moment, he lost his chance when she demanded to see a picture of him.

Damon also has encounters with Chinese couples, where both partners have an amount of control over the meeting. In one of those encounters, a man wanted to be "cuckolded" in front of his wife. He got very turned on when seeing his wife have sex with Damon, and took pictures and videos: "I myself didn't take pictures as I was the actor. I was the one who was doing the fucking. We met for three times over the last months and we went on for hours. And she was quite submissive. I asked her to change her clothes and put her on her knees. He wanted me to tie her up. But I cannot be like that right away. I need some basic physical contact first. I first wanted to fuck her properly."

Damon continues to go out with couples who are looking for an extra male: "Now I am having a similar situation with a Chinese man and his Filipina wife. We have met up but have not gone to bed yet. But I really like this woman so much I just want to kiss her. So far we have only been able to meet in restaurants." The AFF profile of this couple is written by the male who introduces himself as Hong Kong Chinese (British), 53 years of age, a Christian, and working in the financial field. He writes that his wife is "36 years of age, came from the Northern part of the Philippines. 5 ft. 1 inch in height, weighs between 90–95 lbs, petite. Long hair. Beautiful, bold and sexy. She is bi-sexual and a bit of an exhibitionist. She is also into having sex in public places. She works in administration." The husband attached photographs of his wife naked, posing and bathing in an outdoor rock pool.

Their requirements are quite high, as people (and preferably Christians) are asked to send a recent facial picture and to volunteer their real names: "We will not reply if otherwise. Incidentally, there is no point in sending us an old picture, for we will simply walk out of the preliminary meeting." They also do not want married people who arrange meetings behind the backs of their spouses, which is very unusual in the AFF circles. She is perhaps the more poly-amorous person in their relationship, but he is the engine behind the operation who writes the profile. They are Christians and they are also a socially engaged couple who actively do volunteer work. They are into exploring sex as friendships and have been devoted swingers for six years. They stopped counting their lovers when they reached one hundred.

Even though AFF requires a membership, Damon believes that it has had a democratizing effect in society. He himself has been able to find and go out with Chinese and white people from very different class backgrounds. He sees a clear difference between the AFF class and the traditional high society of Hong Kong. As he explains: "It is perhaps expat-dominated but it is very different from the social upper crust of Hong Kong. Hong Kong is a very money-driven city, not just for those very rich people. The upper crust have sexual affairs with each other, but they really don't need the Internet or digital technologies. They have the extremely high-class prostitution and escort networks."

The large presence of travelers and local expats shows that the business class in Asia is now using the Internet to get access to both swingers and commercial sex workers. These men use commercial sites and blogs to share information about their sexual pursuits. They also post images of their Chinese girls, which are often taken without permission. The website www.internationationalsexguide.com is strategically divided into the different countries where business travelers may look for sex services. The site has special areas for paying members, but many forums have detailed information available to nonmembers. A message written by "Asian Gambler" talks about sex workers in China's province of Guangdong: "I checked with mama san of CP, Houjie, Shenzhen she indicates that the biggest groups of visitors during the weekends are the Hong Kongers, next to Taiwanese. These people come up after winning the horse/dogs race in Hong Kong or Macau. So that explains why you should arrive there early if you want to have the best choice of girls before they finish the horse/dogs race. It's so easy to get to this town from HK or Macau, just an hour bus ride!" The people who post information on www.internationationalsexguide.com carefully hide their identities by using an alter ego but talk openly about how and where to meet sex workers.

These commercial encounters with sex workers are different from AFF encounters in which the parties volunteer to have sex together. When I ask Damon to explain the swinger's lifestyle, he compares it to a special-interest group where people meet because they enjoy a certain lifestyle, perhaps they are into a type of cuisine, or they are wine tasters, or they go to concerts together. But these people are interested in having sex. A crucial transition then takes place when people actually get to know each other and may become friends. But according to Damon, they are often unable to maintain friendships and often switch back to petit bourgeois lifestyles. And of course, the fact that people can gather around the AFF lifestyle is highly taboo in Chinese culture.

Conclusion

I did not notice any type of sexual revolution while conducting my case study in Hong Kong, only a real need for people to enter hidden sex spaces and act out secret sex lives or double lives. Hong Kong is indeed a city of hidden romance and p2p porn excess, but it does not have a well-organized public sphere to sustain the disparate needs of the many cultural groups and sexual minorities. There is an immediate bias from traditional Chinese culture and from the mass media about alternative sexual lifestyles and sexual minorities. There seems to be a lack of concern from within the family authorities and the Hong Kong government to take the twilight zone more seriously, to accept the rules and games of a new breed of sex seekers. The eyes of Hong Kong are still fairly closed to these new profiles, to the needs and powers of people regulating sex and pornography. The Hong Kong twilight is pervasive and trendsetting, attracting not only expats but also Chinese people who criticize the nuclear family—the twilight zone continues to break through gender and power molds of the nation-state that were rooted in the colonial hangover and the more recent handover trauma.

Some people in the post-1997 era have migrated to foreign countries in order to avoid the Chinese climate of crime and punishment, but this fear has dwindled and people are starting to paint their "free-speech HK" cultural identity and autonomy from the mainland. Hong Kong people also seem to recover quite quickly from selective arrests and raids by the local police. For instance, despite the new anti-pornography laws and anti-copyright laws for Hong Kong, there are "healthy" mobs of porn consumers who keep using the p2p platforms in an alternative and illegal economy of products. A selective and historically unprecedented physical arrest of a BitTorrent user, Chai Nai-Ming, was made in 2005, which spread a tide of fear and paranoia through the BitTorrent networks, but that lasted only for about six weeks. Chai's arrest made international news headlines and was followed by state-controlled anti-piracy campaigns in high schools and universities. BitTorrent is now illegal in Hong Kong and blocked by the primary ISPs and most schools and universities, but people have found ways to keep using the p2p technology.

Besides the file-sharers who share products and masturbate like George Bataille's industrious busy bees, there are young crowds who use the web to develop fantasy cartoon characters and arrange virtual marriages and wedding ceremonies. After going through virtual divorce, they may mature into other types of web-based sexual affairs and end up on one of those very popular dating and swingers sites. I have tried to show that there are clear racial and gender divisions on these English-speaking sites, but there are also examples of people who proudly break the mold. The ability of Chinese people to take pornographic pictures of themselves and try to seduce each other is a liberation from the commercial industries that still mostly, if not exclusively, cater to white men. These are the points that became more obvious to me in Hong Kong when Lizzy Kinsey was chased mostly by expats in the yellow-fever pause, or by the occasional very serious or too delicious Chinese man.

Notes

1. Don Anderson, "The Force That through the Wall Drives the Penis: The Becomings and Desiring-Machines of Glory Hole Sex," *Rhizomes* 11/12 (Fall 2005/Spring 2006), www.rhizomes.net/issue11/anderson/index.html (November 17, 2006).

2. Grace Ho, City University Group Research Projects, Qualitative Research Methods (Spring 2006), "How Do Filipina Domestic Workers (FDWs) in Hong Kong Get Involved in Virtual Communities?"

3. Dr. Man Lune Ng, "Hong Kong," *International Encyclopedia of Sexuality*, Humboldt University, Berlin, www2.hu-berlin.de/sexology/IES/hongkong .html (November 15, 2006).

4. Ng, "Hong Kong."

5. Gina Marchetti. *Romance and the "Yellow Peril": Race, Sex, and Discursive Strategies in Hollywood* (Berkeley: University of California Press, 1993), 123.

6. Michael Berry, "A History of Pain: Literary and Cinematic Mappings of Violence," doctoral dissertation, University of California–Santa Barbara, 2006.

7. In commenting on an early draft of this manuscript, Berry mentions that Angie Chan's 1985 movie *Huajie Sidai* or *My Name Ain't Suzie Wong* and Peter Chan's 1996 handover film, *Comrades: Almost a Love Story* are Hong Kong's most vocal protests of *The World of Suzie Wong*.

8. Ng, "Hong Kong."

9. Hsi Lai, *The Sexual Teachings of the Jade Dragon: Taoist Methods for Male Sexual Revitalization* (Rochester, VT: Destiny Books, 2002), 25.

10. Gudrun Wacker, "The Internet and Censorship in China," in *China and the Internet: Politics of the Digital Leap Forward*, ed. Christopher R. Hughes and Gudrun Wacker (London: Routledge Curzon, 2003), 78.

11. "China's Unrepentant Bare-Assed Blogger," *Asian Sex Gazette*, www .asiansexgazette.com/asg/china/china05news92.htm (November 12, 2006).

12. "Mu Mu: China's Nude Breed of Blogger," *Asian Sex Gazette*, www .asiansexgazette.com/asg/china/china05news86.htm (November 11, 2006).

13. "China's Sexual Blogolution," *Asian Sex Gazette*, www.asiansex gazette.com/asg/china/china05news31.htm (November 19, 2006).

14. "China: Reporting Porn Websites Can Bring Money," *Asian Sex Gazette*, www.asiansexgazette.com/asg/china/china05news42.htm (November 15, 2006).

15. Josephine Ho, "Queer Existence under Global Governance: A Taiwan Exemplar," keynote speech delivered at Beyond the Strai(gh)ts: Transnationalism and Queer Chinese Politics Conference, Institute of East Asian Studies, University of California at Berkeley, April 29–30, 2005.

16. Ho, "Queer Existence under Global Governance: A Taiwan Exemplar."

17. Michael Chase, James Mulvenon, and Nina Hachigian, "Comrade to Comrade Networks: The Social and Political Implications of Peer-to-Peer Networks in China," in *Chinese Cyberspaces: Technological Changes and Political Effects*, ed. Jenns Damm and Simona Thomas (New York: Routledge, 2006), 95.

18. Sharalyn Orbaugh, "Shojo," in *Encyclopedia of Contemporary Japanese Culture*, ed. S. Buckley (London: Routledge, 2002).

19. H. Fong, *Hong Kong Connection: Pretty Bizarre*. RTHK (Hong Kong Public Television), Hong Kong, 2005.

20. Personal interview with Cynthia at Hong Kong Game Fair, August 2006, unpublished text.

21. Case study based on interview with and research project conducted by Huang Li and Voramon Damrongsinsakul, Anime Community Animation Garden, unpublished research project for Masters of Arts and Communication and New Media, City University of Hong Kong, Fall 2005. Anime Garden is located at www.dmhy.net and Nongfu Mountain: http://bbs.dmhy.net/index.php?proc=forum:category&forumid=327.

Conclusion

The pornography users in this book utilize electronically networked spaces for developing sexual identities and building social or sexual affairs in *twilight zones* far away from publicly sanctified zones of entertainment. It is shown that despite rigid nation-state surveillance, their attitudes and working methods are mutating into porn-as-bedroom-philosophies for the twenty-first century. What do we mean by bedroom philosophies? Jon McKenzie argues in *Perform or Else: From Discipline to Performance* that performativity is a contemporary mode of living with technologies and schizoid or fluid agencies, as bodies and desires move about alongside spaces of technology and experience them as glittering disorders. Hence, we find ways to express our multiple desires, and our porn fantasies, and internalize the mechanisms of nation-state repression. In the bedroom we become a mediated organism of disjunctive voices whose paths mingle, collide, and perhaps even transform one another.[1] The organism is schooled in material-technological competencies that differ from consumerist agency in sex shops, TV lounges, motel rooms, or the masturbation theaters from bygone areas. Therefore, old-school disciplinary methods of rating and punishing cannot be easily applied, but of course they are.

For instance, netporn legislation and recent police raids against web users in Taiwan and mainland China have shown that governments will go as far as monitoring entire web-based porn-friendly bulletin boards and all their strata of sexual communication. In China's great Internet trial against bbs99.com, the entire network was disciplined and eleven of the most active administrators were sent to jail. One could argue that the Chinese custom of these random arrests and severe punishment will not manage to eradicate the emerging porn culture, but it does strike terror into the very heart of the fuzzy organism. It is harder for web users to be media activists when their site managers are disciplined by the law. Nonetheless, one cannot think of twenty-first-century web users as victims of porn, but as agents skilled in technological networking. Netporn spaces will allow people to play with representation while being part of an ephemeral cultural organism. The organism lives by fluctuating regulations as it matches and connects people who live in geographically and mentally different sites, linguistic zones, and dispersed locations, with clashing values and incompatible sexual orientations. Despite these glittering disorders, the network will continue to push people to communicate and exchange porn. Having its roots in the era of cybersex and disembodied socialization, the organism wants its uncanny couplings and artful possibilities. Politically speaking, previously marginal groups are actively feeding data into the network, such as the feminist or artistically inclined pornographers of altporn and indieporn, the activist ethnic pornographers, and the autonomous queer and transgendered producers who manage to assemble an audience of queer, straight, male, and female viewers.

Those porn vanguards have indeed copulated and are unable to fathom an ethics of discipline and punishment. Have they intoxicated the masses with their platforms for porn fantasies and exchange? Or have they just built spaces for our liquid minds and bodies? As Foucault already foresaw in "Of Other Spaces," our modern sense of place is eternally unfolding as spaces, surreal alleyways, and strange festivals where we wander and contemplate bodily rituals and displays. Administrators try to mediate between the ephemeral organism and obscenity laws that are mostly predicated on older cultural histories, morals, and sexual behaviors. Admins are critical of puritanical nation-state laws but also aware of the necessity of, or even taking pleasure in, the act of imposing restrictions on members. The responsibilities of administrators to monitor and reward members, to ban all kinds of illegal porn, to marry those who have fallen in love while exchanging porn, and to give credit to members who are more productive uploaders all result in the cultivation of a general economy.

These netporn spaces breed abundant or obsessive behaviors—lurking, seducing, up/downloading, blogging, mutual masturbating, dating, and swinging. But the general economy only mimics the exchange economy and people get hooked as they engage in free trading and act out sexual desires. Netporn users have loyal libidos and perform well within these symbolical intensities of web life. As Bataille said, general economies are based on the notion of the unreturnable gift where a surplus of data and information can only be channeled in a performative manner. Hence, we see modes of mimicry as a self-aware and ritualized enactment of a culture's high point of exuberance, ecstasy, or intensity.

For instance, the Hong Kong BitTorrent (BT) forum uwants.com is regulated by admins who regulate members in the p2p porn zone. Even though these p2p file-sharing activities are prohibited by Hong Kong law, the BT forums have their own specific laws. They do not declare anarchy but live by the quirks and opinions of the admins, who take their jobs very seriously. They usually ban certain types of porn from forums, such as child porn or bestiality; they also rate porn and reward the active uploaders and endow them with the status of "e-cock." The Hong Kong government issued a clear warning to the BT community by making the first-ever BT arrest in January 2005, but the trading communities are thriving and continue to negotiate a climate of porn excess and punishment. Even though it would be difficult for the "e-cocks" to display their social status in public, since it carries the double stigma of trading illegal products and avidly consuming porn, this title does have positive meaning within the male-dominated network.

It would be perhaps easier to act as if we were only nation-state citizens conditioned by clearly defined social practices and laws, but recent conflicts and arrests have stirred legislators to take into account the specific qualities of pornography's cybergeographies. Take for example the case of Chris Wilson of Orlando, Florida, who was arrested for running the amateur porn site www.nowthatsfuckedup.com (NTFU). What exactly was so *fucked up* about Wilson's porn site? It was one of many amateur pay sites that allowed members to post sexy pictures of themselves

and their partners. As a side-effect of these regulated amateur exchanges, the site attracted a specific group of porn users, U.S. military
personnel who started using the site for posting images of their war trophies interlaced with sexual poses. For instance, a female soldier shows
off a huge gun between her legs and elsewhere shows a bra made of
whipping cream on her naked breasts. The eroticization of her body
merges into a love affair with emblems of military culture and actual violence, as the site also showed the real gore of U.S. soldiers as war machines and the remains of dead Iraqis.

Wilson's lawyer Lawrence Walters was clever in outlining the intricate material-technological qualities and the philosophies of netporn
culture. He was reported to be well known for dealing with conflicts between erotic entertainers and the conservative residents of Polk County.
Echoing the outlines of a 2002 debate between the ACLU and U.S. Attorney General John Ashcroft on the issue of restricting child pornography, Walters argued that NTFU exceeds the moral boundaries of Polk
County.[2] More generally, he argued that the community standards of the
most conservative U.S. counties or states are insufficient to judge Wilson's web community: "This is created by the users. . . . These people
have chosen to submit pictures of their activities, whether they are sexual in nature, whether they are war-oriented, whether they're everyday
activities. For Polk County to claim that images are obscene is essentially saying that the human condition is obscene. You can try to claim
that this is obscene all you want, but this is the world we live in. Sooner
or later, Polk County's going to have to come to terms with it."[3]

Bataille believed that the cultivation of a general economy in industrial nations would entail a reversal of normative values. As he
writes in *The Accursed Share, Vol. 1*: "Changing from the perspectives
of restrictive economy to general economy actually accomplishes a
Copernican transformation: a reversal of thinking—and of ethics. If a
part of wealth (subject to a rough estimate) is doomed to destruction or
at least unproductive use without any possible profit, it is logical, even
inescapable, to surrender commodities without return." Are these recent floods of images of war or violent sex still a legitimate way for people to regulate excess energy, cultural traffic, and opinions? Or do we
have to admit that the porn web has become too messed up? Accord-

ing to Bataille, war is a primary means for any culture to expend its excess energy, but he wanted people to see other possibilities. As he wrote: "We can ignore or forget the fact that the ground we live on is little other than a field of multiple destructions. Our ignorance only has this incontestable effect: it causes us to undergo what we could bring about in our own way."[4] We have to try to find a mechanism to spend the data surplus and engage in symbolical love and war activities. As ancient cultures found ways to relieve trading mechanisms through festivals or symbolical monuments or rituals of sacrifice, modern societies and citizens are led to reabsorb excess energy by means of performativity and leisure time.

However, as we have seen in the cultural logic of netporn spaces, those individuals who squander their collections as illegal uploaders, or as active artists or exhibitionists, and who do not wish for money in return, are of course more punishable by the law and social stigmatization. Alternative porn spaces and web users as "sex workers" are some of the most sophisticated societies to have dealt with Bataille's nagging question of how a culture can deal with its excess energy. Their efforts at progressive self-regulation and bodily aesthetics are challenged by tendencies toward violent representation and porn wars; hence we cannot return to the era when porn was more innocent, less hardcore, and merely a relief for horny males. Take for instance Anna the Nerd, who uploads daily softcore images for paying members. Anna designs herself as a nerd: a person who is condemned to wear glasses, who seeks pleasure among philosophy books and dusty bookshelves, and a computer engineer who gets ecstatic when installing operating systems. She pleases her members with a self-conscious enactment of these stereotypes, even though she radiates a typical female sex worker's youth and nastiness.

Anna is a sexy blonde who posts citations from her philosophy books and who writes essays about her porn experiences; hence the icons of nerdiness are integrated into her agency. When I ask her what kinds of clients she attracts, she says she does attract mostly male nerds:

> If I'm having a little trouble banging out a PHP script, I can hit them up for a little advice. They like to chat with me about typical nerdy subjects—my M:TG cards, the comics I'm reading, that type of thing.

There are definitely the ones that ask lots of nosy questions about my sex life but there are an awful lot of guys (and a few chicks!) who just want to talk about nerdy shit with a girl, and that's cool. I've also talked to a couple that aren't nerdy at all and have problems stringing together a sentence properly, and for a while it baffled me. I think there is also a contingent of people who aren't nerdy at all and are signing up because they think I'm cute—the way that people normally sign up for pay-sites—but those are definitely in the minority. If I did videos, or hardcore more than once in a blue moon, I'd probably get more 'regular' members than nerdy members. Every now and again I do [find] a member that is so extraordinarily stupid, [so] it took me a while to come up with a working theory for them: I suspect that something like 10% of my membership is ex-bullies who used to beat up nerds like me in high school and now get off on seeing pics of nerds naked. But that's just an unsubstantiated theory.;)[5]

Anna the Nerd rides the economies of profit and excess; she is a witty porn star who designs herself toward a new niche of male and female porn users. Needless to say, she likely operates as a fringe producer within a certain educated class of people. But Anna also challenges the gendered premise of porn, which is a male gaze fixed on a point of female agency. She invites her male clients to open up their repertoire of excitability. Moreover, she attempts to attract women who are less prone to slide into the binary of male lurker versus female performer.

Hence, we have witnessed a feminization of the notion of porn agency, not only because straight, lesbian, and transgendered producers try to cater to women, but because consumerism now involves acts of gender morphing and cross-voyeurism. I define a *cross-voyeur* as a person of a peculiar sexual taste or subculture who is tempted to try out an odd or incompatible taste or subculture. Why would we see a rise of these kinds of disorderly tastes and desires? Rather than seeing porn culture as driven by a cult of smooth loving, it could be a continuation of the philosophical traditions of Bataille and de Sade, both of whom meticulously evoked sex scenes that would have vigorous or painful/shocking effects in partners. In *Eroticism* and *Tears of Eros*, Bataille shows how erotic sensibilities have an undercurrent of attraction to scenes and rituals of sacrifice and death. In the writings of de Sade, we witness detailed descriptions of hyperbolic actions that bewilder females, or simply undercut the known positions of female psychology. The young sex bomb is assaulted but stays afloat among a circus of dark eccentricity, perhaps even starts dancing along in modes of hardcore pornographic seduction. Alfonso Lingis describes these reactions to seductions as deadly pleasures or voluptuous emotions, that is, "a kind of vibration produced in our soul by shocks . . . our voluptuous transport—this indescribable convulsive needling which drives us wild, which lifts us to the highest pitch of happiness . . . is ignited . . . by the sight of a lubricious object undergoing the strongest possible sensation."[6]

In his essay "21st Century Schizoid Bear," Francesco Palmieri depicts a similar voluptuous pleasure as a sublime moment when as a gay man he is turned on by somebody he would normally not consider. He describes an encounter with a fat and hairy person who turns him on yet, upon closer investigation, turns out to be a female-born person or transbear. He describes this encounter as a sublime moment in which the transbear's complex appearance lifts him into a high of terror and pleasure. Palmieri said he wonders if and how this process of finding others ever comes to an end. Or does it reach a limit? Alongside developments of cross-voyeurism, FTM porn stars such as Buck Angel have taken an active part in appropriating porn stardom and making seductive appearances for males and females. Buck's growing success among males and females is not only a new networking of porn zones but a call for average straight viewers to question and design their own genders and sexual tastes. As Barbara DeGenevieve writes in "The Hot Bods of Queer Porn," a reflection on her experiences as an administrator of a Chicago-based transgendered porn site, these sex acts engage viewers with performative mutations or multilayered parodies of gender.

These are examples of netporn producers and consumers who trade services while developing novel chemistries. When confronted by the law or capitalist economies, they could argue that their activities are not merely obscene but have added value. For instance, in defining obscenity and pornography in the United States, judges have traditionally used the *Miller* test, which stipulates that "pornography portrays sexual conduct in a patently offensive way in violation of acceptable state laws, and which, [when] taken as a whole, lacks serious literary, political, or scientific value."[7] Hence the law recognizes a type of pornography that has a different cultural function. In his comparative analysis of developments in netporn legislation, Dr. Zhou He writes that Hong Kong porn legislation equally protects articles that are intended for the public good. These articles include "those that were made in the interest of science, literature, art, learning, or any other object of general concern." However, one has to be careful presenting porn to the Hong Kong public, as the Hong Kong law also states "that a person is not supposed to circulate, sell, hire, or lend an indecent article or pornography to the public or a section of the public."[8] Several people accused of distributing obscenities in Hong Kong have meanwhile argued that they actually do not intend to distribute products to the public but only to specific members of a specific club or group. As progressive pornographers or sex educators, we thus have to position ourselves somewhere between the mission to contribute to the public good and the mission not to distribute at all to the public.

The pornography law in mainland China, Temporary Rules on the Identification of Pornography and Obscene Material, issued by the State Press and Publication Bureau, also protects materials that have artistic or literary value. However, the criminal law of China has a special section on computer information networks and Internet security, Protection and Management Regulations, which states that no unit or individual may use the Internet to create, replicate, retrieve, or transmit materials that "promote feudal superstitions, sexually suggestive materials, gambling, violence, and murder." Moreover, as Dr. Zhou He argues, the Chinese government uses those cutting-edge digital technologies to do everything from blocking thousands of websites to closing actual cybercafés. They also monitor and censor the content of individual emails and practice online hijacking—replacing existing sites with government-approved ones. As Hughes and Wacker explain in *China and the Internet: Politics of the Digital Leap Forward*, the censorship practices in China have indeed created a schizophrenic climate of technology hype and mistrust of new technologies. Since neither China nor Hong Kong has netporn industry lobbies that distribute materials through well-organized pay sites, Chinese netporn users are more vulnerable while acting out porn exchanges.

During China's great Internet trial of 2005, eleven defendants were charged with distributing obscenities through the Internet forum 99bbs.com. Most of the defendants were schoolteachers and university students who used the forum to engage in chat and exchange products.

When they climbed up the ranks to become admins of the site, they also took on symbolical roles such as school principal, which gave them higher status in the community. Even though only certain areas of the bulletin boards were porn sites and a brothel directory, the entire site and all the admins were arrested by the Chinese government. The main administrator, Wang Rong, was the only admin to have made some money, and he allegedly fled to the United States before he got arrested, while most of the other ten defendants received harrowing jail sentences. They were punished for riding the high tide of a general economy and moderating China's growing need for online porn excess.

Is it necessary for nation-state governments to start understanding the rules and behaviors of the general economy? Or do we accept that they need to be delegated to an ephemeral underground zone? To keep these exchanges underground is to accept the repressed or shameful nature of the pornographic unconscious. As it currently stands, nation-state governments and nongovernmental organizations are networking toward their anti-porn feminism and homophobic reactions, as they try to glue together the epoch of schizoid sex, that is, consumer excess and draconian legislation. For instance, the networked anti-porn powers are infringing on the vitalities of emerging porn zones in Taiwan. As Josephine Ho explains, conservative women's groups are networking to introduce a campaign against sex workers and for more rigid netporn legislation. Taiwan's awakening queer and cyberqueer climate has suffered from continuous and slanderous media coverage of gay or sex-related happenings and from a series of new laws, litigations, and rules banning all—and any—sex-related information, contacts, and inquiries on the Internet. Ho believes that despite the upsurge of queer activism, Taiwan has a dangerous undercurrent of networked sex-phobia.

For instance, in order to block the channels through which youths may learn about possible job opportunities in the sex trade, a law was amended in 1999 to ban all Internet-related transactions. Those who now potentially fall victim to the law are all sexually active web users, including the more marginalized sexual subjects who depend on the Internet for information, communication, and contact. The moral panic around Internet sex and porn has grown after more than 2,500 cases were sent to court, among them the web users who were playing in clearly marked sexuality chat rooms.

To conclude, the Taiwanese law does not successfully target commercial profit-making porn but hunts down the noncommercial general economies of the Internet. If other nation-states or NGOs decide to follow the example of Taiwan, it will have a huge impact on the nascent netporn cultures and discourses described in this book. One could argue that web users will always find ways to filter excess, but the active or self-conscious within the general economy will be hit harder. There is always a good chance that the sex-positive and activist or sexually active professor will also suffer to some degree from his/her affiliation with the netporn cause, that the academic response to these lines of inquiry has been or will be tenuous, and that the various anti-porn factions will forever have the popular vote after centuries of silence, hypocrisy, and/or discretion—but the chemistry will still invade our bodies.

Notes

1. Jon McKenzie, *Perform or Else: From Discipline to Performance* (New York: Routledge, 2001), 187.

2. See discussion of the 2002 issue of *Supreme Court Debates* on Internet pornography in this book's chapter 1, "Netporn in Small Places and Other Spaces."

3. J. Billman, "Gore? Ok. Sex, No Way!" *Orlando Weekly*, October 13, 2005.

4. Georges Bataille, *The Accursed Share: Vol. 1*. Cited in *The Bataille Reader*, ed. Fred Botting and Scott Wilson (New York: Blackwell, 1997), 185.

5. Anna the Nerd, personal interview with the author, unpublished text, October 10, 2006.

6. Alfonso Lingis, "Deadly Pleasures," in *Must We Burn Sade*, ed. Deepak Sawhney (New York: Prometheus Books), 32.

7. Supreme Court Justice Warren E. Burger in *Miller v. United States* (1973).

8. Zhou He, "Obscenity and Pornography On and Off Line," unpublished text, p. 1.

9. Josephine Ho, "Queer Existence under Global Governance: A Taiwan Exemplar," keynote speech delivered at Beyond the Strai(gh)ts: Transnationalism and Queer Chinese Politics conference, Institute of East Asian Studies, University of California at Berkeley, April 29–30, 2005.

Bibliography

Books and Articles

"Abu Ghraib Files." Photographs and videos compiled and annotated by Michael Scherer and Mark Benjamin for Salon.com. http://www.salon.com/news/abu_ghraib/2006/03/14/introduction (July 19, 2006).

Airaksinen, Miko. *The Philosophy of the Marquis de Sade*. New York: Routledge, 1995.

Appadurai, Arjun. *Modernity at Large: Cultural Dimensions of Globalization*. Minneapolis: University of Minnesota Press, 1996.

Asher, Bill. "Interview with PBS *Frontline*." *Frontline* program website, "American Porn," http://www.pbs.org/wgbh/pages/frontline/shows/porn/interviews/asher (May 16, 2002).

Barlow, John Perry. "Censorship 2000." Posted on Internet mailing list *Nettime*, July 12, 2000, http://www.nettime.org (May 14, 2004).

———. "A Declaration of the Independence of Cyberspace." 1996. http://www.eff.org~barlow/Declaration-Final.html (May 10, 2004).

Bataille, Georges. *The Accursed Share. Volume 1: Consumption*. New York: Zone Books, 1991.

———. *The Tears of Eros*. San Francisco: City Lights Books, 1989.

Berardi, "Bifo" Franco. "The Obsession of the (Vanishing) Body." Posted on the Internet mailing list *Netporn-List*, August 15, 2005 (October 14, 2006).

Berry, Michael. "A History of Pain: Literary and Cinematic Mappings of Violence in Modern China." Doctoral dissertation, University of California, Santa Barbara, 2006.

Butler, Judith. *Bodies That Matter: On the Discursive Limits of Sex.* London: Routledge, 1993.

Carey, Benedict. "Long after Kinsey, Only the Brave Study Sex," *New York Times,* November 9, 2004.

Carter, Angela. *The Sadeian Woman and the Ideology of Pornography.* London: Penguin Books, 1979.

Castonguy, Louis Georges, Jean Proulx, Jocelyn Aubut, Andre MacKibben, and Michael Campbell. "Sexual Preference Assessment of Sexual Aggressors: Predictors of Penile Response Magnitude." *Archives of Sexual Behavior* 22, no. 4 (August 1993): 325–34.

Cheah, Peng, David Fraser, and Judith Gerbich, eds. *Thinking Through the Body of the Law.* Sydney: Allen and Unwin, 1996.

Cheah, Peng, and Bruce Robbins, eds. *Cosmopolitics: Thinking and Feeling beyond the Nation.* Minneapolis: University of Minnesota Press, 1998.

"Child Pornography Is Readily Accessible over Peer-to-Peer Networks." U.S. government document issued by the General Accountability Office, GAO-03–537, http://216.239.37.104/search?q=cache:bViQIv32s48J:www.gao.gov/new.items/d03537t.pdf+gao-03–537T&hl=en&ie=UTF-8. (June 15, 2003).

Copier, Marinka, and Joost Raessens, eds. *Level Up! The Proceedings of the Digital Games Research Conference at Utrecht University.* Utrecht: Universeit Utrecht, 2003.

Cramer, Florian, and Stewart Home. "Pornographic Coding." Paper delivered at the Crash Conference, February 11, 2005.

Culp, Samantha. "First Porn Son: Asian-man.com and the Golden Porn Revolution." *Wake: Journal of Contemporary Culture* (Spring 2004).

Damm, Jenns, and Simona Thomas, eds. *Chinese Cyberspaces: Technological Changes and Political Effects.* New York: Routledge, 2006.

Dasgupta, Rana. "Sexworks/Networks: What Do People Get Out of Internet Porn?" http://www.sarai.net (May 6, 2002).

Defert, Daniel. "Foucault, Space, and the Architects." In *Politics/Poetics: Documenta X—The Book.* Ostfildern-Ruitz: Cantz Verlag, 1997.

DeGenevieve, Barbara. "Hot Bods of Queer Porn," Posted on the Internet mailing list [Netporn-l], October 17, 2005 (June 2, 2006).

Dery, Mark. *Escape Velocity: Cyberculture at the End of the Century.* New York: Grove Press, 1996.

———. "Sex Organs Sprout Everywhere: The Sublime and Grotesque in Web Porn." Keynote lecture delivered at Art and Politics of Netporn conference, Amsterdam, October 2005. Abbreviated version of the lecture available at http://www.markdery.com/archives/news/index.html#000048#more (January 8, 2006).

De Waal, Frans. *The Ape and the Sushi-Master: Cultural Reflections of a Primatologist*. New York: Basic Books, 2001.

Engelhardt, Tom, and David Swanson. "War Porn and Iraq." Lewrockwell.com blog. 2006. http://www.lewrockwell.com/engelhardt/engelhardt197.html (July 15, 2006).

Foucault, Michel. "Of Other Spaces." *Diacritics* 16, no. 1 (1986): 22–27.

Frow, John. *Time and Commodity Exchange*. Oxford, UK: Clarendon Press, 1997.

Goldberg, Vicky. *Light Matters: Writings on Photography*. New York: Aperture, 2005.

Gordon, Max. "Abu Ghraib: Postcards from the Edge." October 14, 2004, Open Democracy website, http://www.opendemocracy.net/media-abu_ghraib/article_2146.jsp (July 15, 2006).

Gray, Chris Hables. *The Cyborg Handbook*. New York: Routledge, 1995.

Hamamoto, Darrell Y. "The Joy Fuck Club: Prolegomenon to an Asian American Porno Practice." *New Political Science* 20, no. 3 (1998). A web-based excerpt of this essay can be found at http://www.mastersofthepillow.com/written.html (October 30, 2003).

Haraway, Donna. *Simians, Cyborgs, and Women: The Reinvention of Nature*. New York: Routledge, 1991.

Hersh, M. Seymour. "Torture at Abu Ghraib." *The New Yorker*, April 5, 2004. http:// www.newyorker.com/fact/content/?040510fa_fact (July 15, 2006).

Ho, Josephine. "Queer Existence under Global Governance: A Taiwan Exemplar." A keynote speech delivered at Beyond the Strai(gh)ts: Transnationalism and Queer Chinese Politics conference, Institute of East Asian Studies, University of California at Berkeley, April 29–30, 2005.

Hughes, Christopher R., and Gudrun Wacker, eds. *China and the Internet: Politics of the Digital Leap Forward*. London: Routledge Curzon, 2003.

Hunt, Lynn. *The Invention of Pornography: Obscenity and the Origins of Modernity, 1500–1800*. Cambridge, MA: MIT/Zone Books, 1997.

Hsi, Lai. *The Sexual Teachings of the Jade Dragon: Taoist Methods for Male Sexual Revitalization*. Rochester, VT: Destiny Books, 2002.

Jacobs, Katrien. *Libi_doc: Journeys in the Performance of Sex Art*. Ljubljana, Slovenia: Maska, 2005.

———. "Pornography in Small Places and Other Spaces." *Cultural Studies* 18, no. 1 (2004): 67–84.

Janssen, Eric, Deanna Carpenter, and Cynthia A. Graham. "Selecting Films for Sex Research: Gender Differences in Erotic Film Preference." *Archives of Sexual Behavior* 32, no. 3 (June 2003): 243–51.

Janssen, Marije. "We Are So Much More Than Our Naked Boobies! The Use of Sexual Agency by Young Feminists in Online Pornographic Communities." Master's thesis, University of Utrecht, Spring 2006.

Kendrick, Walter. *The Secret Museum: Pornography in Modern Culture.* Berkeley: University of California Press, 1996.

Kolko, Beth E., Lisa Nakamura, and Gilbert Rodman, eds. *Race in Cyberspace.* New York: Routledge, 2006.

Kunkel, Thor. *Endstuffe.* Frankfurt: Eichborn, 2004.

Lane, Frederick S. *Obscene Profits: The Entrepreneurs of Pornography in the Cyber Age.* New York: Routledge, 2000.

Levine, Judith. *Harmful to Minors: The Perils of Protecting Children from Sex.* Minneapolis: University of Minnesota Press, 2002.

Lessig, Lawrence. *Code and Other Laws of Cyberspace.* New York: Perseus Books, 1996.

Loviglio, Joan. "Librarians Resist Filtering Technology to Block Adult Sites." *Boston Globe*, March 2, 2002.

Lovink, Geert. *Dark Fiber: Tracking Critical Internet Culture.* Cambridge, MA: MIT Press, 2002.

Lumby, Catherine. "Panic Attacks: Old Fears in a New Media Area." *Media International Australia* 85 (November 1997): 40–47.

Lunenfeld, Peter. *The Digital Dialectic: New Essays on New Media.* Cambridge, MA: MIT Press, 1999.

———. *Snap to Grid: A User's Guide to Digital Arts, Media, and Cultures.* Cambridge, MA: MIT Press, 2000.

MacKinnon, Catherine. "Vindication and Resistance: A Response to the Carnegie Mellon Study of Pornography in Cyberspace." *Georgetown Law Journal* 83, no. 5 (1995): 1959–67.

Manovich, Lev. *The Language of New Media.* Cambridge, MA: MIT Press, 2001.

Marchetti, Gina. *Romance and the "Yellow Peril": Race, Sex, and Discursive Strategies in Hollywood.* Berkeley: University of California Press, 1993.

Massumi, Brian. *Parables for the Virtual: Movement, Affect, Sensation.* Durham, NC: Duke University Press, 2002.

McKenzie, Jon. *Perform or Else: From Discipline to Performance.* New York: Routledge, 2001.

McLelland, Mark. "No Climax, No Point, No Meaning? Japanese Women's Boy-Love Sites on the Internet." *Journal of Commercial Inquiry* 24, no. 3 (2000).

———. "Out and About on the Japanese Gay Net." In *Mobile Cultures: New Media in Queer Asia*, ed. Chris Berry, Fran Martin, and Audrey Yue. Durham, NC: Duke University Press, 2001.

Miller-Young, Mireille. "'Because I'm Sexy and Smart!' Black Web Mistresses Hack Cyperporn." *Cut-Up Media*, September 26, 2005. http://www.cut-up .com/news/detail.php?sid=416 (November 16, 2005).

Milne, Carly, ed. *Naked Ambition: Women Who Are Changing Pornography*. New York: Carroll and Graf, 2005.

Nakamura, Lisa. *Cybertypes: Race, Ethnicity, and Identity on the Internet*. New York: Routledge, 2002.

O'Brien, C. "Boom Times Have Passed for Online Porn." *Siliconvalley.com*, May 4, 2002 (August 6, 2002).

Open Net Initiative. "Internet Content Filtering in India." http://www.open netinitiative.net/bulletins/003 (June 1, 2004).

Orbaugh, Sharalyn. "Shojo." In *Encyclopedia of Contemporary Japanese Culture*, ed. S. Buckley. London: Routledge, 2002.

———. "Busty Battlin' Babes: The Evolution of the Shojo in 1990s Visual Culture." In *Gender and Power in the Japanese Visual Field*, ed. Joshua S. Mostow, Norman Bryson, and Marybeth Graybill. Honolulu: University of Hawaii Press, 2003.

O'Toole, Lawrence. *Pornocopia: Porn, Sex, Technology and Desire*. London: Serpent's Tail, 1998.

Paasonen, Susanna. "Lust and Disgust: Affect and Online Pornography." Paper delivered at ISEA conference. Helsinki, August 2004.

Palmieri, Francesco. "21st Century Schizoid Bear: Masculine Transitions through Net Pornography." Unpublished manuscript, March 2006.

Pasquinelli, Matteo. "Warporn! Warpunk! Autonomous Videopoesis in Wartime." Posted on the Internet mailing list *Nettime*, August 30, 2004. http://www.nettime.org (August 30, 2004).

Paul, Pamela. *Pornified: How Pornography Is Transforming Our Lives, Our Relationships, and Our Families*. New York: Henry Holt, 2005.

Phillips, Dougal. "Can Desire Go On without a Body? Pornographic Exchange and the Death of the Sun." http://culturemachine.tees.as.uk/Interzone/ dphillips.html (January 8, 2006).

Plant, Sadie. *The Most Radical Gesture*. London: Routledge, 1992.

———. *Zeros + Ones: Digital Women and the New Technoculture*. New York: Doubleday, 1997.

Rahim, Babak. "Social Death and War: U.S. Media Representations of Sacrifice." *Bad Subjects*, no. 63, April 2003. http://bad.eserver.org/issues/2003/63/rahimi.html (August 15, 2006).

Rorive, Isabelle. "Strategies to Tackle Racism and Xenophobia on the Internet: Where Are We in Europe?" *International Journal of Communications Law and Policy* 7 (2003): 110–18.

Schleiner, Anne-Marie. "Open Source Art Experiments: Lucky Kiss." Posted on Internet mailing list *Nettime*, November 26, 2000 (November 25, 2005).

Sex: The Annabel Chong Story. DVD. 1999. Produced and directed by Lewis Gough.

Shaviro, Steven. *Connected, or What It Means to Live in Network Society*. Minneapolis: University of Minnesota Press, 2003.

Shirky, Clay. "Weblogs and the Mass Amateurization of Publishing." Clay Shirky's writings about the Internet, Economics & Culture, Media & Community, Open Source. http://shirky.com/writings/weblogs_publishing.html (November 15, 2005).

Show-n-Tell. *webAffairs*, with an essay by Allucquere Rosanne Stone. Boston: Eighteen Publications, 2005.

Slade, Joseph W. *Pornography and Sexual Representation*. Westport, CT: Greenwood Press, 2001.

Soja, Edward W. *Thirdspace: Journeys to Los Angeles and Other Real and Imagined Places*. Oxford, UK: Blackwell, 1996.

Spinello, Richard. *Cyberethics: Morality and Law in Cyberspace*, 2nd ed. Sudbury, MA: Jones and Bartlett, 2003.

———. *Regulating Cyberspace: The Policies and Technologies of Control*. Westport, CT: Quorum Books, 2002.

Straayer, Chris. *Deviant Eyes, Deviant Bodies: Sexual Re-orientation in Film and Video*. New York: Columbia University Press, 1996.

Theweleit, Klaus. *Male Fantasies*, vols. 1 and 2. Minneapolis: University of Minnesota Press, 1987.

Ulmer, Gregory. *Internet Invention: From Literacy to Electracy*. New York: Longman, 2003.

Van Veen, Tobias. "Affective Tactics: Intensifying a Politics of Perception," *Bad Subjects*, no. 63, April 2003. http://bad.eserver.org/issues/2003/63/vanveen.html (March 16, 2006).

Ven-Hwei Lo and Ran Wei. "Third-Person Effect, Gender, and Pornography on the Internet." *Journal of Broadcasting and Communication* 46 (2002): 13–46.

Virno, Paolo. *A Grammar of the Multitude Semiotexte*. Los Angeles: Semiotext(e), 2004.

Waismann, Rogeria, Peter B. C. Fenwick, Glenn. D. Wilson, Terry D. Hewett, and John Lumsden. "EEG Responses to Visual Erotic Stimuli in Men with Normal and Paraphilic Interests." *Archives of Sexual Behavior* 32, no. 2 (April 2003): 135–44.

Weiner, Annette B. *Inalienable Possessions: The Paradox of Keeping while Giving.* Berkeley: University of California Press, 1992.

Williams, Linda. *Hard Core: Power, Pleasure, and the "Frenzy of the Visible."* Berkeley: University of California Press, 1989.

———, ed. *Porn Studies.* Durham, NC: Duke University Press, 2004.

Wright, Les. *The Bear Book: Readings in the History and Evolution of a Gay Male Subculture* Binghamton, NY: Haworth Press, 1997.

Wyatt, Sally, Flis Henwood, Nod Miller, and Peter Senker, eds. *Technology and In/Equality: Questioning the Information Society.* London: Routledge, 2000.

Zaretsky, Adam. "USSMEAC as S/M Response to Atrocity." Posted on the Internet mailing list *Netporn-List*, September 19, 2005 (October 15, 2006).

Zittrain, J. "Internet Points of Control." *Boston College Law Review* 43 (2003): 118–39.

Zittrain, J., and B. Edelman. "Empirical Analysis of Internet Filtering in China." http://cyber.law.harvard.edu/filtering/china (May 31, 2004).

———. "Documentation of Internet Filtering in Saudi Arabia." http://cyber.law .harvard.edu/filtering/saudiarabia (May 31, 2004).

Zizek, Slavoj. "What Rumsfeld Doesn't Know That He Knows about Abu Ghraib." http://www.inthesetimes.com/site/main/article/what_rumsfeld_ doesnt_know_that_he_knows_about_abu_ghraib (January 8, 2006).

Zook, Matthew. "Underground Globalization: Mapping the Space of Flows of the Internet Adult Industry." *Environment and Planning* 25 (2003): 1261–86.

Zornick George, "The Porn of War." *The Nation*, September 22, 2005. http:// www.thenation.com/doc/20051010/the_porn_of_war (July 19, 2006).

Pornographic Websites

Alt/Indie Porn

Altporn Film Star Eon McKai: http://www.eonmckai.com

Combo blog/portal covering "altporn," "alt.porn," "alternaporn," and "subculture erotica": http://www.altporn.net

Dana Dearmond: http://danadearmond.com; http://danabound.com

Dedicated to the Beauty of Human Orgasm: http://www.beautifulagony.com

Erotic Storytelling by and for the Masses: http://www.literotica.com

Fatal Beauties: http://fatalbeauty.com

Joanna Angel: http://burningangel.com/
Indienudes archives of art and porn sites: http://www.indienudes.com/main.html
Punk Porn: http://punkfever.com
Sexy Star with Body Hair: http://furrygirl.com
Some artsy weird-ass porn: http://supercult.com
Somewhere between Art and Porn. Site run by the couple Mr. Lind and Alex
    Lamarsh: http://erotiquedigitale.com
Suicidegirls: http://www.suicidegirls.com
Young and artsy model-type girl: http://www.apneatic.com
Young feminism in netporn: http://www.toxywonderland.com; http://seecandy
    bleeding.com; http://candyposes.com

Nerds
Anna the Nerd: http://www.nerdpron.com
Nakkid Nerds community run by Cloei: http://www.nakkidnerds.com

Queer Porn Sites
Bears dating sites: http://www.bearwww.com; http://www.silverdaddies.com
Bulls newsgroup: http://groups.yahoo.com/group/bullempire
Buckangel FTM porn star: http://www.buckangel.com
Cyberdyke, lesbian porn collective: http://www.cyber-dyke.net
Gay Arab and rascal website: http://www.citebeur.com
Emilie Jouvet, lesbian porn *One Night Stand*: http://onenightstand-thefilm.com
Kelma, online community for gay Arabs and Black gays in France and North
    Africa: http://www.kelma.org
Lesbian erotica, book reviews, and other cool stuff: http://www.cynicaldog.com
Maria Beatty, lesbian s/m porn: http://www.bleuproductions.com
Morty Diamond Trannyfags: http://www.Trannyfags.com
Phag Off Collective Rome: http://www.phagoff.org
Queer and transgender indie: http://www.nofauxxx.com
Queer and transgender porn by Barbara DeGenevieve and Terry Pirtle
    (archive): http://www.ssspread.com
Sex workers news and literature: http://www.whorenet.net

Sex/Porn Blogs

Audacia Ray, "Waking Vixen": http://www.wakingvixen.com/blog
Fleshbot, "Pure Filth since 2003 Because the Internet was Made for Porn":
    http://fleshbot.com

Girls Who Like Porno: http://www.girlswholikeporno.com
Gram Ponante: The Porn Valley Observed: http://gramponante.com
Mark Dery's Shovelware: http://www.markdery.com
Melissa Gira, Web-Based Woman of Pleasure: http://www.melissagira.com
Regina Lynn Online: http://www.reginalynn.com/wordpress/
Sex Blogs Archive: http://www.sexblo.gs.com
Sex Kitten: Women and Pornography: http://www.sex-kitten.net
Slashdong: http://www.slashdong.org/
Tiny Nibbles: http://www.tinynibbles.com/links.html

Magazines, Porn/Sex News

Asian Sex Gazette: http://www.asiansexgazette.com
The Adult Video Industry Online: http://www.avn.com
Jane's Net Sex Guide: Quality Reviews of Alternative Porn Sites and Movies: http://janesguide.com
Nerve: Smart, honest magazine on sex, with prose, fiction, and photographs of naked people that capture more than their flesh: http://nerve.com
Other politics, sex, and technology news: http://Salon.com; http://www.wired.com

Conferences and Festivals

Adult Online Europe Trade Fair: http://www.aoexpo.com
Art and Politics of Netporn: http://www.networkcultures.org/netporn
Porn Ar(t)Ound the World, with afterword by curator: http://www.libidot.org/katrien/tester/happenings.htm
Porn Film Festival Berlin: http://www.pornfilmfestival.com
Post Porn Politics Volskbuhne Berlin: http://www.postpornpolitics.com

Porn and Netporn Research Initiatives

Albert Benshop on cybersex, cyberporn, media addiction, and more: http://www2.fmg.uva.nl/sociosite/websoc/regulation_porno.html
The Berkman Center for Internet and Society at Harvard Law School: http://eon.law.harvard.edu/ilaw/speech
Censorship on the Internet: A Bibliography: http://library2.usask.ca/~dworacze/CENS.HTM
Feminists Against Censorship: http://www.fiawol.demon.co.uk/FAC

Harris Poll, "No Consensus among American Public on the Effects of Pornography on Adults or Children or What the Government Should Do about It," October 7, 2005: http://www.harrisinteractive.com/harris_poll/index.asp?PID=606

International Committee on the Rights of Sex Workers in Europe: http://www.sexworkeurope.org

Kinsey Institute for Research in Sex, Gender, and Reproduction: http://www.indiana.edu/kinsey

The Philip Mak Shoujou-ai Archive: http://www.shoujoai.com/

Sergio Messina Realcore and Realblog: http://www.radiogladio.it

Sexuality and the Internet Psychology: Bibliography: http://construct.haifa.ac.il/~azy/refsex.htm

Sexual Content in Games: http://www.igda.org/sex

Artist Erotica/Pornography

Accidental Video Game Porn Archive: http://www.derekyu.com/avgpa/gallery.html

Adam Zaretsky and Barbara Groves: http://www.ovarium.org

Annie Sprinkle: http://www.anniesprinkle.org

The Aphrodite (Sexworkers) Project: http://theaphroditeproject.tv

Artists and Cloning: http://kloone.anjeroosjen.com/engels/ukindex.htm

Bruce La Bruce: http://www.brucelabruce.com

Francesca da Rimini: http://sysx.org/gashgirl/arc/index.html

Homemade Sex Toys: http://www.homemade-sex-toys.com/case

Ian Haig: http://www.ianhaig.net

Isaac Leung : http://5sps.com/orientalwhore.html

Libidot: Dr. Jacobs's Archive of Sex Art: http://www.libidot.org

Liquid Generation: Pop Star or Porn Star: http://www.liquidgeneration.com

Piepke: http://www.piepke.org

Sexmachines: Photographs and interviews by Timothy Archibald: http://processmediainc.com/press/mini_sites/sex_machines; http://www.timothyarchibald.com/sexmachines.html

The Sex Machines Diaries: http://thesexmachinebook.blogspot.com

Tanya Bezreh: http://newcenturyschoolbook.com; http://www.tanyabezreh.com

Terre Thaemlitz: http://www.comatonse.com

Tobaron Waxman: http://www.artic.edu/~twaxma/frameset.html

Todd Verow: http://www.bangorfilms.com

Vaginal Davis: http://www.vaginaldavis.com

Zoot and Genant: http://www.zootengenant.com

Social Networks
(for Youngsters, Adults, and Midlife Crisis)

Online Swingers and Dating (Vanilla): http://Adultfriendfinder.com
Online Swingers with Kinks: http://Alt.com
P2P Porn Groups: http://empornium.us
Social Networks: http://myspace.com; http://flickr.com; http://friendster.com;
   http://Youtube.com; http://Livejournal.com

Censorship Files

Electronic Frontier Foundation: http://www.eff.org
Electronic Frontiers Australia: http://www.efa.org.au
The File Room: http://www.thefileroom.org
Index on Censorship: http://www.indexonline.org

Feminist Sex Shops

Love Piece Club: http://www.lovepiececlub.com
Good Vibrations: http://www.goodvibes.com
Grandopening: http://www.grandopening.com
Toys in Babeland: http://www.babeland.com

Index

About the Author

Katrien Jacobs is assistant professor in new media at City University of Hong Kong. She has lectured widely on gender, sexuality, new media art, and pornography. She was born in Belgium and received her Ph.D. degree in comparative literature and media from the University of Maryland, with a thesis on dismemberment myths and rituals in 1960s and 1970s body art and performance media. She has published in renowned journals such as *Parallax* and *Cultural Studies* and her book about art, sexuality, performativity, and digital media, *Libi_doc: Journeys in the Performance of Sex Art*, was published in 2005. As a curator and artist, Jacobs has organized several exhibits in different countries. She was the guest curator of the international conference Art and Politics of Netporn, organized by the Institute of Network Cultures in Amsterdam.